VIRGINIA,

ESPECIALLY

RICHMOND,

IN BY-GONE DAYS;

WITH A GLANCE AT THE PRESENT:

BEING REMINISCENCES AND LAST WORDS OF

An Old Citizen.

BY SAMUEL MORDECAI.

"HÆC OLIM MEMINISSE JUVABIT."

Second Edition,
With many corrections and additions.

RICHMOND:
WEST & JOHNSTON, PUBLISHERS.
1860.

<u>Notice</u>

In many older books, foxing (or discoloration) occurs and, in some instances, print lightens with wear and age. Reprinted books, such as this, often duplicate these flaws, notwithstanding efforts to reduce or eliminate them. The pages of this reprint have been digitally enhanced and, where possible, the flaws eliminated in order to provide clarity of content and a pleasant reading experience.

EXTRACT of a letter from WASHINGTON IRVING to the author, dated Sunny-Side, July 6, 1856.

"I had especially intended to thank you for your little volume, for it was particularly acceptable to me. '*Richmond in By-Gone Days*' was Richmond as I knew it in the days of my youth, nearly fifty years since. Every page of your volume brought up some delightful recollection of scenes and characters long since passed away; for at Richmond, at the time of my visit, there was a rare assemblage of the talent and beauty of Virginia; and the impressions I received then have ever made the 'Old Dominion' dear to me.'"

———

Letter from Dr. JOHN W. FRANCIS to the author, dated New York, May 13, 1857.

"*Dear Sir*,—Your interesting volume of men and things, (your reminiscences,) came safely to hand. I had already read the work with much gratification. It is such books that help to make up history, when writers like Macaulay take pen in hand. I shall preserve the volume, and I hope to have some notice taken of it. With many, many thanks, &c."

———

From the New York Observer, Nov. 20, 1856.

"This volume is full of pleasant reading, even for a stranger, but much more interesting to those who know the Capital of the Old Dominion. It is the work of leisure hours, delightfully spent in gathering up the threads of past days, and preserving the records that would otherwise be left to perish."

CONTENTS.

PREFACE TO THE FIRST EDITION.

THE unpretending character of this little book will probably disarm criticism, except from the attacks of such literary prowlers as make their assaults on the weakest, that they may be safe from resistance or retaliation.

These reminiscences were commenced at a period of illness, to while away the tedium of a sick chamber, and would not have extended beyond the few pages thus penned to kill time, had not some friends urged the extension of them, to serve as a slight memorial of men and things and events, of which there were few or no records, and which must soon pass into oblivion if not rescued by one of the survivors of them.

The reader may doubt whether a large portion of the contents deserve to be thus rescued; and should this be the general opinion, the judgment will be carried into execution, by the book being consigned to the oblivion it merits.

What portions of these reminiscences are to be ascribed to false impressions on the memory, I must refer to my cotemporaries, being unconscious of them myself. In old age, the memory like the

2

sight, discerns remote objects, while those which
are near become indistinct, or imperceptible. But
the imagination sometimes plays tricks with both.
Memory becomes so strongly impressed with what it
had frequently heard or frequently narrated, as to
convert legends into facts, and phantoms into real-
ities; and the eye is also deceived by outlines and
shadows, into seeing objects, which have neither
form nor substance—

> " Giving to airy nothings a local habitation and a name."

The writer trusts that there is nothing in these
pages to wound the feelings of any one living
person mentioned, or of the descendants of one;
he can conscientiously assert that there is no such
intention, and express his regret if his motives
should be misinterpreted.

P. S.—When the following pages were penned,
the writer had not seen the volume entitled "History of Richmond, by Dr. John P. Little; " and
having not yet perused it regularly, he is unconscious of any encroachments on the Doctor's
manor, and *he* will be the first probably to excul-
pate the writer from any such charge. The Doctor's work appears to be one of historical research,
to which this lays no claim.

MARCH, 1856.

PREFACE TO THE SECOND EDITION.

THE appearance of this volume is prompted solely by a wish to leave, instead of its predecessor, a more correct and complete record of the writer's reminiscences. Ever since the publication of that volume, the author has been conscious of its errors and imperfections, which, if they were overlooked by his friends, were not by himself; and he has felt it a duty to both to leave a fairer record, unimportant as it is. If he succeeds in this, his object will be attained, without any other reward than the approbation of the public, and especially of his fair friends, whose kind reception of the first edition is an additional inducement to test their indulgence and that of the public by the issue of a second.

Having now confessed his errors, for which he seeks to atone, he trusts to obtain absolution. He seeks not only to merit this, but to obtain favor by the amplification of former subjects and the introduction of new ones.

A slight change has been made in the title, partly to distinguish this from the first edition, and partly because some subjects outside of Richmond are introduced.

New flounces have been added to the old dress, and patches or new breadths (like those in ladies' dresses of to-day), are inserted where it was necessary to tear out the former texture, in order to substitute better materials. Indeed, the old dress should be entirely discarded, and the new one substituted. Those who possess the former, are therefore advised, if a gentleman to use it for lighting cigars, if a lady for curl-papers (it will put no wicked thoughts in her head), and obtain a copy of the "second edition, corrected and enlarged."

Whether any persons will be tempted to follow this advice is a risk to be incurred by the publishers, and if not followed, the public will also be the losers. Warm weather prevails, when light diet is best, and such this volume furnishes.

Should there be found an infusion of garrulity, the influence of seventy-four summers on the writer must plead his excuse. Age is more apt to have a profusion of words than of ideas. Pray, dear reader, proceed to the perusal with an indulgent spirit, and if a lady, with a sweet voice, to atone for rough composition. May it at least induce gentle slumbers and pleasant dreams. Good night.

Or to change this levity to a serious and softer tone, for these are parting words to many friends—
FAREWELL.

MAY 1, 1860.

INTRODUCTION.

It may not be amiss to prefix to these recollections of the City of Richmond a short notice of its origin.

The name originated from the fancied resemblance of its site to Richmond, on the Thames, which is noticed at the present day by persons who have seen both, and if *Rougemont* gave a color of adaptation to the latter, it might well have done so to our city, whose hill-sides glow with a rich red tint.

A grant of 7,351 acres of land, "beginning at the mouth of Shoccoe's Creek," and running up the river several miles, and north of it a considerable distance, was obtained by Capt. William Bird from Sir William Berkeley, Governor, on the 15th of March, 1675–6, in consideration of the introduction of 122 persons into the Colony, the names of whom are recited in the grant, and subsequently for introducing some negro slaves. In 1687, a patent was granted to the same gentleman for 956 acres, beginning on the east side of Shoccoe's Creek at its mouth, and extending up the creek and down the river. On a part of this latter grant, Richmond first sprung up and subsequently spread over a portion of the larger grant west of Shockoe Creek.

[These grants were confirmed by an act of the "Grand Assembly, held at James City " in 1679, which "granted to Capt. William Bird within these bounds, beginning on the south side of James River, one mile and a half below the Falls, and so continuing five miles up the river in a straight line, and backwards one mile into the woods," "and on the north side of said river, beginning half a mile before the Falls, and thence continuing five miles up the river and two miles backwards into the woods, all which he accounts and presumes to be his own land,"—"and he shall become bound and obliged to seat the whole number of fifty able men armed and constantly furnished with sufficient ammunition and provisions, together with such number of titheable persons not exceeding 250 in the whole, on both sides of said river, within the space of half a mile along the river on each side and a quarter of a mile backwards into the woods."

A similar grant on Rappahannock river, was made to Lawrence Smith, and offered to any other persons, at or near the heads of any other of the great rivers, on condition of their placing military forces and other persons, "for the protection of his Majesty's country against our barbarous enemies, the Indians."]

The following extract from a manuscript volume of Col. WM. BYRD, OF WESTOVER, the founder of the City, was written in the year 1733, in his journal:

"Sept. 19, 1733.—When we got home we laid the foundation of two large cities, one at Shacco's, to be called Richmond, and the other at the Falls of Appomattox river, to be named Petersburg. These Major Mayo offered to lay out into lots without fee or reward. The truth of it is, these two places being the uppermost landing of James and Appomattox rivers, are naturally intended for marts where the traffic of the outer inhabitants must centre. Thus we did not build castles only, but also cities in the air." [The Westover Manuscripts, Petersburg.—Printed by Edmund and Julian Ruffin, 1841.]

It was to PETER JONES, not to *Peter the Great*, that Petersburg was indebted for its name—Jones little thought that the claims of the Czar and himself would ever conflict for any honor or distinction, although, like his great name-sake, he also founded a city on marshy ground, as the old part of our Petersburg originally was. But great geniuses often jump together.

In the year 1742, the Assembly of Virginia passed " an act establishing the town of Richmond, in the county of Henrico, and allowing Fairs to be held therein " in the months of May and November, " on the lands of Wm. Byrd, Esq., at the Falls of James river." Shockoe's Creek was the northern and eastern boundary. The river and a line therefrom along First street to the creek, (probably Bacon Branch) was the southern and western.

In 1744, an act was passed to prohibit the building of wooden chimneys, " by reason of the imminent danger of fire."

In 1769, "an act for establishing towns at *Rocky Ridge*, (Manchester), at Gloucester Court House, and Layton's Ware-house."

In 1779, " an act for the removal of the seat of

government" to the town of Richmond—which includes a section authorizing an enlargement of its limits by the addition of two hundred lots, or one hundred acres.

In 1780, "an act for locating the public squares, to enlarge the town, and for other purposes"—locates the *Capitol*, Halls of Justice, State House for Executive Boards, and a house for the Governor, on Shockoe Hill, and a Public Market below the hill, on the *same side* of the creek. "Thomas Jefferson, Archibald Cary, Robert Carter Nicholas, Richard Adams, Edmund Randolph, Turner Southall, Robert Goode, James Buchanan, and Samuel Du Vall, Esquires, were appointed to lay off in such form and of such dimensions as shall be convenient and requisite." Two hundred more lots of a half acre each were added, and authority given to clear the navigation leading to Shockoe landing, "which was much obstructed of late by freshets, the natural course of the creek being altered, by which large banks of sand have been thrown up, which if not quickly removed, may render the navigation to the upper landing useless," *i. e.* the late site of the Gas Works, on Cary street.

In 1781, "an act to secure to persons who desire titles to lots, lands and tenements, under the lottery, or under a deed of trust of the late Wm. Byrd, Esq., a fee simple estate therein."

The WM. BYRD here spoken of, was a son of the founder, and was as industrious in losing a fortune, as his father had been in making one. The sale of lots in Richmond was perhaps not so rapid as his expenditures required, and from the recital in this act, it appears that in 1756 he made a *lottery of lots in Richmond and Manchester.* He may have sunk metal more precious by working a Lead mine in the county of Augusta wherein he was concerned with John Robinson and John Chiswell.

Augusta may then have been the frontier county in Virginia, bounded on the west, it may be presumed, by the Pacific. I have seen a large map mouldering on the ruinous walls at Eltham, at the head of York river, where Albemarle county had such an illimitable boundary.

In 1757 a deed was made by Wm. Byrd, premising that he intends shortly to leave the Colony and is desirous to provide for the maintenance of his wife and mother, and for the payment of his debts, and conveying to and placing under the management of Peyton Randolph, John Robinson, John Page, Presley Thornton, Charles Carter and Charles Turnbull all his lands in Chesterfield, Henrico, Lunenburg and Halifax, with the slaves and live stock thereon. Part of the property conveyed in this deed was the subject of his lottery, which was drawn before the act of 1769 for suppressing private lotteries. The plan of the lottery was put on record in the court of Henrico county.

At the date of the act of 1781, CHARLES CARTER was the only surviving trustee, and he was authorized by it to execute the deeds.

In 1782, an act was passed which conferred on Richmond the title of *City*, and incorporated it as such.

In 1788, the city was allowed a Representative in the House of Delegates.

The name and deeds of Nathaniel Bacon, called the rebel, but meriting the title of patriot, are recorded in history, and are retained in the eastern and western limits of Richmond.

Bloody-Run by tradition obtained its name from a sanguinary battle with the Indians, where his conquest terminated hostilities with them, and *Bacon's Quarter Branch*, also by tradition, derives its name from his occupancy of the banks of that stream with his troops, when opposed to those of the Governor in 1676, and when his resistance to oppression preceded by a century that which resulted in Independence.

Bacon's Castle in Surry is a strongly built house which bears the marks of port-holes for musketry, and it is still a comfortable dwelling.

VIRGINIA,

ESPECIALLY

RICHMOND, IN BY-GONE DAYS.

CHAPTER I.

LONG TIME AGO.

> " Should auld acquaintance be forgot,
> And never brought to min' ?
> Should auld acquaintance be forgot,
> And days o'lang-syne ?"

THERE are few residents of Richmond at this day whose reminiscences of its localities, &c., have a more remote retrospection than mine ; impressed on my childhood, perhaps on my imagination ; and as the latter may occasionally prevail, I will not venture to assert that my descriptions and anecdotes are literally correct,—they are so, as the qualification in court goes, "to the best of my knowledge and belief."

As far back as the year 1792, I think I remember the *market-house* occupying the site of the one just rebuilt (1855) on Main and

Seventeenth streets. The first edifice was an open shed supported on wooden posts, and the slope from it down to *Shockoe Creek* was a green pasture, and considered a common, much used by laundresses whereon to dry the clothes which they washed in the stream. A spring of cool water arose in the common on the south side of Main street, but the spot is now occupied by a building where fountains of *fire-water* are substituted for the natural and pure element, and, I fear, it may be added, that the combined elements attract more thirsty bodies than the simple one did of yore, although the thirst is more apt to be increased than allayed by the fiery substitute.*

The creek was crossed by foot passengers on a narrow bridge, raised a few feet above the surface of the water, but horses cooled *their* feet by fording it. When freshets occurred, the planks were removed from the bridge and a ferry-boat was substituted, which conveyed vehicles, as well as man and horse, across the wide and sometimes deep stream.

At the mouth of the creek, where the gas holders now rise and fall, was a wharf, built around a broad, flat rock (which has been blasted to accommodate the gas), and this place was called the *Rock Landing*, where oyster boats and small craft resorted.

---

* This fountain has found a different outlet, 1860.

Along the then elevated bank of the river, from about the rear of the present *Union Hotel,* a grassy walk, shaded by elm and other trees, extended for a considerable distance, down to where *Foster's rope-walk* afterwards stood, and this was the fashionable promenade. Of late years, the clay which nourished those trees has been converted into bricks, the surface lowered many feet, and a large portion of it covered with buildings. Below this bank was a small branch of the river, separated from the main stream by a narrow strip of land, an island, on which grew a few large sycamore trees, about the site of the present dock. I remember a vessel, grounded probably in a freshet, in this narrow stream, and converted into a place of refreshment, which was reached by a platform from the shore, and resorted to by promenaders. Its position was peculiarly favorable for the sale of oysters to those who sought recreation there.

The eastern end of this shaded walk terminated in a high and steep cliff, overhanging the river, which washed its base at high water, but at low tide admitted of a narrow walk on the sands. On the occasion of a severe ice freshet once, a great deposit of drift-wood, soil and sand formed a small island some hundred feet from this cliff. A German, named Widewilt, whose trumpet called the troops to horse, procured a land warrant and

3

located it on this new-found land, and, to secure
it against becoming a floating island, he drove
stakes all round his slippery domain, and wattled
them, so that future freshets might add further
deposits; and thus *Widewilt's Island* became a
possession of some value as a fishery and a sand
mart. The island remained above water longer
than its founder did above ground; but a similar
accident to that which formed the island recurred,
and destroyed the work of its predecessor. An
ice freshet consolidated the river, and so obstructed
the current that the ice borne over the Falls continued to accumulate in height until it rose to the
level of Mayo's Bridge. An unfrozen current
flowed underneath, but was not visible for many
miles. The immense mass of ice slowly disappeared, and with it disappeared Widewilt's Island.

A similar loss of territory happened to Great
Britain some years before. A volcanic island rose
in the Atlantic off St. Michael's, one of the
Azores, in 1811, and when it became cool enough
not to scorch shoe leather, the captain of the British frigate *Sabrina*, then cruising on that station,
landed on it, and coolly took possession in the
name of his sovereign, and gave to it the name
of his ship. It was my fortune, or misfortune,
during the war in 1814, soon after passing the site
of this new British territory, to be captured by
one of his Britannic Majesty's ships. I was on

board an American vessel commanded by a Scotchman, and was captured by a British vessel commanded by a Yankee, and to complete the strange
antithesis, a Yankee prize-master was placed over
my Scotch captain. The Yankee was a well disposed—I should rather say a good-natured man—
for his disposition to fight against his country was
not *well*, but he had been a carpenter in the British
service "long before the fight begun." I inquired
of him about the island, and was told he could
show me what remained of it. Thereupon, opening his sea-chest, he handed me a lump of lava,
and said he was present at the birth of the island,
and acted as one of its godfathers. That he took
this memento of his bantling, who did not survive,
or rather *sur-wave*, but about eighteen months;
and he bestowed on me one-half of the British
dominion he had rescued from the other dominion
which is claimed in that boastful song, "Britannia
rules the waves."

An ephemeral island has risen and subsided
several times near the same spot. Should "Sabrina," or one of her *ascendants*, venture again to
raise her head above water, she will probably be
claimed by Great Britain as a deserter; nor is such
a claim likely to be disputed, except in the lower
regions, whence these islands seem to emigrate.

Widewilt and his successors in various projects,
forced the river from its natural bed, and such has

been the encroachment of Richmond on its passive opposite neighbor, that a large rock, formerly on the southern margin of the river, to which the Manchester anglers could step, with the aid of a fence-rail, now shows its rugged head in mid-channel. The present margin of the river is not its natural one along any portion of the entire length of the city; but the latter may be traced along the inner banks of Haxall's canal, of that portion of the James River Canal which extends from Haxall's to the Dock, and of the north side of the Dock throughout its whole length. Many acres of land have been made by encroachments on the water, embracing a new territory below Haxall's mills, the site of the Danville Railroad Depot, that of the new tobacco warehouse of Messrs. Mayo, and the long extent of embankment betwixt the dock and the river on which a street is made and a number of buildings erected. In old times the river would probably have attempted to repel this encroachment, but it does not rise in its wrath now as formerly. There is no knowing what it may yet do when highly excited.

The *Rock Landing* has had a singular succession of occupants. When vessels of some size could no longer float there, and when even the oyster boats had to abandon it in favor of a wharf which was extended to deeper water, a shot-tower was erected on it. Although founded on a rock, it had not attained to its full altitude, when it fell to the ground, proving that bad bricks and weak mortar were unfit for high pressure, or perhaps the rock on which it was based may not have been dressed to a true level, and the tall structure slid off side-wise. The materials served to form a less aspiring structure, to use a gentle term, for a block of buildings in the Valley not always in very good repute.

Thus dead to any useful purpose, the Rock Landing was buried under the accumulating mass of earth and rubbish, which was carted from foundations for houses and from less pure sources. After many years interment it was exhumed, and like some other subjects, whose graves are violated, its still firm body was dislocated, and the members scattered abroad or used in the erection of a huge monument (the gas holders) which cover its grave, but a bright and subtle spirit arises from it, which serves to enlighten our citizens in the most be-nighted times.

"*The Cage*" is, I believe, a term peculiar to Richmond as applied to the receptacle for offend-ers. It originated from a structure so called, erected at the north-east end of the market bridge, some fifty years ago, when it terminated close to the market-house; its long parapet wall of brick was surmounted by a coping of free-stone, which extended west to the store now and for many years

occupied by Mr. Palmer, and an equal length on
the opposite side of the street. In the rear of
Mr. P.'s was the first iron foundry in Richmond,
erected by the Brothers Dunlop. This cage, of
octagonal form, had open iron gratings on three
sides, about ten feet above the street, and the floor
of this open prison was arranged amphitheatri-
cally, so that each occupant could see, and what
was worse, be seen from the street.

Here were encaged, when caught, the un-
feathered night-hawks that prowl for prey, and
screeching owls that make night hideous, and black
birds, who had flown from their own nests, to nestle
elsewhere, like cuckoos; and some birds, both black
and white, who had no nests at all were brought to
roost here until that official ornithologist the police
master should examine into their characters. This
was a somewhat convenient arrangement to the
citizen, who on rising in the morning, missed the
attendant on his household comforts, and as he
went to market had only to look into the cage for
his flown bird.

A structure made memorable to future ages by
the author of Hudibras, stood in rear of the cage.

> "———————— In all the fabrick
> You shall not see one stone or brick,
> But all of wood, by powerful spell
> Of magic, made impregnable :
> There's neither iron bar, nor gate,
> Portcullis, chain, nor bolt, nor grate:

And yet men durance there abide,
In dungeon, scarce three inches wide,
With roof so low, that under it
They never stand, but lie or sit;
And yet so foul that whoso is in,
Is to the middle-leg in prison;
In circle magical confin'd,
With wall of subtile air and wind;
Which none are able to break thorough,
Until they're freed by the head-borough."

This mystical prison—the *stocks*—surmounted the *whipping-post*, and was an awful warning to the foul birds; some of whom were occasionally condemned to roost in the upper part and others to become acquainted with the twigs in the lower.

Another mode of punishment, derived from the mother country, was " whipping at a cart's tail." I saw this inflicted, when a child, in Petersburg. The culprit on foot, naked to the waist, was tied to the rear of a cart, which was driven slowly along the street. A constable with a whip walked near the miserable offender, and at short intervals applied the lash to his bleeding back. The limits of the town were the limit to his punishment. His hands were then untied, and he was admonished never to repass those limits, under the penalty of a similar infliction.

There was yet another mode of punishment adopted in Virginia for offenders of another class, viz: those whose tones were too high and discordant for the peace and comfort of their neighbors.

The implement for inflicting this was called a cucking or ducking stool. The occupancy of it was an exclusive privilege of the fair and gentle sex, so called, and never contested by the rougher one. It was thus constructed: a post was planted in the ground on the margin of a pond or stream; on the top of this post a long pole fixed at its centre on a pivot, was made to revolve; at one end of the pole a chair was fastened in which the privileged party entitled to the seat was placed so securely that she could not abdicate it. The pole was then turned so as to bring the incumbent over the water and was depressed sufficiently to dip her beneath the surface. This plunging bath was repeated until the patient was cooled—externally at least. "Common scolds" were thus silenced—pro tem.

This bathing machine fell into disuse many years ago, whether because the offence ceased to be committed, or that instead of an offence it became a venial privilege, can be decided by members of the Caudle Club. The last revolution of the stool recorded in our history, was excited by an old lady of literary renown, and of a Royal family, who exacted black mail for exemption from her scurrilous pen—perhaps this also has become a privilege, for scurrility prevails unpunished. The water of the Potomac gave ablution to this victim.

In Philadelphia, a case is recorded of the cucking stool being put in requisition as late as 1824, when Nancy Jones was convicted of being a common (query, uncommon ?) scold and sentenced " to be placed in a certain engine of correction, called a cucking or ducking stool and being so placed to be plunged three times in the water."

In 1661-2, it was enacted by " the Grand Assembly of Virginia," that there should be erected in each county (then seventeen in number) a pillory, whipping post, ducking stool and stocks.

CHAPTER II.

BRITISH MERCHANTS AND COMMERCIAL QUACKS.

THE term " British merchants " is here used *not* in its general acceptation, but as it was formerly applied in Virginia to those who had establishments here and who in fact had the monopoly of trade in most of the Southern States. Far be it from me to impugn the integrity and liberality of so truly noble a class as the British merchants, or to reflect on any nationalities, classes or sects.

On another page it is stated that supplies of goods were imported into Virginia previous to and

for a score of years after the Revolution chiefly by
English, Scotch and Irish merchants. The principals of these mercantile houses resided in Great
Britain and junior partners conducted the business
in Virginia. Some of these concerns branched out
like polypi to the villages and court-houses, and
some of them also like polypi consumed the substance of all that came within their grasp. There
were, however, many honorable exceptions to this
rule.

It was said to have been one of the stipulations
between the principals of those houses and the
young men they sent to Virginia as clerks, that
they were not to marry in Virginia. They came
with the prospect of being admitted as partners in
some branch of the central establishment, and it
might weaken the sordid attachment to their patrons if they formed one of a purer and tenderer
nature to the fair daughters of their customers.
They might make less stringent bargains, or be
more indulgent in requiring payments; or perhaps
their friends in Scotland had conscientious scruples, imagining that the only wives they could find
in Virginia were Indians or negroes, and that they
were thus saving their proteges from the embrace
of the Heathen. This might well have been their
mistake, for it is but recently that a Scotch gentleman carried his fair and beautiful wife on a visit
to his relations in a remote part of Scotland, and

their first exclamation on seeing her was, "Gude save us, she is white !"

This monkish system tended to prevent that social intercourse between merchant and planter which the hospitable disposition of the latter would have encouraged, and this exclusion of the former from good society and from the benign influence of virtuous woman led to low habits and to intemperance, to which many of them became victims.

With a moderate share of prudence and industry, the acquisition of a fortune was almost certain. Competition did not interfere to reduce the profit on goods below forty or fifty per cent., nor to raise the price of tobacco, which was generally taken in payment, above sixteen shillings and eight pence ($2.78) or eighteen shillings ($3) per hundred pounds, and at that time the sale of no tobacco other than good leaf or stemmed was permitted— such as was not merchantable, if presented for inspection, was burned. Previous to the Revolution a convention of the (Virginia) British merchants was semi-annually held at Williamsburg, when the prices they would allow for tobacco was fixed for the ensuing year, after the crops were pretty well ascertained. This was trading on a safe basis, as the partners abroad could control the prices there in a great degree. Those planters who lived extravagantly were apt to fall in debt to their merchants and would give bonds, renewed from year to year with interest added, until a mortgage or deed of trust ensued, and thus some fine estates changed hands from planter to merchant.

Loans were also made to the planters which were apt to prove ruinous to the borrowers. One mode of evading the usury law was by buying from the planter a bill of exchange drawn by him on some person *or thing* in London, at a very low rate of exchange, which bill would of course be protested and returned, subject to damages, and to a refund at the current rate of exchange, thus involving a loss of twenty-five per cent. or more for six or eight months' use of the money.

An instance is recorded of a loan being made to a gentleman at the rate of 5 per cent. per annum, on condition that he would draw a bill for the amount on London where he had no funds, which would incur 10 per cent. damages, on being returned protested. He drew on a London firm with whom he had no correspondence, but his respectability was known by them, and confiding in his integrity, and moreover expecting that he intended to make them the consignees of his to-bacco, they accepted and paid his bill. The lender was sorely disappointed and complained that the gentleman had sold him a good bill instead of a bad one, viewing it as a breach of faith. The faith of the London house was no doubt rewarded.

I have heard that such bills had been drawn on

"the pump at Aldgate," and that on one occasion, when the planter was at a loss for a name to .draw on, the pious merchant suggested " the Bishop of London," which was adopted. When the bill was presented to his reverence he was much surprised, but thinking there must be some good ground for it, he consulted a friend as to the course to be pursued, stating that he did not know the drawer, nor any cause for such a bill, and wished to be advised how to act. A protest was of course the result and no grace was given to the graceless parties.

This system of evading the usury law gave rise to an enactment by the Legislature of Virginia, requiring that after the sum in sterling on the face of the bill, it should also express in currency the amount actually received for it, and if this was omitted the holder could recover no more pounds in currency than were drawn for in sterling.

The British merchants had drawn the Virginia planters so deeply in debt to them, and the cessation of trade during the Revolution had caused such an advance in the price of imported goods and so great a depreciation in produce, that to save the planters from ruin and to punish the merchants for Toryism, the Legislature passed an act confiscating British debts and authorizing the treasurer to collect them. The effect of this was annulled when peace took place.

4

The monopoly of the trade of Virginia, in a
great degree, was retained by the British merchants many years after the peace of 1783, but
adventurers from the Northern and Eastern States
gradually made good their footing and created competition, and even some Virginians condescended
to stand behind the desk or the counter. Some
of the imported celibates relinquished their vows
and became engrafted on society, and thus an
entire change was brought about in our commercial
system.

When all our goods were imported directly
from abroad and our produce exported to Europe,
we paid dearly for the honor of such direct trade
and found it to our interest to encourage Northern competition, which increased by slow degrees.

One of the first bold innovators who dared to
compete on a large scale with the importers was
Bartlett Still. He purchased his goods in the
Northern cities, priced them in dollars and cents,
instead of pounds, shillings and pence, and sold
for cash. His fancy articles were more stylish and
his store more showy and brilliant than those of
the old fogies and he attracted the fashionable
custom. His deeds were celebrated in rhyme,
which gave increased notoriety to his establishment.

His example was soon followed, and "*new* store"
was succeeded by "NEW *new* store," which latter
throve so well that those of the next generation

became stock-jobbers, millionaires and bankrupts in New York in rapid succession.

Thus by degrees the purchase of goods in New York and Philadelphia became the rule and direct importation the exception. Of late years the largest portion of our tobacco crop is manufactured at home and in that state sold at the North, but the quantity shipped in leaf direct to Europe is usually equal to the demand, now that the Western States furnish so large a supply to markets abroad.

The system which formerly existed prevented an accumulation of commercial capital in Richmond, or in any town in Virginia, and thus stinted their growth. The profits on trade went in the first instance chiefly to the principals in Great Britain, and when their Virginia partners had amassed a comfortable capital, having no family ties here, they would retire to "the old country" as they called it, with the capital they had accumulated, and this continual drain kept the new country poor.

Many adventurers from the Northern States, after making money here, would return to spend or increase it there. It is of late years comparatively, that a large mercantile capital has become stable in Virginia. Millions might be counted up that were abstracted from Richmond and Petersburg in former days to establish those merchants, who had accumulated it here, in London, Liverpool and New York, while scarcely any capital came from those cities to replace it.

The foreign trade of Virginia was very extensive subsequent to the Revolution and for some years after the beginning of the present century. Manchester even imported largely, as did Fredericksburg, Falmouth and Alexandria. The commerce of Norfolk was very extensive—especially with the West Indies. During the wars that succeeded the French Revolution, her fine harbor was frequently crowded with vessels of all nations, including ships of war which put in there for supplies, for repairs or for safety from an enemy of superior strength; the position of the Capes, of Hampton Roads and of the Bay rendering it the most convenient and desirable harbor along our whole coast. Merchant vessels would also resort to Hampton Roads in great numbers, in search of freight from any of the ports within Chesapeake Bay, through the agency of Norfolk merchants and they were also large ship owners. Alexandria had a considerable West India trade. Such are facts. Political economists may investigate the cause of the disappearance of most of this trade.

The old Scotch merchants had known so little of liberty at home, either political or social, that few of them could appreciate our Republican institutions, and on returning to the Land of Cakes, they were prepared to become dutiful subjects under the comparative despotism that existed there even as late as fifty years ago, as recorded in Lord Cockburn's Memorials of his times.*

COMMERCIAL QUACKS.

It was not only to foreign monopoly of our trade and the consequent abstraction of capital, that the tardy growth of the commercial towns of Virginia and of the country, consequently, is to be attributed. The action of the legislature has always been adverse to the mercantile class, inheriting perhaps from their ancestors a prejudice against it. Was increase of revenue required, merchants and inhabitants of towns were taxed far higher than agriculturists. The exactions for licenses to sell, per centage on sales, tax on insurance, &c., are greater than in any community that has thriven; besides which, antiquated and useless regulations and restrictions were, and still are retained and even new ones introduced, which are clogs on trade, and cannot but re-act, though imperceptibly, on the agricultural interest, for the benefit only of a few office-holders or sinecurists, and of the *political* patronage of appointment; qualification for the duties required being overlooked. When the present Constitution was formed, equality of taxation was to be one of its

---

* The subsequent part of this chapter was written in 1857.

features, but a keen member contrived to introduce, at a favorable moment, a special exception for licenses, which would enable the legislature to tax merchants higher than planters.

But while the most onerous burthens are laid on commerce, and useless obstructions placed in her track, there is professed at the same time a great desire to promote her interests, to open for her new channels, "to encourage direct trade, and render ourselves independent of the North." Such is the *slang*—and slang is the appropriate word, where actions contradict professions. If commerce were rid of the practices, maugre the professions of politicians, and left to take care of herself, she would probably thrive much better, and so would all the interests connected with her, which she is constantly accused of oppressing. She could dispense with the assemblages of dry-nurses, who meet at stated periods in various Southern cities, each trying to concoct pap for her own babe, and some of them seeking to nourish foreign bantlings on Southern pap, but contending whether Virginia, Carolina or Georgia shall be the foster-mother and obtain the remuneration. A member of such a convention, and also of the legislature, after listening to and engaging in discussions on free trade, in the African church, and suggesting impracticable plans to promote it, will the next moment, in the legislative body, aid in framing laws which would counteract such plans, were they practicable. These "Commercial Conventions," as they are called, composed more of planters, lawyers and politicians than of merchants, assemble to discuss subjects of which few of them have any practical knowledge. They would regulate not only our own trade, but that of Europe, and dictate to the nations there, how they should relinquish one of their most important sources of revenue, for our benefit.

If commerce is ever to thrive in Virginia it will be when her shackles are struck off. At present free trade is not permitted. Useless inspections and costly licenses obstruct it, and among other antiquated fetters, usury laws are retained as betwixt individuals (perhaps on Scriptural grounds), while corporations which have no souls to be d—d, and certainly none to be saved, are in many instances specially exempted from their operation. The consequence of this restriction is, that money flows from Virginia to Northern cities where interest is higher, and while we thus contribute to their prosperity at the expense of our own, we complain that they outstrip us.

P. S.—April, 1860. The legislature that has just adjourned took the first step toward the emancipation of trade from the trammels that have so long obstructed it, by exempting from compulsory inspection, flour shipped to foreign ports in Virginia vessels. It is to be hoped that this entering wedge will be driven home in a few years, and trade be unobstructed.

CHAPTER III.

MODERN ANTIQUITIES.

OUR antiquities are so modern, compared even with European (and they are but mere upstarts in comparison with the Egyptian and Asiatic), that the term scarcely seems applicable in America, except with respect to the mounds and ruins discovered in the West and South-west.

Among the most respectable in point of age and appearance of which Richmond can boast, is the *old stone house* of one story, on Main street, which dates probably A. U. C. 1.—and what is more remarkable has always been in the Egé family. May it long remain in its primitive and respectable condition, or according to the Spanish benediction, "may it live a thousand years." *

A steam corn mill and several other steam

---

* The benediction was vain. The melancholy announcement "To Rent" appears for the first time on the old door in 1858.

engines have lately intruded themselves as near
neighbors to the ancient and honorable stone
house. These mere upstarts are puffing and
blowing, and making all sorts of noises in the
very ears of Mr. Egé's descendants. It is enough
to arouse the old patriarch from his grave when
his old mansion is thus besieged—but if he were
to come, he would be astonished by the whistle
of the locomotive on one hand, and the blowing
off of a steamboat on the other, by lights in his
house without oil or candle, by the water of the
river flowing in his yard, and above all, by portraits of his great-grand children, taken " in no-
time " without pencil or brush; and when he turned
from these pictures, painted by sunbeams, and
looked through the deep casements of his window,
he would see something like a high clothes-line in
the street, along which people carry on a conversation with Boston or New Orleans—things never
dreamed of in his philosophy.

On the very summit of the high and steep hill
north-east of the Egé house, stands the old *Adams
Mansion*, a cotemporary probably, erected by the
ancient proprietor, whose domain was separated by
Shockoe creek from that of Col. Byrd, the founder
of Richmond—from whom he purchased it. That
mansion retains its primitive and picturesque appearance, and is kept in fine preservation by its
present worthy owner, Mr. Loftin Ellett. The

old *Parish Church of St. John's*, which was entitled to precedence for its sacred character, if not for its age, is preserved in its ancient simple architecture, with only the addition of a tower and belfry, which rising in pure white among the tall trees around it, presents one of the most beautiful and conspicuous objects in the many beautiful landscapes of which Richmond can boast.

The *Masonic Hall* deserves also to be mentioned among the "ancient and honorable" edifices. Its proportions are creditable to the architect, as its good preservation is to the brethren.

The oldest public house in Richmond was "*the Bird in hand*," on Main street, at the foot of Church hill, lately a ruinous hovel, but now embellished with a new front of brick-bats..

Dickens' eyes might even yet be relieved from the glare of new houses, by the sight of some moss-covered roofs of old wooden ones, cotemporaries of their neighbor, "the Bird in hand"—such as in Fredericksburg, reminded him of home.

A more modern, and a splendid house in its day, was the *City Tavern*, erected by Mr. Galt, of Williamsburg, and known as Galt's Tavern. "*Hotel*" was no more known then than in Meg Dod's palmiest days. But the old tavern having almost miraculously, as a wooden building, escaped conflagration, is now degraded to a workshop: The smoke-stack has succeeded the smoke-jack,

the table is displaced by the work-bench, and
wheels, bands and pullies revolve where minuets,
reels and congos were danced at a ball given in
honor of General Washington. *

A successor to the City Tavern rose on the
opposite side of the street, under the title of the
Union Hotel, but now called the "United States ;"
for taverns like rogues change their names when
they lose their characters, and this is a case of
reformation under new rulers, and frequent changes
of administration.

Bowler's Tavern stood where afterwards was
" the *Bell Tavern*," named after its Quaker
founder, and where now stands the *City Hotel*,
or of recent sanctification (Query: the appro-
priateness ?) the "*Saint Charles Hotel*."

Bowler's was a one story wooden house of an L
shape, standing on a bank some six feet or more
above the street, and reached by a flight of steps,
beneath which ran the gutter—sometimes a mill
stream in volume.

On some occasions the river, much more aspiring
than of late years, would submerge the street and
obstruct the approach to the house. An old
citizen who died some years ago, said that he had
paddled a canoe into Bowler's tavern—and a living

---

* It has shared the fate of most of its cotemporaries, having been destroyed by fire in 1858, while in the full exercise of
an industrious and useful old age.

one tells me he has crossed the street there in a boat.

The landlord was a figure to attract notice as a living model of departed fashions. His tall and burly form arrayed in fair-top boots, buff shorts, scarlet vest, green coat decked with large gilt buttons, a cocked hat; his rubicund face, surmounted by a carrot-colored wig, to the rear of which hung a long and thick queue stiffly enwrapped in black ribbon, except a short brush of hair peeping out at the lower end to show what it contained.

This queue oscillated like a pendulum half-way down his back, marking a section of a circle on his coat. A worthy and kind old gentleman was Major Bowler, and I have introduced him with no feeling of disrespect, but as a fine specimen of the fashion in his day.

In the rear of this tavern, on a steep hill-side, now cut down and occupied by livery stables and slave dealers, were the *Falling Gardens*, extending down to Shockoe Creek, and the residence of their proprietor, Mr. Lowndes, a fine type of the Quaker in garb and in personal appearance—with his broad-brimmed hat, drab suit, the coat of plainest cut without a superfluous button, waistcoat in same style, both of ample length and breadth, knee-breeches, gray stockings, and silver knee and shoe buckles. Many such figures were then to be seen in our streets; now not one, though some of the sect remain.

Just above his residence, and where now stands the *Odd Fellows' Hall*, on Franklin street, there stood on a hill nearly as high as is that Hall, two small brick buildings, with as much decoration of cornice and panel work as could well be displayed. These were traditionally (but incorrectly I am told) called the Auditor's and Treasurer's offices. They were erected by Henry Banks, as wings to a grand centre, which was designed to connect them; but some of Mr. B.'s speculations fell to the ground, and his palace never rose above it. He had the reputation, well-earned, of being a very litigious man, and on one occasion, meeting a gentleman of his acquaintance on horseback, he accosted him and remarked casually, "that horse, Mr. P., is very much like one that I had." "O, Mr. Banks," replied Mr. P., at the same time making a movement to dismount, "if you mean to claim the horse, do not bring suit, I will relinquish him rather than go to law."

The *Treasury* was a wooden house, afterwards occupied as a dwelling by Mr. James Brown, Jr., in the rear of his (now Mr. Webb's) large store. Its security must have rested more on the absence of temptation, than on the strength of the building. On the summit of the high hill, overlooking the Treasury, was the *Council Chamber*, which

5

until lately gave name to the hill. Attached to it was a piece of ground called the *Governor's Garden*, on the north-east side of Ross street, of which more anon. But the plain brick building in which "the potent, grave and reverend seignors" of the State assembled in the early years of the Commonwealth, has disappeared, as has the summit of the hill on which it stood. Ross street, and Mayo and College streets have bored deeply into it, exposing to view the impressions of vast beds of scallop and other shells, a few shark's teeth, and various unmistakable indications, that this lofty hill, overlooking the surrounding country, had once been at the bottom of the now distant ocean. In this, if in nothing else, we may lay claim to high antiquity.

The only other house on Ross street stood nearly opposite to the Council Chamber and had no claim to antiquity, but it excited admiration by the beauty of its elevated position and its Italian aspect. A centre building with wings, and a portico in the rear fronting the river displayed an arcade in the entire length of the edifice, commanding an extensive view of the city beneath, of the country around, of the river, its islands and its falls and its smooth water; with the sails of vessels glancing through the trees in the sinuosities of the stream; of yellow fields of wheat and green fields of corn, with a back-ground of forest, all

changing their dress with the changes of the
seasons; these combined to form an exquisite landscape. The residence here mentioned coated in
white, embosomed amid tall Lombardy poplars,
and the hill-side terraced as far down as Franklin
street, presented a charming aspect from the city
below. The first occupant of this spot that I remember, was James Strange, a Scotch merchant,
but an American citizen, with a majestic Virginia
wife. Their son was a conspicuous man in public
life in North Carolina. Their successor was
Thomas Gilliat, an English merchant, whose wife
and her sisters rendered the spot more attractive;
one of them has long graced the society of Norfolk.
The last occupant was Joseph Marx, a merchant of
German birth, but of pure American feelings; and
the attractions though changed, still continued.
While occupied by him, but during his absence, the
whole establishment was consumed by fire. A
block of brick dwellings now occupies the site
above, and the Metropolitan Hall, with other buildings and shanties, have supplanted the garden
below.* The pencil should depict such scenery as
this, to which the pen is entirely inadequate.

---

* A view of Richmond taken in 1805, is given as an embellishment to Bishop Madison's Map of Virginia. In that picture
this house and garden are conspicuous as are the Old Council
Chamber, Harris' tall house and various other objects recorded
in these pages.

The Council Chamber, and a portion of the beautiful hill on which it stood, became the property of Col. John Mayo: converted into a dwelling, it was his occasional city residence, when by way of variety his family left their country seat, north-west of the city, called the *Hermitage*, which was anything but a hermitage in point of seclusion; for there the reigning belle of the day, as well as other members of the family, attracted many visitors, and General Scott proved, by carrying her off against all competitors, that "none but the brave deserve the fair."

Bellville, the beautiful country-seat, named after the gentleman who built it, also became, in 1816, the property of Col. John Mayo at the price of $31,000 (far below the cost), and $28,000 for fourteen additional acres, and was thereafter the residence of the Mayo family; but both the Hermitage* and Bellville now present a melancholy aspect. Time and neglect have preyed on the one, and fire on the other, leaving bare walls only to mark the spot.

Another branch of the Mayo family has occupied, for nearly a century perhaps, a country-seat south-east of the city, called *Powhatan*, and reputed, no doubt correctly, to have been the site

* The Hermitage house was burnt in 1857, and part of the grounds were purchased in 1859, by the Agricultural Society, as an eligible spot on which to hold their fairs.

of a royal residence of the king whose name it bears; but it was not the scene of Pocahontas's romantic rescue of Captain Smith.

The Council-chamber residence was particularly convenient to Colonel Mayo, for with a spy-glass he could see from thence all that was passing on his bridge, a structure which—like the Pyramids of Egypt, each the work of the life-time of the Pharaoh who was to occupy it—kept the Colonel employed from the prime of youth to a ripe old age, and left a similar occupation to his successor.

The first *Capitol* in Richmond occupied a very humble site below this hill, and the homeliness of the building was adapted to its locality; but it may be questioned whether, in that mere wooden barn, more high talent, more political wisdom, and more polished gentility, were not assembled, than have been since in the marred copy of a beautiful Grecian temple, which, in its coat of shabby stucco, crowns the commanding summit of Capitol hill.

The *Old Capitol*, as it was called till it was demolished, was on Fourteenth (or modern Pearl) street, below Exchange alley, where Mr. Fry has erected some fine stores. The house was a plain one-story building, originally of small dimensions. From halls of legislation it was converted into counting rooms,—bills of exchange were drawn in place of legislative bills—bargain and sale superseded motions and enactments—for I dare be sworn that bargain and sale never polluted those Halls when occupied by the Fathers of the Republic, and I hope it cannot be truly charged on their successors. It is lamentable that the same cannot be predicated of the splendid Halls for all purposes at the seat of the Federal Government. There corruption stalks abroad in open day, and finds open doors and open hands to welcome her baseness and partake of her bounty, portending ruin to the republic.

An English firm, Donald & Burton, occupied the old Capitol, as did their successors, carrying on a very extensive business. The name of the last one, James Brown, being common to several other residents, caused the soubriquet of " Old Capitol Brown " to be applied to him, while others were variously distinguished. The last survivor of these synonymes still retains the designation of *Junior*, though he has nearly reached four score, and I hope his juniority will continue for many years more.* With him I will close this chapter of Modern Antiquities.

---

* This worthy gentleman died in his 79th year, Jannary 3d, 1859, in consequence of an injury received from a locomotive engine, while crossing the side-walk of Broad street.

CHAPTER IV.

MAIN STREET.

THE earliest impression on my mind of the appearance of the *Main street*, (and it was the only one on which the buildings were not " few and far between,") is that the houses were of wood, and generally of one or two stories in height. On the west of Shockoe creek two of these yet remain. One is a few doors below the spot where Bowler's, the Bell, the City, and St. Charles, have successively offered their accommodations to travellers; a small two story house, for many years past a tinner's shop, but very many years previously the property of the worthy " *Minton Collins, seedsman*," who showed his gratitude by bestowing it on the daughters of his hospitable friend Mr. Wiseham. The other wooden structure, which has escaped demolition—though time has nearly effected it—is the house at the corner of Main and Fourteenth or Pearl streets, and this, like some folks, artfully conceals its natural complexion and its antiquity, under an artificial exterior, a coat of plaster and paint, though it is sometimes betrayed by the laths. *

The Brick Row, thus distinguished of old for its exclusiveness, commenced at this spot, and extended up to what *was Crawford's Corner, now* the Dispatch office, corner of 13th street; where the same cannon has stood guard against the assaults of drays and wagons at least sixty years. The square diagonally above the old gun was, I think, the next that could boast of brick fronts, and these, where not replaced by new ones, now show marks of antiquity. The opposite square was the third to obtain such distinction, and its most conspicuous edifice was the *Eagle Tavern*. Pursuing an angular course from the upper corner of the *Eagle Square*, as it is still called, though the eagle has flown, we see the last of the brick rows that stood, at the beginning of the present century, on

---

* Half of this ancient edifice disappeared soon after it was recorded in these pages, and one of brick rose on the site, mounted on wooden stilts, between the legs of which a splendid display of jewelry shone through large windows of plate glass. But the most marked and to us novel distinction which this corner house presents, is "the Town Clock," for such name it merits, being the only public time-piece in the city that informs the eye and ear of the progress of time.

The State time-keeper retains its pristine simplicity after half a century's constant use. It is the only clock whose hand is one of flesh and blood, and which, without showing its face, strikes the hour all the year round, unless the operator should happen to be wound up instead of the prompting time-piece.

Main, between 11th and 12th streets, and that row
has risen a story, by an Irish process of depres-
sion; the street having been cut down until the
cellars were brought to light and converted into
shops. The only *four story* house in the city was
"*Harris's building,*" at the upper corner of the
square, and this grew up, or rather down, to be of
five stories, when its elevation (like Cardinal Wol-
sey's) caused its downfall; it had aspired above
the reach of its protectors, the fire engines, even
aided by the great Fire King, Sewall Osgood, and
it expired in a blaze, not more glorious than the
cardinal's, though like him, resigned to its fate, *i. e.*,
if as well insured in "The Mutual," as the cardinal was in the monastery. Seawell Osgood shall
also go down to posterity if I can carry him there.
He was more useful to the city than a host of
loud-mouthed, pot-house politicians, and served it
by a fluency and a use of liquids different from
theirs. Osgood was a Yankee blacksmith, and a
most prompt and efficient fireman. With the activity of a monkey, he would, in an instant, be
perched on the peak of a roof, or wherever the fire
was hottest and his efforts could be most available.
But Osgood's talents were adapted to every occasion. One for example: at the muster of a militia
company no musician was present. Osgood slung
the drum over his shoulder, and, with drum-stick
in his left hand and the flute in his right, he

tooted and rub-a-dubbed at the head of the company, which marked and kept time as correctly as
if they had the Armory band before them.

Nearly opposite to the present *Exchange Bank*
stood a large wooden building, which, in my youthful days, was *Mrs. Gilbert's Coffee House*; not a
news-room, but truly what its name imports; and
here tea, coffee and chocolate were dispensed to
customers, seated around the fire in winter, or at
the open windows in summer.   In after years, and
under other occupants, it assumed the name of the
Union, and afterwards the *Globe Tavern*, and it
closed its career, a few years ago, as an "oyster
and beef-steak house, with other refreshments,"
under a skillful mulatto woman, whose canvas
backs, soras and other delicacies of the season
attracted many customers.   The great Globe is
"dissolved, leaving not a wreck behind," and the
splendid store of Kent, Paine & Co., the first
specimen in Richmond of the Broadway style of
dry goods palaces, has risen on the spot.

Main street was then not a smooth road to travel
either on horseback or on foot.   No portion of the
carriage-way was paved, and the side-walks only
here and there, and with ups and downs.   The
dealers, who wished to entice the ladies to their
shops (stores, I beg pardon), would present a
paved entrance; those who sought rougher customers offered a rough reception, over gravel or

cobble stone. Dust in summer was insufferable, and in winter the mud would be ankle deep, and in some places "up to the hub." By way of making crossings, a narrow mound of ashes and cinders would be raised across the street, and woe to him or her who, on a dark night, deviated from the right path.

A small stream used to flow rather diagonally across Main street; its source was a spring or springs flowing from the hill which terminated below the present *Metropolitan Hall*, formerly the First Presbyterian Church; it passed in a trunk through *Byrd's warehouse*, and flowed along an alley, the entrance of which is now spanned by a wide arch at what lately was Mr. Womble's store, above Fourteenth street. Its course continued openly and boldly across Main street, but was then concealed until it emerged in Exchange alley, and flowed along Virginia and across Cary streets to the river. Sometimes with its affluents from the gutters, after a rain, it would spread over the entire surface of Virginia street, and convey to the river a liberal contribution of gravel and mud. All these vagaries are now hidden by a culvert, concealing, like the under-ground railroad, many foul movements.*

---

* This book certainly produced a sensation, as is noted in several instances. On its first appearance, as if to verify its statement, the culvert, which had lain concealed for fifty years,

A somewhat successful attempt was made by the residents on Main street, at about the close of the last century, to beautify it by planting trees; and Mr. Jefferson's (recently introduced) favorite exotic, the Lombardy poplar, which was then all the rage, was chosen above all the trees of the forest. It flourished, as many of its countrymen have on our soil, and its towering summits soon aspired to, and even overtopped the height of the chimneys; but pride must have a fall. The national plant of Virginia (unjustly stigmatized as a weed) may naturally be supposed to have become jealous of the foreign upstart that towered above her near her native fields at every homestead, and it is as natural to imagine that she induced the insects she had nourished to make an attack on the invader, and a successful one it proved. The great caterpillars were not recognized by the people as native tobacco worms, but were stigmatized as poisonous foreigners, and as being ungratefully introduced and nourished by the exotic themselves had cherished. The rage now took an opposite course. Evidence as strong was adduced against the caterpillars, as of yore against the witches, and the decision was equally just and fatal to both. The axe was put to the roots of the trees, and scarcely

caved in, and disclosed the stream, which should have been ashamed to expose itself in so filthy a condition.

one in all the region around survives to show the injustice of the sentence.

Main street did not extend far beyond Harris's house (Eleventh street) in habitable guise, in those days. Gullies and swamps crossed its path. Where *Tan-bark-hall* stood, and Bosher's row stands,* were the tan-yards of Bockius and McKechnie. A path of tan bark or of boards enabled pedestrians to reach the nearly uninhabited regions beyond, but carriages rarely ventured through the swamp or up the ascent beyond it. The eaves of the houses used by the tanners were not so high as the present foot-way. There was a good skating pond in winter on the lot on the north side of the street. The family of McKim owned and resided on the property where Corinthian Hall and other buildings now rear their tall heads, in place of the ancient and lowly structures lately removed. This portion of the city from Fifth to Eleventh street has undergone great transformations—it was originally hills, valleys and even morass; indeed similar inequalities existed everywhere except on the summits of the hills. The levelings recently made or now in progress north of Marshall street, are an illustration of those made south of Grace street. Indeed the original and the present sur-

---

* This row was demolished in 1859, to make room for a large hotel and other extensive edifices—being the 3d edition or erection of them, (1860).

6

face of the city may be compared to the contrast
of the waves in a storm, and their subsidence
during a calm.

Quite a rural and romantic spot was the square
on the north side of Main street, between Sixth
and Seventh—a steep hill, and a little valley
shaded with forest trees ; a spring, the water of
which formed a pond for fishing and skating—the
silence broken only by the singing of birds, the
croaking of frogs or the sports of children.

Now it is one of the noisest spots in the city—
filled with work-shops, with machinery propelled
by steam for preparing all sorts of building materials in wood, iron, stone or stucco, as are the
adjacent squares.

I ought to apologize for pursuing a devious
course, for I now descend from the upper end of
Main street to the south-west end of the market
bridge, where was the parterre of Mons. Didier
Colin, Perruquier, extending from his house down
to the margin of Shockoe creek. Looking over
the parapet of the bridge, the pedestrian might
have his senses regaled with the sight and smell of
various flowers in their season. The spot on which
they grew is now covered with brick buildings, but
the creek, not reconciled to the encroachment,
sometimes rises in its wrath and drives the invaders
from their watery regions.

A place of great public resort during many

years after about 1810, for politicians, quidnuncs, stock-jobbers, and in general those who had nothing else to do, was *Lynch's Coffee House*, two doors below the Globe, which Mr. Lynch had vacated. Here all the news, foreign and domestic, rumors true or false, scandal and tittle-tattle centered, and from hence it was diffused, with increased vigor at each corner round which it circulated. Here windy talkers would blow their bellows, and tedious ones tire their listeners; but here also men of note might frequently be listened to, and here Mr. Lynch held his stock auctions. The most difficult thing at this reading-room, was a quiet perusal of the papers; but with all its disadvantages, it was an useful place of resort, where a-body could meet a-body; and it does no credit to Richmond, that a reading-room cannot now be well sustained; it must be ascribed to the great industry of its merchants and professional men, who have no time to spare.

At Lynch's during times of political excitement, as soon as the papers were obtained from the post office, he would open the most important one and read the news aloud to the assembled multitude. During the war with Great Britain, and when General Scott was on the Canadian frontier, he read aloud " the army is *in statu quo*." " Indeed!" said one of his hearers, "how far is that from Montreal?" And on another occasion he announced "Congress is to be called together *instanter*." "Dear me!" said a listener "are they afraid to meet in Washington?" The site of Lynch's Coffee House and the adjacent buildings, was previously that of John Graham's cottage and vineyard.

A ludicrous incident occurred on the Main Street near "The Bell," one fine spring morning. A horse took fright in the street and rushed into the passage of a house, at the rear of which was the stair-way. Terror urged him on, and up he went till he reached the front room on the second floor. There he became composed, walked round the breakfast table, and may have helped himself to a roll, then to the open window, where he put out his head and looked (as idle and curious folks are apt to do) to see what was passing in the street. No fair face that ever looked from that window excited such general admiration.

Whether the aspiring steed took breakfast before he took leave, or whether he said *neigh* to the invitation, is not recorded in the Chronicles, but after offering his back to the ladies, he did not turn it on them, but backed out in courtly fashion.

CHAPTER V.

BROAD STREET.

Some sixty years ago or more, *Broad street* (or rather, broad road,) contained few houses, except at its two extremities, which were First and Twelfth streets. The trade with Staunton and from both sides of the Blue Ridge was carried on by means of large four or six-horse wagons; and as they entered the city at the head of Broad street, small dealers established themselves there to meet the trade. The name of one of them yet remains in the identical spot occupied by that of his grandfather James Bootwright in the last century, on the first house on First street, and when he recently died, we then lost "the oldest inhabitant." * His cotemporary, Gathwright, at the opposite corner, was his friendly rival in trade during some thirty or forty years. The wagons came laden with flour, butter, hemp, wax, tallow, flaxseed, lead, feathers, deer and bear skins, furs, ginseng, snake-root, &c.; and I once saw a bunch

---

* The name of Bootwright, which had held its place over the door longer than any other in the city, was removed in 1859.

of dried rattlesnakes, which I was told were useful
to make viper broth for consumptive patients.
Rattlesnakes seem to have been considered a delicacy, even amongst the higher classes, in olden
times; for Col. Byrd, in his "Journal to the Land
of Eden," (on Roanoke river,) says: "We killed
two very large rattlesnakes, of fifteen and twelve
rattles; they were both fat, but nobody would be
persuaded to carry them to our quarters, although
they would have added much to the luxury of
our supper." As they had venison and wild turkey, they could not have been in a starving condition.

A portion of the wagoners traded on Broad
street, but by far the larger number, and especially of those who brought loads from country
merchants, drove down town. That trade was
chiefly in the hands of four or five city merchants;
and the fleets of wagons that would assemble, in
brisk times, near their stores, looked like the bag-
gage train of a small army. Many of the wagons,
however, came by another road, through the
Southern Valley, from Abingdon, and that region
was even then a wealthy one, from its mineral and
agricultural products. As specie *only* circulated
in that remote country, one of the expedients
resorted to by the merchants there to make remit-
tances to Richmond, was, to place a bag of gold or
silver in the centre of a cask of melted wax or

tallow, or to conceal the silver within a large bale of hemp.

Such a journey, over such roads as were then travelled, was a work of time and toil. Almost a month then, for what is accomplished in one or two days now, from the Salt Works in Wythe (now Washington) county, to Richmond.

To reach Broad street from Main street, was almost as difficult a task as the ascent of a small mountain. Thirteenth, or Governor street, was at the same base then as now, but the present (reduced) height of the Governor's grounds, on that street, indicate its former ascent, which was furrowed with gullies. The only other route was across the Capitol square, diagonally from Eleventh to Ninth street, near where St. Paul's Church now stands. This road, as well as the other, was usually washed into gullies by every hard rain, and the stiff red clay would sometimes form almost a compact mass between the spokes of wagon wheels.

A most dilapidated old wooden house on Broad street, west of Sixth, or a portion of it, is now (1856) in course of demolition. It has long been an eye-sore to passengers. Of late years the upper part has been the nestling place of families of the *plebeian* class of free negroes (for they have their grades,) and the class of the occupants was obvious at the windows, which were decorated, and also

protected against the intrusion of light and air, by
old hats and bundles of rags. The cellar was also
sometimes a receptacle for rags, besides old iron,
broken glass, and other commodities, destined, in
regenerated forms, possibly, to aid in the decoration of a palace. Between these upper and lower
regions, (the one not tenanted by angels nor the
other by devils,) was the ground floor, on which
were shops for the sale of old raiment for the outer
man, some of it almost fit for the window blinds of
the upper or the rag-bags of the lower tenants;
and, for the comfort of the inner man was presented a cheap repast of cow-heel, tripe, and
hoe-cake, or a refreshing dram, whose spirit was
not betrayed by its color. To complete the conve-
niences of this bazaar, there was a receptacle for
dilapidated furniture—tables and chairs, scarcely
able to stand on their own legs, much less to sustain the dishes that were to be served, or the
guests that were to be seated on them—cradles
without rockers, and bedsteads already occupied.
This description applies, however, to only two-
thirds of the extensive premises—the other third
may perhaps be a dower right, and, consequently,
if a lady's property, much better cared for.
Whilst the rest of the ancient edifice has been the
victim first of disgrace, and now of demolition, the
remaining portion seems to be occupied as a thriving shop for the sale of all sorts of commodities for

daily use and consumption. Its neat block cornice
and ancient front only require a coat of paint to
restore its good looks—like some other faded
antiquities.* The gutter in front was sometimes
enlivened by the prattle of ragged and dirty and
happy children, who were busily employed in
making dirt pies, and baking them in dirt ovens,
moulded on their bare feet; while a few chickens
pecked and scratched on the unpaved sidewalk,
unless frightened off by a hungry dog, who en-
vied them the invisible repast, which they seemed
to enjoy.

My first recollection of this populous habitation,
was when the sign of *Richard's Tavern* swung
before the door; the portico occupied by inveterate
tobacco chewers, who kept the footway well
sprinkled for some yards before them, but this was
in the middle age of the ancient structure, which
was probably coeval with the survey of the street
on which it stood, near the entrance of the town
and on the great highway to it of the "outer inhabitants," as Col. Byrd designated the people of
the upper country. It was originally, no doubt,
the principal "house of entertainment" for those
outsiders. The dusty or more generally miry

---

* The hint was taken and the paint applied, but the spirit of
improvement has now gone further, and the last remnant of
Richard's tavern and a row of adjoining old houses are razed,
and new ones are being raised. 1860.

street in front of it, was made lively by the fleets of wagons from the Blue Ridge, and vocal with the jingling of the peals of bells, attached to the harness of the stout horses, who seemed proud of the music, as well as of the bear-skin mantillas which protected their withers, of the rosettes of red and yellow galoon which decorated their bridles, and of the same gaudy materials with which their plaited tails were tied—when not in fly time.

Now-a-days, we occasionally see one of these mountain ships; but the muddy road they toiled through in former days, is now traversed by the iron horse, and his piercing screams have silenced the grateful neighings of his noble predecessor.

In the early days of the house last described, Main street was not practicable west of Eleventh, nor was Ninth street a highway, or rather, it was a *high way*, not to be ascended to Broad street by wheels. The formation of Broad street across the valley is in the memory of many of my readers, if many I shall have; formerly it was practicable only to goats, which were then numerous, but it is now being built up with wooden houses, thero being no foundation for brick ones.

CHAPTER VI.

THE CAPITOL AND THE SQUARE.

THE *Capitol Square* was originally as rugged a piece of ground as many of our hill-sides in the country exhibit, after a ruinous course of cultivation. Deep ravines furrowed it on either side, and May and Jamestown weeds decorated and perfumed it in undisturbed luxuriance. On either side of the capitol was a long horse-rack, for the convenience of the public and to diversify the odor. In front of the portico stood an unpainted wooden belfry, somewhat resembling the dairies we see at good farm-houses. The portico might then be reached by a narrow, winding stone stairway, now closed, which gave to the goats and kids, who sported in numbers about the grounds, a convenient access to the portico, where they found shelter in wet weather. A few of the original forest trees, oaks and pines, which had escaped the barbarous refinement of clearing away native growths to be supplanted by exotics, constituted the only relief to the dismal aspect of the grounds, except a few chinquepin bushes, which served to prick the fingers of boys in due season, and a copious and luxuriant growth of thistles, whose down, in a good breeze, resembled a snow storm.

Between the Governor's house and the Capitol was a high stone wall, near the line of the street, built to close the upper end of an immense ravine (now a shady dell), and over this wall, after a heavy fall of rain, flowed a great body of water, forming a fine rose-tinted cascade.

The *Guard-house* and belfry, now rather disfiguring the square, was preceded by a much uglier edifice: a shabby, old second-hand wooden house, occupied as barracks by the Public Guard, under the command of Captain Quarrier. The grounds immediately around it were bedecked with the shirts of the soldiers and the chemises of their wives, which flaunted on clothes-lines, and pigs, poultry and children enlivened the scene.

The *Capitol* itself, not then stuccoed, exposed its bare brick walls between the columns or pilasters. The roof was once flat, if I mistake not, and paved with tiles, and, like Noah's Ark, "was pitched without, with pitch." But as a hot sun caused the pitch to flow down the gutters, and the rains to enter the halls, an elevated roof was substituted. In process of time, the attic thus formed was converted into an arsenal, the building and the fire-arms being perhaps considered fire-proof, or the risk not considered at all. Even at this day, a most valuable deposit, the *State Library*, is at risk in the combustible upper part of the Capitol, and the inestimable *statue of Washington*, by *Houdon*, may one day be destroyed, as was Canova's splendid one at Raleigh, N. C. A handsome fire-proof building should be erected for the preservation of both, and of other objects of value.*

The *Governor's House* preceding the present one, was a very plain wooden building of two stories, with only two moderate sized rooms on the first floor. It was for many years unconscious of paint, and the furniture was in keeping with the republican simplicity of the edifice, and of its occupants, from Henry and Jefferson down to Monroe and Page. The palings around the yard were usually in a dilapidated condition, and the goats that sported on the steep hill-sides of the Capitol Square, claimed and exercised the liberty of grazing on his Excellency's grounds.

The cows are now endeavoring to establish a similar claim to the grass and onions on the public square in the very face of the sentry.†

---

* Governor Wise has followed up this suggestion and wisely recommended the erection of such an edifice (1857), but to no purpose.

† Since writing the above, posts have been planted at each gate, about twelve inches apart, which, while they exclude the cows, may also practically exclude fashionable ladies from the Capitol Square, now that the *Eugénie hoops* have become in vogue, and are adopted indiscriminately by those who have or have not the same motive that induced the Empress to intro-

7

The old residence of the Governors of Virginia might usually have boasted that, if it had in itself no claims to distinction, its occupants had many.

Two articles of furniture of the colonial times are extant in the Capitol, namely: the *Speaker's chair* of the House of Burgesses, originally decorated with the royal arms; this was removed from Williamsburg, and is now, though shorn of its regal emblems, occupied by the Speaker of the House of Delegates:—and secondly, the tall *stove* which warmed those colonial and independent halls, in succession, for about sixty years, and for the last twenty-five has served to warm the central hall, in which stands Houdon's statue of Washington. This stove, a work of note, bears the old Virginia colonial arms and other embellishments in relief, and they remain perfect, being as indestructible as the structure they decorate, for the stove is truly a structure of three stories.

The founder of it, Buzaglo, was proud of his work, and when it was shipped from London, he thus writes to "My Lord," (Botetourt,) dated August 15th, 1770: " *The elegance of workmanship does honour to Great Britain. It excels in grandeur anything ever seen of the kind, and is a master-piece not to be equalled in all Europe. It*

---

duce them. It is impracticable for a fashionable hoop, without considerable coaxing, to pass between the barriers which are placed to obstruct the entrance of the cows. 1856.

has met with general applause, and could not be sufficiently admired"!!! The reader is advised to draw a long breath, and pause awhile, till his admiration subsides.

This "warming machine," as Buzaglo called it, this master-piece of art and science, doomed to carry his name to posterity, was presented to the House of Burgesses by the Duke of Beaufort. It has survived three British monarchs, and been cotemporaneous with three kingly monarchies, two republics and two imperial governments in France—but of only one constellation of republics in the United States,—I hope and trust "*one and indivisible, now and forever!*"

The grounds of the Capitol Square were originally laid out by Mons. Godefroï, a French gentleman of skill and taste, according to the formal style, where

"Grove nods at grove, each alley has its brother,
And half the terrace just reflects the other."

He certainly reduced chaos to order, and made the grounds very handsome, and wonderfully uniform, considering their original irregularity. But now "half the terrace" does not "reflect the other;" The west side has been modernized according to an irregular plan, adapted to it by Mr. Notman, of Philadelphia. Some dozen flights of stone steps are dispensed with; the straight lines of trees are

being gradually thrown into disorder. But the
east side, like a prim old maid, retains its formality
for the present, and serves to show the contrast
between the formal and the picturesque styles.*
But the great and striking embellishment of the
square will be the *Washington Monument*,† now
ready for the erection of the statuary on their
pedestals.

The succeeding generation will have no idea
of the original surface of Richmond, from that
which will be presented to their view. Besides
the changes noted elsewhere, there existed a few
years ago a complete barrier to the progress of
man and horse, north of Leigh street from Fourth
to Fourteenth, by the intervention of a deep
ravine, which has now (1860) been filled up on
Fourth and Fifth, and is being filled on the higher
numbers. Another ravine cut off the communication between Clay and Leigh streets from Sixth to
Fourteenth or further. The intercourse is now
opened on Sixth, Seventh, Eighth and Ninth, and
a stack or chimney (for water, not fire), about 100
feet high, is now being erected on Tenth, down
which the water will flow from Clay and from
Leigh streets, when the chasm between them shall

---

* The east side has also been changed and beautified.

† The incomparable equestrian statue of Washington, by
Crawford, was erected and inaugurated February 22d, 1858.

be filled. Marshall street, a few years ago, was closed at Twelfth by a profound ravine, which is now overcome as far as College street—but the heaviest work yet executed, has been the present easy connection of Shockoe hill with Church hill along the line of Broad street, which seemed almost impracticable. The extension of Franklin street from Fourteenth to Seventeenth along precipices and deep gullies is another strong case. It would be wearisome, if not so already, to describe the changes south of Broad street. In a word, the city was all hills, valleys and deep ravines, and had a most forbidding aspect. This page is written for readers in Richmond in 1900.

In the days of my boyhood springs of cool water flowed from various spots at the base of Shockoe hill, along its whole extent from Fifth to Fourteenth streets, and the number of them was considerable, as was their utility. It is but a few years ago that one which discharged itself on Thirteenth street, below the Governor's house, was condemned to flow under the pavement into the culvert; one of the two in the Capitol Square is permitted to discharge its waters near the Court house, far from the spot where they formerly rose. Its brother on the west side of the Capitol was condemned a few years ago and buried alive. On almost every square (west of the Capitol) that sloped to the foot of the hill there was a spring—

Hay's, Blair's, Dobie's, Graham's and Hay's again. They all continue to flow in obscurity, no doubt, but the kindness of Nature in bestowing them on thirsty man and beast, and on the arid earth, is no longer estimated—like benefactors whose gifts are forgotten, when no longer enjoyed.

BLACK COCKADES AND TRI-COLORED.

I have a faint recollection of seeing cockades mounted in the hats of many gentlemen, toward the close of Washington's administration.

A black rosette denoted the attachment of the wearer to the policy of Washington; that of strict neutrality toward England and France, when the latter violated our nationality by fitting out privateers from our ports and sending prizes into them; and when the former had very unwisely espoused the cause of her old enemies, the dethroned Bourbons.

The partisans of France decorated their hats with the tri-color (as if they had no nationality of their own), sung *Ca Ira* and *Carmagnole*, and accused their opponents of being monarchists or aristocrats, because they did not rejoice with them and make bonfires, when Louis and Maria Antoinette were guillotined, and because they supported Washington when he no longer recognized the French minister and consuls, who had violated our laws; as another minister and other consuls of another power have done more recently.

Such was, if I am correct, the origin of the opprobrious epithet "Black Cockade Federalist," applied by their political opponents, in after years, to those who had been the advocates of law and national rights and the supporters of Washington.

It may be asked, why is this subject introduced in a volume on Richmond? The reply is that Richmond was one of the strongholds of Federalism, and black cockades were the prevailing fashion, and when the emblem disappeared, the principles remained unchanged through more than one generation.

CHAPTER VII.*

OLD RESIDENCES AND THEIR OCCUPANTS.

WHEN *Shockoe hill* began to change its aspect from fields and forests, to streets and squares, the

---

* Kind reader, if you have no local nor personal attachment to Richmond, pardon for the sake of those who have, a portion of this and the next chapter, which to you may seem mere twaddle, but to them, (and for them it is written,) and to their children it may be an interesting record.

I have, however, to relieve the extreme dryness of some of the pages, ventured to intersperse occasionally an anecdote, which though stale to my old readers, may be fresh to the younger ones.

larger portion of the latter were held by wealthy and by professional gentlemen. The bar of Richmond toward the close of the last century possessed a greater number of members of distinguished talent, than almost any other in the Union, and many of them resided on Shockoe hill.

To each residence, with few exceptions, was attached the ground of an entire square of two acres, or at least that of half a square. A strong contrast to what may now be seen, when the old domicile and its appurtenances are supplanted and occupied by twenty or more tenements. If the crowding system continues to contract our space, we may presently emulate the bee-hive system of some parts of Baltimore, where a man can scarcely stand with his arms a-kimbo on his front steps, without jostling his neighbor, should he happen to be in a similar position.

Among the oldest and most respectable of the occupants of Shockoe hill was the Ambler family, of which the *Treasurer, Jaquelin Ambler* was the head *—his own residence yet stands, between

---

* The name of Jaquelin, was derived from the celebrated Huguenot family of La Roche Jaquelin of La Vendée. Edward Jaquelin, came to Virginia in 1697, settled in Jamestown, and married a Miss Cary. Their eldest daughter, Elizabeth, married Richard Ambler, an emigrant from Yorkshire, who settled in Yorktown as a merchant. His son Jaquelin, the Treasurer, married Rebecca, daughter of Lewis Burwell, and their daughters were the ladies here mentioned. Their son, John Ambler, inherited the estate of Jamestown, a large farm.

Marshall and Clay streets, and is occupied by his last surviving son-in-law.

A letter written by one of the daughters of Treasurer Ambler, on the removal of the family to the new seat of Government at Richmond, gives a lively description of it in that day:

"It is indeed a very lovely situation, and may at some future period be a great city, but it will at present afford scarcely one comfort of life. With the exception of two or three families, the little town is made up of Scotch factors, who inhabit small tenements here and there, from the river to the hill, some of them looking, as Col. Marshall observes, as if the poor Caledonians had brought them over on their backs; the weaker of whom were glad to stop at the foot of the hill, others a little stronger, proceeded higher, while a few of the strongest and boldest reached the summit, which once accomplished affords a situation beautiful and picturesque. One of these hardy Scots has thought proper to vacate his little dwelling on the hill, and though our family can scarcely stand up together in it, my father has determined to rent it, as the only decent tenement on the hill."

The house here spoken of stands next to St. James' Church on Fifth street, in larger dimensions than it originally possessed, in perfect preservation and neat in appearance.

The writer is indebted to Bishop Meade's History of Old Churches in Virginia for this letter of the lady, who was afterwards Mrs. Carrington, and the gentleman she speaks of, was afterwards Chief Justice Marshall, her brother-in-law.

Mr. Ambler's daughters were married to gentle-

men who built their dwellings not far from the
paternal mansion, and a distinguished circle they
formed. *Chief Justice (then General) Marshall*
is entitled to priority. His residence yet stands
on the street named in his honor, the only house
on that street coeval with the present century,
except one or two ruinous wooden ones, but the
grounds have been reduced to a fraction of their
original extent, and a number of fine dwellings
have been erected in his former garden, between
Eighth and Ninth streets. Of Judge Marshall I
will not presume to say more than that his personal appearance and deportment as a citizen were
of the most unpretending character—of true
republican simplicity—but natural, not assumed—
his dress was plain even to negligence, of which he
seemed unconscious. He marketed for himself,
and might be seen at an early hour returning
home, with a pair of fowls, or a basket of eggs in
his hand, not with ostentatious humility, but for
mere convenience. His style of travelling to and
from Raleigh, N. C., about 175 miles each way, to
preside at the Federal Court held there, was for
many years, in that primitive sort of vehicle, a
stick gig (or chair as it was then called), with one
horse and with no attendant. The modest and
unassuming simplicity of his character is evinced to
the last, in the inscription which he directed for
his tombstone :

"John Marshall, son of Thomas and Mary Marshall, was born the 24th of September, 1755. Intermarried with Mary Willis Ambler, the 3d of January, 1783. Departed this life the 6th of July, 1835."

During many of the latter years of her life, Mrs. Marshall was unable to attend Church; and on every Sunday before he went there, Judge Marshall read the morning service to her. After her death, he continued to perform the same devotion, seated in the same chair, near to the one which she had occupied, as if her spirit accompanied his to the Heavenly Throne.

When his will was opened there was found within its folds an euloguim on his wife, from which I am permitted by one of her neices to make the following extract; it was written in his own hand December 25th, 1832:

"This day of joy and festivity to the whole Christian world is, to my sad heart, the anniversary of the keenest affliction which humanity can sustain. While all around is gladness, my mind dwells on the silent tomb, and cherishes the remembrance of the beloved object which it contains.

"On the 25th of December, 1831, it was the will of Heaven to take to itself the companion who had sweetened the choicest part of my life; had rendered toil a pleasure, had partaken of all my feelings, and was enthroned in the inmost recess of my heart. Never can I cease to feel the loss and to deplore it. Grief for her is too sacred ever to be profaned on this day, which shall be, during my existence, marked by a recollection of her virtues.

"On the 3rd of January, 1783, I was united by the holiest bands to the woman I adored. From the hour of our union, to that of our separation, I never ceased to thank Heaven for this its best gift. Not a moment passed in which I did not consider her as a blessing from which the chief happiness of my life was derived. This never dying sentiment, originating in love, was cherished by a long and close observation of as amiable and estimable qualities as ever adorned the female bosom. To a person which in youth was very attractive; to manners uncommonly pleasing; she added a fine understanding, and the sweetest temper which can accompany a just and modest sense of what was due to herself. She was educated with a profound reverence for religion, which she preserved to her last moments. This sentiment, among the earliest and deepest impressions, gave a coloring to her whole life. Hers was the religion taught by the Saviour of man. She was a firm believer in the faith inculcated by the Church (Episcopal) in which she was bred.

"I have lost her!' and with her, have lost the solace of my life! Yet she remains still the companion of my retired hours; still occupies my inmost bosom. When alone, and unemployed, my mind still recurs to her. More than a thousand times since the 25th of December, 1831, have I repeated to myself the beautiful lines written by General Burgoyne under a similar affliction, substituting 'Mary' for 'Anna:'

"Encompassed in an Angel's frame,
    An Angel's virtues lay;
Too soon did Heaven assert its claim,
    And take its own away!
My Mary's worth, my Mary's charms,
    Can never more return!
What now shall fill these widowed arms?
    Ah, me! my Mary's urn!
    Ah, me! ah, me! my Mary's urn!"

Judge Marshall erected a dwelling immediately opposite to his own, for his eldest son, Thomas, who did not long occupy it. He and his brothers preferred to reside in Fauquier county, on farms obtained from their father, who bought part of the great Fairfax estate there. Thomas, in the prime of life and of usefulness as a good citizen, was killed in Baltimore by the fall of a brick from the walls of the Court-house.

Col. *Edward Carrington*, also a soldier of the Revolution, married another of the Misses Ambler, a most excellent lady, as was each of her sisters. He was a member of the Old Congress in 1785–6. The high estimation in which Col. Carrington was held by his personal friend General Washington, is shown by his connecting him with Gen. St.Clair and Alexander Hamilton, in 1780, in a commission to meet commissioners on the part of the enemy for settling a general cartel; by his offering him in 1795 the department of War, and consulting him as to persons proposed for other departments, and by selecting him to be Quarter-master General, when in 1798 war with France was expected, and an organization of officers formed for the crisis.

Under John Adams's administration, Colonel Carrington held the office of Commissioner of the Revenue of the United States for Virginia; direct taxes being then resorted to, in consequence of the depredations on our commerce.

8

The very humble edifice, yet standing, shaded
by an old Catalpa tree, at the north-west corner
of Marshall and Eleventh streets, was the office
of the Commissioner.* His residence, which was
demolished a few years ago, was on the same
square, fronting on Clay street. Col. Carrington
was a man of dignified deportment, which was well
sustained by his tall and massive figure. He was
a pure patriot, and pure in all the relations of life.
He died October 28th, 1810, aged 61.

Daniel Call, a distinguished lawyer, married
another of the sisters Ambler, and his residence on
the square between the Capitol and Broad street,
was also taken down a few years ago to be substituted by Mr. Valentine's large store.

Mr. Call was a very tall, thin man, loosely
jointed, so that when he walked his arms had a
great swing, and his head moved from shoulder to
shoulder; when he sat, his legs would be twisted
round each other, and his jaws even seemed to partake of the general relaxation—but not so with his
mind. His high position at the bar, and at such a
bar as Richmond possessed, was a sufficient proof
of the strength of his mental powers. To give a
little variety to what the reader may find dull, the
following anecdote may not come amiss: A client
entered Mr. Call's office, and found him writing.

---

* Demolished in June, 1858.

He took a seat and told Mr. Call he wanted his legal advice—(let us put it in dialogue form):

Client—"My father died and made a will."

Mr. Call—(Writing steadily)—"You say your father died and made a will!"

Client—"Yes, sir, my father died and made a will."

Mr. Call—(Still writing and paying no attention)—"Humph."

Client—"I say, Mr. Call, my father died and made a will."

Mr. Call—"Very strange!" (writing and not noticing the man.)

Client—(Taking out his purse and laying a fee on the table)—"Mr. Call, I say again, my father made a will and died."

Mr. Call—(All attention)—"O, now we understand each other; your father made a will before he died. Why didn't you say so at first? Well, now go on, let's hear."

George Fisher married a fourth sister, and he, a retired merchant, and one of our oldest citizens, was the survivor of all that I have mentioned, and the occupant of the patriarchal mansion of Treasurer Ambler, on Marshall, between Ninth and Tenth streets.*

---

* Mr. Fisher died on the 25th March, 1857, in his 82d year. The old homestead is sold, and the grounds around it are covered with handsome houses, but it still retains its ancient air of respectability (1860).

One brother, *Major Ambler*, had his residence on Clay, between Eleventh and Twelfth streets, nearly opposite to Col. Carrington's, on the brow of the hill commanding a splendid landscape, where Mrs. Bruce's fine mansion has supplanted its ruinous predecessor.* Previous to Major Ambler's occupancy, it was the residence of Lewis Burwell, a gentleman of the old school in dress and style of living.

On the western half of the same square *Dr. Brockenbrough* built a large house, (now Mr. Caskie's,) but not being satisfied with it, he built a much more costly one, (now Mr. Crenshaw's,) at the natural terminus of Marshall and Twelfth streets. Dr. B. was for many years Cashier, and for many subsequent ones President of the Bank of Virginia. He became proprietor of the Warm Springs, where he died in 1853.

On the opposite square resided Judge *Philip Norborne Nicholas*. He married Miss Byrd, a lineal descendant of the founder of Richmond. The death of her brother, Colonel Francis Otway Byrd, late a resident of Clarke county, is just announced (May, 1860.) He served under Gen'l Scott, in the war of 1812.

The distinguished jurist and statesman, *Benjamin Watkins Leigh*, lived for some years in this

---

* Since the death of that excellent lady it has passed out of the family (1859).

neighborhood (corner of Clay and Tenth), in a house built for Dr. McClurg, whose granddaughter, Miss Wickham, was Mr. L.'s third wife. J. M. Gregory, Esq., is now the occupant. A much more stately edifice has arisen near it.

Mr. Leigh was a politician of unswerving principle and of spotless purity. One of a class less rare in by-gone than in later days, but not yet entirely extinct. Not to be met with, however, in the crooked and devious paths which now lead to office, if not to honor; and into which so many of all parties have strayed from the broad high road of disinterested patriotism.

On the square east of Treasurer Ambler's, was the mansion of Col. John Harvie, Register of the Land office. He removed to the fine country seat Belvidere, built by Col. Byrd, the son of the founder of Richmond, beyond its western limit, and commanding an extensive view of the surrounding country. After passing through various hands, its last occupants were a number of families of iron workers, and thus, "fallen from its high estate," it was recently destroyed by fire.

Burnaby, an English clergyman, who published a book of travels a century ago, speaks of Belvidere as *a* beautiful seat of Col. Byrd in 1759.

The city residence of Col. Harvie, shaded by noble elms, became that of the celebrated lawyer, *John Wickham*, the eloquent, the witty and the graceful. After him, it had many successive occupants.

TO A FAIR FRIEND, WHO WAS AMONG THE LATEST
OF THESE, AND ONE OF THE BRIGHTEST, GENTLEST
AND FAIREST THAT HAD GRACED THOSE HALLS, AND
WHO GRACED EVERY STATION THAT SHE OCCUPIED,
IN PROSPERITY OR IN ADVERSITY, IN WHOSE VEINS
FLOWS (LONG MAY IT FLOW) THE BLOOD OF A SISTER
OF WASHINGTON, THESE PAGES ARE DEDICATED.

Mr. Wickham sold this residence, and erected a splendid dwelling on the same square. The site of the former one is now occupied by the spacious edifice of the Baptist Female Institute.

The writer feels an unaffected diffidence in speaking of distinguished men with whom he had little or no intercourse, for there was a lapse of twenty-five years, during which he was not a resident of Richmond, yet he trusts to be pardoned for introducing into his pages something, however inadequate, respecting its prominent citizens.

Mr. Wickham was a gentleman of the most elegant and graceful deportment, of the most polished and easy manners; full of wit and reparteee, and whether at the bar or at the festive board, always distinguished—profound as a lawyer, brilliant as a companion.

The following passage between him and Mr. George Hay, in court, is given as a slight instance of his repartee: Mr. Hay was a man of fine per-

sonal appearance, of very dignified manners, and
withal, rather pompous. He also was a lawyer of
considerable eminence. These two gentlemen were
employed as joint counsel in an important suit, and
when it was about to be called Mr. Wickam asked
Mr. Hay to open the case, which he declined to
do. Mr. W. repeated the request in more urgent
terms some two or three times, until Mr. H., in
a somewhat excited manner, said: " Sir, I will not
be made a catspaw of." " O !" replied Mr. W.,
in the most complaisant manner and gentlest tone,
"then, *I* will be the catspaw and *you* shall be
the —" He left the last word to inference.

A son of Col. Harvie, with a higher military
title, and who married a daughter of Judge Marshall, built on and occupies the square north of the
Ambler house.*

On Marshall street, opposite to the Ambler
square, we now pass the former residence of *Benjamin Botts*, a learned member of the bar, who
was one of the victims of the conflagration at the
theatre, in 1811. He was the father of John
Minor Botts, the conspicuous politician. His local
but not his immediate successor, was the eminent
and distinguished lawyer, *Chapman Johnson*, who

---

* This gentleman died since the above was written, and his
mansion has been sold and re-sold. His daughters occupy
that of their grandfather, Judge Marshall, who bequeathed it
to them, (1857).

left Staunton for the more extensive forensic field
of Richmond, where most of the higher courts
were concentrated, and where there was an ample
field for the exercise of his talents ; but incessant
labors in his profession wore out his vision and
indeed weakened his mental faculties, which were
exerted to attain a competency,

> " Not for to hide it in a hedge, nor for a train attendant,
>   But for the glorious privilege of being independent."

His form and features bore Nature's impress of
nobility. His son, Carter Page Johnson, was one of
the professors in the Richmond Medical College,
and was lost in the steamer Arctic, on his return
from a visit to Europe in 1854, and Carter's brother,
George Nicolson Johnson, a lawyer of established
and increasing celebrity, did not long survive him.

On the same square with Mr. Botts's, stands the
many-angled house erected by Alexander McRae,
a lawyer of eminence, but, in the latter part of his
career, Consul at Paris.

Mr. McRae and Mr. McCraw, were both members of the Executive Council under the first and
best Constitution of Virginia. Rotation in that office was then regulated, not by a term of service,
but by a rule, that in each third year, one of the
members should be *elected out*, by a joint vote of
the Senate and Delegates. The least popular
member would of course obtain a majority; this
ostracising process was termed *scratching*.

When it came to the scratch on one occasion, the unsought contest lay between the two gentlemen above named, who divided the negative popularity between them, and when the ballots were read, the names of McRae, McCraw, McCraw, McRae came in continued succession. The effect was so ludicrous, that a gentleman in the gallery wrote the following parody on one of Swift's coarse effusions, but not like that, obnoxious to decency, running thus—

> " Hurray for McRae and Hurrau for McCraw !
> Hurray and Hurrau for McRae and McCraw !
> Hurrau for McCraw and Hurray for McRae !
> Hurrau and Hurray for McCraw and McRae !
> Hurrau for McRae and Hurray for McCraw !
> Hurray and Hurrau for McRae and McCraw !
> Hurray for McCraw and Hurrau for McRae !
> Hurrau and Hurray for McCraw and McRae !! "

At a popular election, Mr. McRae being present when Mr. Thomas Taylor voted for the candidate whose cause Mr. McRae espoused, he said, " Mr. Taylor, that is the first correct vote you ever gave." "Perhaps it is," replied Mr. T. in his blandest manner, "for I once gave a vote to you, Mr. McRae."

Mr. McRae was elected to the office of President of the Virginia Mutual Assurance Society, which he filled for some years, and he sold to that Institution his dwelling and its extensive appurtenances.

He was not a diffident man, and he was congratulated by Mr. Wickham, " on his election to the Presidency of the Assurance Company, which he was so well qualified to fill." Mr. McRae was subsequently appointed Consul at Paris, which he filled several years until his death.

Continuing up Marshall street we pass the Railway work-shops, where formerly stood the residence of *George Pickett*, and nearly opposite stands that erected by his partner, Robert Pollard —the quiet and peaceable gentleman, who offered, a little sarcastically, to relinquish his horse rather than stand a law-suit with Mr. Banks.

The introduction of Mr. Pickett, reminds me of an instance of Yankee cuteness, which I heard him relate. A Connecticut trader came to Richmond with a cargo of Yankee notions, and in addition to the customary medley he had a few casks of fine Madeira wine, not then, as now, made at the North. In seeking customers for such commodities he would of course call on Mr. Pickett. He proffered to him a bargain in apples, onions, fish and Hingham buckets, at all which, particularly the onions and fish, Mr. Pickett turned up his nose. The trader then mentioned the wine, at which Mr. P. rather smacked his lips, and was invited, with some other connoisseurs, to test its flavor. It proved quite satisfactory and the price was not unreasonable. Mr. P. who was not dull at bargaining, told the Yankee that he had no money to lay out in wine, but he had some Western lands on the Ohio, and if they would serve for payment, he would take a few casks. The Yankee demurred at the barter but would consider of it, if Mr. P. would take the "sarce" and other notions ; which being disdainfully rejected, the chaffering was closed— or rather suspended—for soon after, the trader called at Mr. P.'s counting room in a careless way, and the offer of the lands was repeated and that of the onions, &c., urged as a *sine qua non*. At length the Yankee asked to look at the land warrants and surveys, and from among them, selected one or more, which he said contained as much land as he could take. The prices were after due higgling agreed on, the barter was made and so were the conveyances. After the deeds and the wines had been duly delivered, Mr. Pickett said to "the party of the second part," "Now, my friend, let me give you a piece of advice, don't again buy wild lands unless you have seen them." The Yankee thanked Mr. P. for his advice, and not willing to be exceeded in generosity, said he "would offer some in return, which was, never to *sell* wild lands until you have seen them." "Why," said Mr. P. "what do you know about the land?" To which the reply was "I have traded on the Ohio and looked about the country; examined the soil and the advantages of situation, and found

out who were the owners of such as I liked best.
In fact, Mr. Pickett, I came to Richmond to buy
this tract of land from you. It contains water
power and other advantages, and I would not part
with it for five times what it cost me." This land
was, if I am not misinformed, at the confluence of
the Muskingum and Ohio, and became the site of
Marietta.

Robert Pollard's house nearly opposite to Mr.
Pickett's has for a number of years been the residence of Mrs. Young, whose name will appear on
a subsequent page. The square next to Mr. Pollard, and extending to the market, was built on
and long occupied by *Dr. James Lyons,* and subsequently by his son of the same name, a conspicuous citizen. On the square west of the market, on
the north side of Marshall street, there yet stands
a yellow wooden house in which Peter Tinsley, the
clerk in whose office Mr. Clay wrote, long resided,
until he built the dwelling, now Mr. Goddin's, on
Sixth street. Small houses and small salaries suf-
ficed for officials in that day.

I will also mention a curious circumstance I
heard from Mr. Pollard. A man in Connecticut
wrote to him, requesting that Mr. P. would address
a letter to him, stating his wish to buy a certain
piece of land in the West, for which he would give
a good price, say $10,000, promising that the offer
should not be used to Mr. P.'s injury, nor should

he be considered as committing himself by it. The applicant added, that he wished to use the letter to effect a sale he had in view, and he would on any other occasion render a similar service to Mr. Pollard !

Charles Johnston, afterwards President of the Farmers' Bank in Lynchburg, was a partner with Pickett & Pollard, and these gentlemen dealt very largely in Western lands, which may account for the two affairs I have mentioned, and for the following :

Mr. Johnston, when a very young man, in 1789, accompanied a party in an attempt to descend the Ohio. They were made prisoners by the Indians, most of them killed, and he, one of the survivors, after dreadful sufferings, and once even at the point of being burned at the stake, was, after a long march, sold to a humane Frenchman, an Indian trader from Detroit, who carried Mr. Johnston there, treated him most kindly and furnished him with the means of returning home. Many years afterwards Mr. Johnston had the satisfaction of welcoming in Virginia his deliverer, Mr. Dechouquet. A narrative of these events was published by Mr. Johnston in 1827.

The large and respectable old mansion on the summit of Gamble's hill, overlooking the Armory, and all the country around, was erected, but left unfinished, by Col. John Harvie. The house was

9

planned by Mr. Latrobe, the architect of its neighbor, the Penitentiary; the intermediate ground
embraced Gallows hill, the edifice on which was
rendered in a great measure useless by the Penitentiary—with what good effect this is not the
place to inquire. One small wooden house, with
a shed at either end, stood not far off, in which
service was performed by Baptist preachers, for
want of a better place of worship. Its locality
possessed the advantage of being near the Penitentiary pond—convenient for immersion—for it
was then pure water.

But to return from this digression, Col. Harvie
wished to make some change in Latrobe's plan, to
which the architect would not accede. They
parted—the house stood unfinished for some time,
when it passed into the hands of Colonel Robert
Gamble, after some previous change of ownership.
The Colonel finished and occupied it for many
years, until his death; and after remaining in the
hands of his descendants for some time, it has
passed to others repeatedly.

Col. Gamble, in advanced years, but still an
active merchant, and I should add a most estimable citizen, was accidentally killed by being thrown
from his horse. His sons and partners in trade,
John and Robert, were valuable citizens in both
civil and military capacities. The former commanded the Light Infantry Blues, and the latter

the Richmond Troop of Horse, and were in service in the war of 1812. They were among the first adventurers to Florida, after its cession to the United States, and among its most enterprising and valuable citizens. John died in 1853, and Robert is yet (1859) an active and energetic man. When the Indians were committing depredations around him, he remained unharmed, because he had always been kind to them. One of their sisters became the wife of the distinguished William Wirt, and the other of W. H. Cabell, at one time Governor of Virginia, and afterwards President of the Court of Appeals.

The extensive grounds around the old mansion have been divided and subdivided until but a small portion remains attached to it. It is now flanked on one side by a Gothic tower, on the very apex of the hill; a distant view of which gives to the hill a Rhenish aspect; but in the good old colonel's time the visitor at a nearer view would more likely be reminded of Madeira.

The following ludicrous anecdote is related by Kennedy in his Life of Wirt, concerning some of the personages above named. It occurred in 1803, when Mr. Wirt was awaiting Col. Gamble's sanction to his marriage with Miss Gamble, his second wife :*

---

* This lady died at the residence of her son-in-law, Alex'r Randall, Esq., in Annapolis, January 24, 1857, aged 73 years.

"Colonel Gamble had occasion, one summer morning, to visit his future son-in-law's office. It unluckily happened that Wirt had the night before, brought some young friends there, and they had had a merry time of it, which so beguiled the hours, that even now, at sunrise, they had not separated. The Colonel opened the door, little expecting to find any company there at that hour. His eyes fell on the strangest group! There stood Wirt with a poker in his right hand, the sheet-iron blower on his left arm, which was thrust through the handle; on his head was a tin wash-basin, and as to the rest of his dress, it was hot weather, and the hero of this grotesque scene had dispensed with as much of his trappings as comfort might require, substituting for them a light wrapper, that greatly aided the theatrical effect. There he stood, in this whimsical caparison, reciting with great gesticulation Falstaff's onset on the thieves, his back to the door. The opening of it attracted the attention of all. We may imagine the queer look of the anxious probationer, as Col. Gamble, with grave and mannerly silence, bowed and withdrew, closing the door behind him without the exchange of a word."

The spot fronting the Capitol Square on which the First Presbyterian Church now stands, was formerly occupied by the humble residence of a distinguished man and eminent lawyer, *Edmund Randolph*. He erected and afterwards resided in the mansion now Mr. Fry's, between that church and the City Hall. The first humble dwelling was removed to a dirty alley on Seventh street, opposite the side entrance to the Theatre. Its present shabby aspect is scarcely reconcilable with the idea that it was once the abode of a Secretary of State, and afterwards of his son-in-law, also a distinguished lawyer, Bennet Taylor, and of another son-in-law, Peter V. Daniel, now (1860) a Judge of the (Federal) Supreme Court. Mr. Randolph's only son, Peyton, also a lawyer, died in the prime of life. It was of his beautiful wife, when Miss Ward, that the celebrated John Randolph was enamored.

On the square west of the Capitol, and on part of which stands St. Paul's Church, *Bushrod Washington* built a small office, which is yet standing in rear of the church. I will venture to record an anecdote which I have heard of this distinguished gentleman and his illustrious relative. When practicing law in Richmond, in early life (1789), during the presidency of *Washington*, his friends urged Bushrod Washington to apply for the office of district attorney in the United States Court for Virginia.

He wrote to Washington, asking his opinion whether it would be worth his while to solicit the office, and received a reply in these terms: " Your standing at the bar would not justify my nomination of you as attorney to the Federal District Court, in preference to some of the oldest and most esteemed General Court lawyers in your own State, who are desirous of this appointment."

Such anti-nepotism was not adopted as a precedent by Washington's successors; some of whom pursued a diametrically opposite course, and seemed to consider consanguinity a sufficient qualification for office, without any other. Bushrod Washington was deemed worthy by his uncle's successor to fill a much higher station, and was appointed one of the Justices of the Supreme Court. He resided at Mount Vernon after the death of Washington, but removed from Richmond, I think, prior to that event.

The square on which his office stands was purchased by *George Hay*, a lawyer of eminence, who became district attorney under Mr. Jefferson, and who erected the present residence, afterwards Judge Stanard's, now Dr. Beale's, fronting the Capitol square.

Mr. Hay was prosecuting attorney at the trial of Aaron Burr, and had to encounter an array of talent rarely exceeded at any bar—but he did not fight single-handed, though against great odds.

Mr. Hay's second wife, who became his widow, was the daughter of Mr. Monroe, President of the United States. Her life was one of great vicissitudes. From the high estate she once held she was reduced by misfortune, when in her widowhood, to a state of destitution; and, as I have heard, her address was not known by the party to whose care her letters were sent. In that condition she was found in Paris, (where she had been educated,) and almost at her last moment, by one of her country-women, an acquaintance of her early days. From this lady, the wife of an United

States military officer of the highest rank and distinction, she received every attention and kindness to the fatal close.

On the square south of the Capitol, where the United States has erected a Court Room, Custom House and Post Office, resided one of the most eminent physicians and talented men of his time—which is no faint praise. I mean *Dr. James McClurg*. He served in the medical staff during the Revolutionary War, and was declared to be the most skillful and accomplished medical officer in the division of the army serving in this part of the Union.

Mr. Madison had a great regard for him, and, in 1782, suggested him for the office of Secretary of Foreign Affairs. In 1787, after Mr. Henry, Gen. Nelson and R. H. Lee had successively resigned the place of member of the Convention that formed the Constitution of the United States, Dr. McClurg was appointed, and attended at Philadelphia with George Washington, Edmund Randolph, John Blair, James Madison, George Mason and George Wythe—a glorious communion.

His original domicile in Richmond was a small Dutch-roofed wooden house, recently demolished, (to make room for the United States offices,) as has been a portion of the larger one of brick erected near it by the doctor, and afterwards occupied by the Bank of Virginia. His third, or rather fourth, and most spacious dwelling was built on Grace street, the grounds attached to it extending to Broad street. Now shorn of a large portion of superfluous territory, but retaining a spacious one, it is occupied (1856) by Dr. C. B. Gibson. A short biography of Dr. McClurg, who was the uncle of Dr. McCaw, has been published by a grandson of the latter.

On the square west of the last-mentioned residence on Grace street, stood the old-fashioned, double-winged, triple-porticoed house of *Major Du Val*, one of the last of the cocked hats, satin shorts, and bag wigs.

For the information of my younger readers, I will tell them that a bag wig was furnished with a black silk plaited appendage, something like a lady's reticule, (and entitled to the appellation of a gentleman's ridicule.) The queue or tail of the wig was inserted into this bag, which was drawn tightly at the top to retain the hair, and dangled behind like a pendulum.

The Du Val lot was said to be the scene of Ralph Ringwood's adventure, as told by Washingington Irving. It was afterwards occupied by the celebrated William Wirt; but, like many cotemporary wooden structures, it has of late years changed its location, and retired to one in the suburbs.

On the opposite square stood the unpretending

abode of that learned, wise and excellent man, *George Wythe*, one of the signers of the Declaration of Independence, and whose life is interwoven with the history of Virginia, from his early manhood to his latest years.

He was a conspicuous member of the Convention that formed the Federal Constitution, but he did not sign it; ten years previously to which, on the organization of the Government of Virginia, he was appointed Chancellor of the Court of Equity, which arduous office he filled until his death. This occurred on the 8th of June, 1806, and was caused by poison, administered by a youthful relative whom he had cherished, and who expected to inherit his estate—but no legal convicting evidence was adduced. The miscreant was disappointed in his object, for Mr. Wythe lived long enough to disinherit him.

A fine tulip poplar, (Miss Murray would say Liriodendron Tulipifera,) planted by Mr. Wythe, marks the corner where his house stood, and where now stands the very handsome one of Mr. A. Warwick—but no tombstone marks the spot (where is it?) where this good and wise man and learned jurist was buried.

Henry Clay, when a youth, wrote in the office of Peter Tinsley, clerk of the court in which Mr. Wythe presided, and his attention was no doubt attracted by young Clay's deportment. The judge invited him to his house, and gave him advice and instruction, and it was from this ample source, probably, that Mr. Clay got the first insight of his profession.

It was a pleasure to the kind Chancellor to give instruction to young men who would receive and appreciate it.

A letter from Mr. Clay to Mr. Minor, dated May 3d, 1851, and published in the Virginia Historical Register, vol. v., says:

"My first acquaintance with Mr. Wythe was in 1793, in my sixteenth year, when I was a clerk in his court, and he then probably threescore and ten. His right hand was disabled by gout or rheumatism, and I acted as his amanuensis and wrote the cases he reported. It cost me a great deal of labor, not understanding a single Greek character, to write citations from Greek authors, which he inserted in the copies of his reports sent to Mr. Jefferson, to Samuel Adams, and one or two others; I copied them by imitating each character from the book.

"Mr. Wythe was one of the purest, best and most learned men in classical lore that I ever knew.

"He had a grand nephew, a youth scarcely of mature age, to whom by his will, written by me at his dictation before my departure from Richmond, he devised the greater part of his estate. That youth poisoned him and others (black members of his household), by putting arsenic into a pot in which coffee was prepared for breakfast. The paper which contained the arsenic was found on the floor of the kitchen. The coffee having been drank by the Chancellor and his servants, the poison developed the usual effects.

"The Chancellor lived long enough to send for his neighbor, Major William Duval, and got him to write another will, disinheriting the ungrateful and guilty grand nephew, and making other disposition of his estate. An old negro woman, his cook, also died under the operation of the poison. After the Chancellor's death, it was discovered that the atrocious author of it had forged bank checks in Mr. Wythe's name.

"Mr. Wythe's personal appearance and habits were plain, simple and unostentatious. His countenance was full of blandness and benevolence, and he made, in his salutation to others, the most graceful bow that I ever witnessed."

[P. S.—On this 12th day of April, 1860, the eighty-third anniversary of Henry Clay's birth, an admirable marble statue of him, by Hart, is erected in the Capitol square, and inaugurated in a speech worthy of the theme, in the presence of one of the largest assemblages, from all parts of the country, that ever convened in Richmond. His memory has survived party prejudice, or the statue would not be permitted to occupy that position; but time does justice, and dispels falsehood, the venom of which had done its work many years ago. However high a position his maligners may have unworthily attained, his character is and ever will be held in the estimation of mankind as much above theirs as is the soaring eagle above the mousing owl.

It is to the glory of our country-women that they originated and effected this patriotic work, a token of gratitude to one of our greatest statesmen. To them also is the nation indebted for rescuing from the chance of desecration the earthly

home of her greatest man. Is not the summit of
Bunker Hill Monument also indebted to the ladies
for ascending to its proper elevation?

We had better entrust such works to the ladies.
No misapplication of money stains their hands,
and none of their plans are left unfinished.*

On this same day another statue of Henry Clay
is inaugurated at New Orleans; and in his own
Kentucky, a third! Were such triple honors ever
before paid simultaneously, without preconcert, to
one man, and in cities so remote from each other?]

The square on which Mr. Wythe resided was
pre-eminent as was its owner. It was on the
highest spot in the city, as ascertained by Mr.
Watkins, who surveyed it, and who erected a
small dwelling on the same square, which was
taken down not many years ago, to be replaced
by Mr. Dunlop's residence.

On the square west of the Chancellor's, and at
the corner of Franklin and Fifth streets, lived
John Warden, a Scotchman—one of the best read
and worst-featured, most good-tempered and worst

---

* When this suggestion was made, the writer was not aware
that the ladies were about to attempt the rescue of the monument to Washington, commenced many years ago, in his own
city, from the danger of falling into premature decay, or of
being desecrated to the purposes of party or of peculation, as
many of our public works are, where money is expended and
votes are wanted.

formed, but among the best informed members of the Richmond bar—his mind and body were a bundle of contrasts. His ugliness was so attractive and so strongly marked, that the boys used to amuse themselves in drawing likenesses of his short thick figure, crooked legs and satyr-like features on the walls of the court room. But his talents, wit and humor compensated for the externals, in which nature had been so niggardly.

On one occasion in court, when Mr. Wickham and Mr. Hay were adverse counsel, the former got the latter into a dilemma. On which Mr. Warden whispered to Mr. Wirt, "Habet fenum in cornu,"* who extemporized the following epigram :

> " Wickham one day in open court
> Was tossing Hay about for sport:
> Jock rich in Wit and Latin too,
> Cried "Habet fenum in cornu."

Mr. Warden retained with his broad Scotch dialect his allegiance to the mother country, and looked rather contemptuously on Republicanism in its infancy, and on its rebel representatives. During a session of the Legislature, he was reported to have uttered contemptuous expressions

---

* " He has hay on his horns." The Romans tied hay on the horns of mischievous cattle, both as a caution and as a protection to those who approached them. Hence the term was applied to "a dangerous fellow."

10

concerning that body. The Sergeant-at-arms arrested and brought him to the bar of the House. The Speaker charged him with the offence and required him to retract it on his knees, or he should be sent to prison. The sarcastic Scot assumed the prescribed humble position, and thus apologized: "Mr. Speaker, I confess I did say that your honors were not fit to carry guts to a bear—I now retract that assertion, and acknowledge that you are fit." Then slowly rising, he brushed the dust from his knees—muttered "I dommed dirty hoose," made his bow and retired, amid the mirth and mortification of the members and the bystanders.

The residence of the celebrated and eccentric *Alexander Campbell* was the same that Mr. Warden afterwards occupied. His name appears in the constellation of lawyers that shone in the early days of the Commonwealth. He was a materialist in faith, or rather in the lack of faith, and in the singular will which he made, in 1795, he says, "I hope no tombstone will be raised over me, because it will merely hinder something from growing on the spot. If all men had tombstones erected over their graves, the earth, in a few centuries, would be one entire pavement." Judge Wayne of the Supreme Court of the U. S., married a daughter of Mr. Campbell.

Descending Fifth street from Mr. Warden's

we first pass the house surmounted by a cupola a questionable ornament to a dwelling), once occupied by John Barrett, the father of the gentleman who now lives near the same spot. We now pass the square formerly occupied by the Singleton family, now by Mr. Hobson and other gentlemen, and then we descend to the square of William Hay, on which a tall colonnade is now seen, and many other buildings are erected. Opposite to this is the handsome residence, built and long occupied by *Joseph Marx*, an enterprising merchant, of the strictest probity, a public-spirited, useful and hospitable member of society, who contributed liberally to the prosperity of the city.

Here terminated the residences in old times, except that of *William Munford*, who filled the office of Clerk of the House of Delegates for many years, and left a worthy successor to the station in his eldest son. The metrical translation of Homer, by Mr. Munford, published after his death, is pronounced, by eminent Greek scholars, to be one of the most faithful extant.

CHAPTER VIII.

OLD RESIDENCES AND THEIR OCCUPANTS.

(CONTINUED.)

The house, corner of Main and Third streets, now occupied by John Robertson, Esq., (late Judge,) was, more than fifty years ago, the residence of his father, *William Robertson*, Clerk of the Council, who there reared a large family. T. Bolling Robertson, Governor of Louisiana, was one of his sons, and others were not undistinguished. They are descendants of Pocahontas, as the names of several members indicate. That Princess must have possessed a greater share of beauty than her portraits exhibit, if we may judge by that of her female descendants, who are distinguished for it.

The spacious square on Franklin street between Second and Third, retained its full dimensions during about fifty years' occupancy by its quiet and unaspiring proprietor, Anthony Robinson, except that, in the latter years of his life, he apportioned a part of it to one of his sons, on which to erect a residence. His own yet stands.

In a plain and not spacious wooden building at the north-east corner of Franklin and Third streets, I recognize the residence for several years of *Thomas Ritchie*, the founder and indefatigable editor of the Enquirer. In the office attached to the house was concocted during the small hours before daylight many a furious paragraph against the Whigs or Federalists, as they were then called. A more commodious tenement on Grace, between Fifth and Sixth (Mr. Wythe's square), was in later years the dwelling of Mr. Ritchie till he removed to the head-quarters of politicians at Washington, where he died July 3, 1854.

An antique dwelling, half brick, half wood, with the square on which it stood, on the south side of Main, between Second and Third streets, was the residence, many years ago, of *Major Andrew Dunscombe*, probably a soldier of the Revolution, a gentleman of the olden time.

In 1787 he was appointed by the Executive of Virginia, Commissioner for settling the accounts between this Commonwealth and the United States, which arose during the war of the Revolution, &c. This occupied him several years, after which, I think, he was Master in Chancery of Judge Wythe's court.

He erected Goodall's Tavern (The Indian Queen), now the Central Hotel. The small brick office that he long occupied was taken down to make room for an addition to the Hotel. Major D. married Miss Philadelphia Pope, a sister of Nathaniel Pope, of Hanover. The respected name of Dunscombe no longer exists in our community, but in those of Christian, at Lynchburg, and Horsley, of Nelson, his descendants are found. A brother of his was long ago Clerk of the Federal Court, New York.

Among the broad spaces formerly occupied by old citizens, was the square extending from Franklin to Main and from Seventh to Eighth streets, on which stood on the summit of a high hill, the residence of *Archibald Blair*, Clerk of the Council of State, opposite to where the United Presbyterian Church now stands. At the foot of the hill was a pond, fed by a spring and shaded by forest trees and shrubs. The hill and the trees have been cut down, the pond has been filled up, and Mr. Stewart's row of fine dwellings covers a part of the leveled surface. The front on Main street remains unimproved, except by workshops, and less attractive, except for the hum of industry, than when in a state of nature. Mr. Blair's territories extended over one or two other squares, which have also submitted to the leveling system.

His neighbor, *John Graham*, a Scotchman, and among the first to engage in coal-mining, transplanted his vineyard from Main and Twelfth streets (where some tall and splendid stores now rear their fronts) to the square above Mr. Blair's, now built up chiefly by Mr. W. H. Allen. A portion of this square contains the former resi-

dence of the late *John Robinson*,* for fifty years
clerk of various courts, according to the changes
of organization, and one of his sons became his
successor in that which he last filled. His other
sons are distinguished, Conway† as a jurist, Moncure and Edwin by their connection with railroads.
Another portion of the Graham square contains
the fine edifices erected by the Messrs. James and
occupied as the Arlington House. Such was the
inequality of the ground in this part of the city,
that Mr. Allen had to build *two stories above the
foundations* to reach the surface of the street,
while on the next square the original surface was
as high as the second stories of the present dwellings.

On an adjoining square, Edward Cunningham,
an Irish gentleman, engaged in the milling and
mercantile business, erected a capacious dwelling,
afterwards the residence of the late Dr. Watson,
and still occupied by his family.

The occupant of this lot in the last century was
John Dobie, whose house now forms an office within
the yard. He was the architect of the Capitol, if
not a capital architect, as the want of symmetry
in the columns of that building would imply. A

---

* Demolished (1860) to make room for three others.

† The author is indebted to this gentleman for various useful
hints and corrections in this edition.

fine sycamore tree planted by him flourishes on
Franklin near Sixth, where he resided.

One of the dwellings between the Washington
Tavern and the Catholic Church was the residence
of *John Brown*, who had been the Clerk of the
District Court, General Court and Court of Appeals, in succession, and a most accomplished one in
all that regarded the duties of the station.   In his
office and under his instruction, was formed that
corps of clerks so distinguished for the beauty and
neatness of their records, in many Virginia Courts,
some years ago, before judges, clerks and sheriffs
were elected by universal suffrage ! !   Anthony
Robinson was one and John Robinson another of
that corps.   They were his successors in the Clerk-
ship of the District Court.   The latter served fifty
years after John Brown's resignation of that office.

Mr. Brown accompanied General Marshall as
his secretary, when he went to Paris with Pinck-
ney and Gerry, Envoys Extraordinary to the
French republic.   James Brown, Jr., late Auditor,
is the only surviving member of his father's
family.*

Two fine elm trees on Broad street, planted probably before the introduction of those upstarts, the
Lombardy poplars, are all that remain to designate
the former residence, at the corner of Broad and

---

* His death in 1859 is mentioned in a previous page.

Seventh streets, of John Hopkins, Commissioner of Loans of the United States, and of the distinguished occupant who succeeded him, John A· Chevallie, of whom I shall probably take occasion to speak elsewhere.

Let us look at the other side of the square, where the sycamores grow; for the lot extended through to Marshall street. This front was built on by Mr. H. Moncure, and is made conspicuous by three enormous Turkish cannon balls wrought out of stone and mounted on pedestals at the corners. These balls were quarried and rounded to be served to the mouths of cannon on the shores of the Bosphorus. They were brought from thence by one of our naval officers to be presented to a public institution, and were landed at Rocketts. There they lay, until tired of inactivity, they were about to roll into the river, when Mr. Moncure rescued them from a watery grave and mounted them around his house. These balls are thirty inches in diameter, larger than any used at Sebastopol. When the property changed hands they obtained the name of Duval's pills, from the vocation of the owner, and they would no doubt be very efficacious if skillfully administered. Dr. Wellford is now the proprietor of them, and it is gratifying that they are in such good hands, and that our city has such an accession to the faculty and to its society.

On the north side of Broad, between Fourth and
Fifth streets, yet stands a wooden building* (as
most of that date were), the former residence of
the Braxton family, whose inclosure embraced the
square—now converted into shops, the names on
which would indicate a German colony. Indeed,
the line of Broad street is occupied chiefly by Germans, as is a considerable portion of many other
streets. The Braxtons removed to their estates on
the Pamunky many years ago, and that family
and the community sustained a heavy loss about
two years since, in the sudden death of General
Braxton, of Chericoke, a most estimable man and
useful citizen.

The mansion of the Rev. Mr. Woodbridge, at
the south-east corner of Grace and Seventh was
erected by the father of Mrs. W., Mr. Andrew
Nicolson, and has been for fifty years the abode of
his family. May it long retain its present occupants, in health and happiness, and descend to as
worthy ones.

The dwelling at the south-west corner of Grace
and Seventh streets, with the ground extending to
Sixth, including that now (1856) occupied by the
handsome mansions of Mrs. Cabell† and Mrs.
Stanard, was in 1800 the residence of Mr. Brydie,

---

* Demolished to make room for brick stores (1860).

† This lady, the daughter of Col. Mayo and sister of Mrs.
General Scott, died April 24, 1860.

a Scotch merchant of the firm of McClure, Brydie & Co. Mr. McClure was a gentleman of scientific pursuits, and his name will be found in annals of that character.

Mr. McCredie, who on the death of Mr. Brydie became his successor both in his mercantile and domestic establishments, met with his death in a manner that created great excitement in the city. On occasion of an alarm of fire, he was hastening across the Capitol Square, when the sentry hailed him. He did not hear, or did not heed the challenge, and the sentry most unwarrantably fired and shot him dead.

The commercial house of McClure, Brydie & Co. was one of the first in the city in respectability as well as seniority. It was located near Shockoe Warehouse, and on the steep and now dirty alley extending down to Virginia street, may yet be seen a portion of the stone wall which enclosed their premises of the same extent.

The death of Mr. McCredie reminds me of another that occurred near the same spot. Col. Tatem, an old soldier, and either very eccentric or deranged, and moreover poor, determined to close his life on the fourth of July. He took his station near the artillery, when a salute was being fired, and watching his opportunity, stepped in front of a cannon at the moment the match was applied. His body was blown to atoms.

An unpretending wooden building near the corner of Leigh and Fifth streets was the residence of the *Rev. Richard Channing Moore*, Bishop of Virginia. What would an English Primate think of such a palace?

This worthy minister was invited, in November, 1813, by Bushrod Washington, then residing at Mount Vernon, and E. J. Lee at Alexandria, to take charge of the Episcopal Church then building at Richmond (the Monumental), with the intention to make him Bishop of the Diocese, which was effected, and in 1814, he was consecrated at Philadelphia. This reverend prelate was much beloved, not only by those of his own Church, but by the community generally. He died at Lynchburg, in 1841, while in the performance of his episcopal duties, at the age of seventy-nine.

One of the few residences on L, now Leigh, between Seventh and Eighth streets, was built by Joseph Jackson, and I think occupied by some of the Southall family, a name then and now conspicuous. It was afterwards the residence of Patrick Gibson, a respectable merchant, connected in business with a nephew of Mr. Jefferson. Of late years, Mr. N. Mills has been the proprietor of these extensive grounds.

I must insert a few omissions which I discover in my Shockoe Hill rambles. The Powhatan House, opposite to the City Hall, is an extension and elevation of the former residence, store and strong hold of *Wright Southgate,* once an officer in the British navy. A very high wall, protected against escalade by a capping of broken glass, enclosed the grounds, and each opening on the lower floor was secured by chains, bolts, bars and bells. Two of his nephews were among the most respectable and enterprising merchants in Norfolk, and one of his sons, not submissive to man-of-war discipline, went penniless from home, and attained to eminence and great wealth in Kentucky, and another followed some years later.

Adjoining this castle was the cottage of a worthy old couple, *Jacob Cohen* and his wife, whose residence dates back some twenty years in the last century. Their cottage is supplanted by the handsome block of dwellings erected by Mr. Jaquelin Taylor.

Opposite to this on Twelfth street, was the resi- of *Mr. Samuel Myers* an intelligent merchant and useful citizen, and of his neighbor, Mr. Wiseham, of hospitable memory. The latter house is substituted by Mr. Morson's three fine dwellings, and Judge Crump has embellished Mr. Myers's old mansion.

On the theatre square, north of Mr. Myers', and built after the model of his, were the residences of Mr. Prosser and Mr. Moncure, partners in an extensive auction business. One of these is

11

now "the Carleton House," the other Mr. John
Jones' dwelling. Mr. Myers' son, Gustavus, has
introduced a different style of architecture and an
improved one, in his dwelling adjoining the paternal homestead.

On the lot where the First Baptist Church
stands, and adjoining the residence in old times of
Charles Copeland, attorney, *James Heron*, a retired merchant and worthy citizen, was preparing
to erect a comfortable residence for his old age,
and commenced by building a capacious kitchen.
But just as the walls were erected, he, by the im-
prudent exercise of a close inspection, met with a
fall which proved fatal. The kitchen, converted
into a dwelling, was long occupied by his family,
and by John G. Blair, who married one of the
daughters, who have a long line of descendants.

The square on the south side of Franklin, between First and Second streets, was the residence
of *Charles Ellis*, of the long existing firm of Ellis
& Allan, worthy members of our community for
nearly half a century. This unpretending mansion, now overtopped by those around, is still
occupied by his family. The square opposite to it
was Mr. Ellis's garden, embellished by a row of
fine Linden trees along its front. Most of the
Lindens have disappeared, but have given their
name to the square, now built up with fine residences. A few of the trees have survived the

trimming process, their scarred trunks almost bereft of branches and of beauty. If there are "tongues in trees," as the great poet imagined, each limb would cry aloud "against the deep damnation of its taking off." Those who wantonly or tastelessly mutilate trees can have neither poetry nor "music in their souls, and are fit for treasons, stratagems and spoils." This is a general plea in favor of the groves, not a special one in the case before us. But if the Lindens have disappeared, the square can now boast of superior attractions, in beauties of a more animated nature; and these, while yet in bloom, will doubtless be severed from the parent stem, but not like the Lindens, to disappear, both root and branch.

I fear that my readers will think I am imposing on them an antiquated directory, in which they feel as little interest as in any similar compilations; but I trust that some of the survivors may be willing to take a retrospect of the homes of their parents and more remote ancestors, and of others who conferred distinction on our metropolis. I will therefore venture to continue the subject— indeed, I must do so, in justice to some memorable personages whom I have omitted as yet to mention. Among these is *Albert Gallatin*, the distinguished financier and statesman. He came to Richmond a young man. But we will let him speak for himself, by inserting the following extract of a letter to Wm. Maxwell, Esq., Corresponding Secretary of the Virginia Historical Society, dated New York, February 15, 1848, in his 87th year, and eighteen months before his death:

"It was in Richmond where I spent most of the winters between the years 1783 and 1789, that I was received with that old proverbial Virginia hospitality, to which I know no parallel anywhere within the circle of my travels. It was not hospitality only that was shown to me. I do not know how it came to pass, but every one with whom I became acquainted appeared to take an interest in the young stranger. I was only the interpreter of a gentleman, the agent of a foreign house that had a large claim for advances to the 'State; and this made me known to all the officers of the Government and some of the most prominent members of the Legislature. It gave me the first opportunity of showing some talent even as a speaker, of which I was not myself aware. Every one encouraged me and was disposed to promote my success in life. To name all those from whom I received offers of service would be to name all the most distinguished residents at that time in Richmond. I will only mention two: John Marshall, who though but a young lawyer in 1783, was almost at the head of the bar in 1786, offered to take me into his office without a fee, and assured me that I would become a distinguished lawyer. Patrick Henry advised me to go to the West, where I might study law if I chose, but predicted that I was intended for a statesman, and told me that this was the career which should be my aim. He also rendered me services on more than one occasion. But I must stop; and if there be some egotism in what I have said, the feelings which I have expressed come at least from a grateful heart."

I will venture to relate an anecdote which I have heard concerning Mr. Gallatin, though I cannot vouch for its authenticity. When he came to Richmond, he boarded in the house of Mrs. Allegre, to whose daughter he became attached, and he asked the mother to sanction his addresses. The old lady was quite wroth at his presumption, and seizing a spit, threatened to transfix and baste him, if *he* dare aspire to her daughter! She must have relented, however, for the marriage took place, and I hope the indignant old lady lived to see her son-in-law a member of Congress, Secretary of the Treasury, and Minister Plenipotentiary. In 1794 he married a daughter of Commodore Nicholson, U. S. N.

The taste of Mr. Gallatin, a native of Switzerland, would naturally prefer a hilly to a level surface, and he purchased for a residence the square between Leigh and Clay, and Seventh and Eighth streets, through which runs a deep ravine, or valley rather, for its slopes are well wooded with native growths and still retain the wild aspect of nature. This house was rendered singular in appearance by its tall, round chimneys. Two acres were attached to it, in which was the wooded dell. This property was sold by Mr. Gallatin in 1789, to a French gentleman, Savary de Valcoulon, from whom it passed, in 1792, to Bushrod Washington, who planted a number of sycamore trees in the form of the letter W about the grounds, some of which are still thriving. In 1801 Judge Washing-

ton, after his removal to Mount Vernon, sold the
property to Dr. J. D. McCaw for $3000! and he
resided there many years. In 1842 it passed from
him to Conway Robinson, Esq., who has erected a
new dwelling near to the old one.

P. S. 1860. It is with no slight regret I
record that soon after the preceding paragraph
was written, our city lost Mr. Robinson as a resident—a great loss, for few have rendered her such
important services, and no one has yet replaced
him. He now resides near Washington city. His
new house in Richmond became the property of
Mr. Bresee, and the preceding description no
longer applies to the grounds. The dell has been
filled up, and utility has taken the place of the
picturesque. The melody of the mocking-bird
that has long nestled securely in that dell will be
hushed ere long, and be succeeded by the tones
of the piano, which to the lovers of nature will
scarcely compensate for the loss of the little
songster's imitations and variations.

In my progress down Fifth street, I omitted to
mention the former residence of *Major Gibbon*, an
officer of the Revolution, and distinguished early
in life as a leader of one section of the forlorn
hope at Stony Point, in 1779. He was for many
years Collector of Customs for the port of Richmond, and resided at the corner of Main and
Fifth streets. His enclosure embraced the ground

now occupied by the Second Presbyterian Church and by private residences up to Franklin street.

A son of Major Gibbon distinguished himself in the Navy during the war with Tripoli. He was betrothed to Miss Conyers, a niece of Mrs. Gallego, their opposite neighbor. They were in the Theatre on the night of the fire, and in endeavoring to save Miss C., he perished with her, as did Mrs. Gallego.

Another extensive domicil in the same neighborhood, is opposite to Major Gibbon's, on the south side of Main street. As the property of *David Meade Randolph* it embraced the entire square, on part of which now stand the Second Baptist Church, several handsome dwellings and the extensive carpenter shops of the industrious brothers Gibson.

Mr. Randolph was Marshal of Virginia until the election of Mr. Jefferson, and being one of those federal office-holders who would "neither die nor resign," the only alternative was to remove him. A gentleman, whose propensity for ascertaining and for conferring names was one of his characteristics—Mr. E. W. Rootes—dubbed the Randolph establishment *Moldavia*, after Molly and David, its mistress and master. Mrs. Randolph was one of the remarkable and distinguished persons of her day. When her husband was deprived of the office of Marshal, he found it necessary to

sell his house and to retrench his establisment,
which had not probably been an economical one.
Mrs. R., who lacked neither energy nor industry,
determined to open a boarding-house, feeling assured that those who had, in her prosperity,
partaken of her hospitality, would second her exertions when in adversity. The friend who had
named Moldavia, now conferred on her the title
of Queen, and aided in enlisting subjects for her
new realm. This was on *Cary* street (a name
which she gave it), in a house which now constitutes a small portion of the Columbian Hotel. *
It was then a quiet spot, with very few houses in
its immediate vicinity. The Queen soon attracted
as many subjects as her dominions could accommodate, and a loyal set they generally were. There
were few more festive boards than the Queen's.
Wit, humor and good-fellowship prevailed, but
excess rarely. Social evenings were also enjoyed,
and discord seldom intruded. In the course of
a few years, noise and dust interfered with the
royal comfort, and the throne and its supporters
were transferred to a more pleasant palace, where
they remained until the abdication of the sovereign.

The lovers of comfort and of cool beverages, are
indebted to Mrs. R.'s ingenuity, for the invention
of the 'Refrigerator' as she called it. The first

---

* This portion is razed to the foundation, (1857.)

one was constructed according to her plan, for her own use. It was said that a shrewd Yankee, who was an inmate of her house for a few days, to whom she showed it, carried the invention with him, perhaps obtained a patent, and it soon got into general use.

The Queen's eldest brother, *Thomas Mann Randolph*, (Governor of Virginia) an eccentric and talented man, married a daughter of Mr. Jefferson, a peerless woman, and her descendants have graced society at home and abroad, "to the remotest Ind."

One of the Queen's sisters was the wife of Mr. Hackley, Consul at Cadiz, during the Peninsular War. She is the survivor of her sisters and brothers, and her life has been one of utility to many besides her own children. *

Another of the sisters became the wife of the distinguished *Gouverneur Morris*. In early life he engaged in the strife of the Revolution; in mature years, in that of diplomacy, and, retiring from these, he sought matrimony late in life; but left an heir to his name and possessions.

I have spun out a long yarn for the Queen's web, and will introduce only one strand more, too bright to be left unwoven.

The son of Dr. Chapman, of Philadephia,

---

* This worthy lady died in 1859.

married a neice of my royal heroine; and her
daughter (I hope she will pardon me, if she ever
hears of my presumption) is the most beautiful
woman these old eyes ever gazed on. She has
proved that beauty can subdue *Power*. Her face
and form should be perpetuated in the purest
marble, so that if the Venus de Medici shall be
lost, there may be a substitute for her, if another Praxiteles can be found to mould another
Venus.

Moldavia passed into the possession of Mr.
Gallego, the great miller, whose name and flour
are known to bakers all over the civilized world,
and some portion of the semi-barbarous.

After Mr. Gallego's death, the worthy Scotch
merchant *John Allan*, commonly called Jock, to
distinguish him from his Irish and English
namesakes, became Hospodar of Moldavia, and his
successors retain a part of the territory, having
contracted its boundaries. It was to Mr. Allan
that the poet, Edgar Allan Poe, an orphan, was
indebted for his education—and might have been
for his promotion.

The square immediately above, and west of the
Queen's ancient dominion on Cary street, now
covered with blocks of warehouses, was occupied
by *Andrew Ronald*, a native of Scotland and an
eminent lawyer, who was one of the counsel opposed to Patrick Henry in 1791, in the great suit

arising from the confiscation of British debts during the war of the Revolution. Mr. Ronald's dwelling fronted the Basin, or rather where the Basin now is, and his garden was separated from Shockoe Warehouse by the street and an open space between them. The present aspect of the place is anything but quiet and retired.

South from Mr. Ronald's and beyond a deep ravine which the *supplementary* Gallego mills are now partly filling up, on the summit of a cliff overhanging the river and overlooking Haxall's mills, stands a wooden building,* the former residence of the celebrated *David Ross*, the original owner of the mill, a Scotch merchant anterior to the Revolution. He became the possessor of most valuable lands and mines in various parts of Virginia, when Virginia was bounded by the Mississippi, and some of his descendants now reside, I believe, on a portion of his territories in the western regions, no longer in the Old Dominion. Mr. Ross was remarkable for his unerring judgment of the talents of others, and how to use them.

I must travel beyond the former limits of the city to mention a territory now partly included in them. I mean the lands and former residence of a most worthy citizen and enterprising merchant,

---

* 1860. The cliff is cut down, except the small spot on which the house stands, towering in loneliness and ruin.

the late *Thomas Rutherfoord.* The inclosure originally attached to his dwelling embraced what now constitutes several squares, and his possessions beyond it were very many acres. I have heard that he became possessed of a large portion of this extensive territory by the judicious investment of a thousand pounds, given to him as a wedding present by an uncle in Scotland, on the occasion of his marriage, and by an equally judicious purchase of the rest.

He furnished building-lots to various gentlemen, thus forming a good neighborhood around him, and I can recall, among those who first constituted it, the names of James Penn, John A. Chevallie, Thomas Wilson (mayor), David Bullock (mayor), William Price, Carter B. Page, and Robert Gwathmey; and in later years, General Pegram, President of the Virginia Bank, and that eminent lawyer and excellent man, Samuel Taylor, both victims to casualties. I may also name G. W. Munford, Secretary of the Commonwealth, and J. R. Anderson, of iron fame, truly a man of metal, whose locomotives run on many a Southern and Western road, and whose cannon serve to arm our ships and forts. Mr. Rutherfoord's sons have clustered around the paternal mansion, which was partially destroyed by fire while in the occupancy of Jno. Y. Mason, now Minister to France, who became the purchaser and embellisher of it, but by a subsequent sale it has reverted to a member of the Rutherfoord family.*

I will presume on Mr. Mason's indulgence to give an instance of his coolness during the hot fire that was consuming his effects. The family had escaped in their night clothes and were watching the progress of the conflagration from the porch of an opposite neighbor; Mrs. M. was bewailing their loss, and deeply distressed, when her husband thus consoled her : "My dear, you know you disliked that ugly roof and wished it changed; now your wish will be gratified. The walls will be ready to receive a new roof, and the house be greatly improved." And such was the result. (Mr. Mason died in Paris, in 1859, while filling the office of Minister Plenipotentiary from the U. States.)

The name of *John A. Chevallie* has only been mentioned incidentally, but it merits a more special notice. He was a gentleman of the most scrupulous politeness, of fine literary attainments, and of extensive and varied information. He was brought up in the ante-revolutionary days of French society, and his manners conformed to it. He came to this country as an agent for the celebrated Beaumarchais, who had, either as a secret

---

* I must apologise to the member here alluded to, or rather, to his wife, for saying, in the first edition, he was the *eldest*, as he has senior brothers, but I will not imperil myself with *their* wives by designating the eldest.

12

agent of Louis XVI., or at his own outlay, furnished a large quantity of arms to the United States during the Revolutionary war. After many years of constant exertion, Mr. Chevallie partially succeeded in his object, if my memory serves.

The house of Mr. and the second Mrs. Chevallie, (a daughter of Judge Lyons) was the home of hospitality and cheerfulness, and a favorite resort of old and young. Previous to their residence near Mr. Rutherfoord, they occupied the house of John Hopkins, Commissioner of Loans, on Broad street, corner of Seventh, now demolished, but then embowered in fine elms and sycamores, as already noticed.

I heard this anecdote from Mr. Chevallie, among many others:—Beaumarchais, although an elegant courtier, had been a watchmaker, and of course was not of the old nobility. One of these sought to mortify him at court, by handing an elegant watch to him, saying it did not keep time, and he wished Beaumarchais to see what was amiss. Taking it in his hands and attempting to open it, he let it fall on the floor. He then expressed his regret, adding, that he had been so long out of practice he had become awkward, and bowing politely, retired.*

* "Beaumarchais and his Times," by Leoménil, appeared a few months after the 1st edition of this book was published, and relates this anecdote more fully.

West of Mr. Anderson, and just beyond the line of the city, stands a large dwelling, erected by Peyton Drew in the "flush times," from whom it soon passed to Thomas Richardson, a son-in-law of our old friend Mr. Pollard, and then to John Mutter, the father of Dr. Mutter, Professor of Surgery in the Jefferson Medical College of Philadelphia, which chair he has just resigned (June, 1856), bestowing on the College his extensive museum, and endowing it with a fund for its further extension. After Mr. Mutter's death his house was successively purchased by David Bullock, and its present owner, Mr. George Palmer, under whom it is likely to see its palmiest days in the way of embellishment.

The handsome dwelling at the corner of Leigh and Eighth, with extensive grounds, now the residence of Mr. McCance, was originally, in plain garb, that of Dr. Hayes, from whom it passed to Thomas Green, who decorated it highly and introduced the Heathen Deities into the grounds, where they still preside. During the snowy months of winter, they looked decidedly cool at each other. Goddesses even will do so when they are uncomfortable; but Flora after a while brings about a reconciliation.

It was in a more remote part of the city in old times (the locality is neither here nor there), that a connubial parting scene occurred between a pair of loving birds, as their names denoted. The wife was pious, the husband may speak for himself. "My dear," said Mrs. P. to her husband, on his death-bed, "when you are gone, have you any objection to my marrying brother G.?" "Marry and be d—d," replied her dying spouse—and *he* died and *she* did.

Eastward from Dr. Hayes' (now Mr. McCance's) and at the corner of Leigh and Ninth streets, was the residence of Judge *Spencer Roane*, President of the Court of Appeals, and eminent as a lawyer and politician. He had a controlling influence in the Democratic ranks, which he exercised largely through the columns of "The Enquirer," and thus issued what might almost be called his edicts. He was the autocrat of the Democracy. To look at his stern and commanding aspect, one might think it would be hazardous to disobey them. He removed from Studley, his farm in Hanover, to Richmond, about 1816, after building the house above mentioned, to which were attached extensive grounds. For many years past it has been the residence of Mr. Lewis Webb, and the city has pur-chased an extent of hill-sides south and east of it for a public square—a spot well adapted to test the skill of a landscape gardener.*

---

* Scarcely was the ink dry which wrote the above, when the step-fathers of the city decreed that the grounds should be

I must trespass on the patience of my readers a few moments longer, to mention the residences of some old citizens on Church Hill, &c., which should not be overlooked in story, as they cannot be in eminence of locality.

The *Adams* family, the original proprietors of the eastern portion of the city, occupied several of the squares in their own domain. The three brothers, Richard, Samuel and John, who resided there fifty or sixty years ago, but lived at a later period, have long since gone to their last homes, near to their first; but those they occupied in life have been improved in appearance under tasteful residents, as has that of their distinguished neighbor and connexion, *William Marshall*, a brother of the Chief Justice and a lawyer of almost as great talent, which was partially obscured by his indolence.

Streets were laid out on Adams's, now Church or Richmond Hill (for it is known by all these names), to correspond with those in Byrd's plan, but the very large portion north of Broad street is not included in the city limits, and its numerous

divided in lots and sold, thus healing the pockets at the expense of the lungs ; and instead of opening the streets leading to the grounds previous to the sale, a large portion of the money obtained is expended for that purpose, and the lots thereby much enhanced in value, to the gain of the buyers, but loss to the city.

residents are exempt from city taxes. The city is courting them to its embrace, but finds them very coy.

This hill is divided by little dells into a succession of spurs, forming a cluster of heights overlooking the river, the city and the surrounding country. The proprietor assigned to each of his sons and married daughters one of these prominences. The eldest son, *Richard Adams*, possessed the fine old family mansion, now Mr. Ellett's. *John* erected his mansion east of it, now Mrs. Van-Lew's ; William Marshall, who married a Miss Adams, built yet further east, and his house is now the centre of a row, as it was once of an open square, on Franklin, Grace, Twenty-sixth and Twenty-seventh streets. South-east of Mr. Marshall, another son-in-law, *George W. Smith*, placed his residence, a neat wooden building, on Franklin, Main, Twenty-seventh and Twenty-eighth. This gentleman was Governor of Virginia at the time that the Theatre was burned, and was one of the victims, in consequence of his efforts to save others. *Samuel G. Adams*, the youngest of the sons, erected the building on the western slope of the hill, on Broad street, now the Bellevue Hospital. The possessions of the Adams family in Richmond and elsewhere gave them a prospect of great wealth in the natural course of things ; but impelled by an enterprising spirit, the two younger brothers sought to hasten the event. The chapter on "Flush times" gives the result.

George Nicolson, once mayor of the city (as was also Dr. John Adams), resided on one of the adjacent and most commanding heights overlooking the city and the surrounding country. The land west of it and south of Mr. Marshall's and Governor Smith's, embracing the slope of the hill, has recently been purchased by the city for a public square. Mr. Nicolson's residence was destroyed by fire some years ago. His descendants are among our worthy citizens.

One of his daughters married Carter B. Page, an enterprising man; another was the wife of *Robert Gwathmey,* a merchant of eminence in Liverpool and in Richmond; a third was the wife of the distinguished lawyer and politician, *Chapman Johnson;* and the fourth and surviving one has been a mother to the orphans of her sisters.

On Main street, near the foot of Church Hill, stood in old times and until lately, the residence of *Friend Couch*—a neat house, with a large garden attached. In my younger days this square was shaded on two sides by a number of spreading elms, the only row of trees on a mile of street. It was like an oasis in a desert, and furnished a refreshing shade to the pedestrian on a hot summer day—of which I can speak from experience. It was said that there were attractions also within the walls, but these it was not my good fortune to discover till late in life. The house, the elms, the spacious garden with its flowers and bee-hives, have all disappeared; even the soil itself on which they stood, has been deeply excavated, to furnish bricks for the erection of other structures. But some of the former occupants who cultivated those flowers still flourish, if not in immortal youth, in ripened years, engaged in social and benevolent avocations.

John Foster, a useful public servant, was one of their nearest neighbors; his residence yet stands, partially restored from the dilapidations of time and fire. John Strobia, a worthy father of a worthy and yet surviving son, * Friend Clarke, and Col. David Lambert, father of the late Mayor, were also their neighbors, but more remote. Their residences may yet be traced, and also some of their descendants, in other parts of the city.

A short distance east of where Seabrook's Warehouse is built, was the pleasant and rural-looking residence of *Adam Craig*, Clerk of the Hustings Court. The green slope in rear of the house was washed at its base by a clear rivulet, which now flows, mixed with less pure waters, through a culvert to Shockoe creek; but the house remains with its fine trees and hedges of box. The Clerk's

---

* This gentleman died in October, 1856.

office was in the small Dutch-roofed house, at the corner on Grace and Eighteenth streets. Here *Andrew Stevenson*, who was successively Speaker of the Virginia House of Delegates, of the Congressional House of Representatives, and Minister to Great Britian, acquired the elements of legal lore. *Robert Stanard*, his cotemporary, a distinguished lawyer and a Judge of the Court of Appeals, married a daughter of Mr. Craig. Mr. Stevenson died in 1857. Judge Stanard in 1846.

A most worthy couple, residing at the foot of Church hill near Rocketts, should not be forgotten. The home and good works of *Mr.* and *Mrs. Wm. Rowlett* are coeval with the century, and while I write this, his good works have just ceased, and he has gone to his reward, after attaining to nearly fourscore and ten years. He was the first to engage in the occupation of ship-broker in Richmond, and pursued it for more than half a century; but his charitable offices were of longer duration.

A neighbor of Mr. Rowlett at Rocketts, was *Richard Young*, City Surveyor, but who did not limit his investigations, to the surface of the earth. He was an instance of the pursuit of knowledge under difficulties. He would have been a Geologist, Zoologist, and all the other logists from A. to Z., had his education and opportunities favored such acquirements. His desire to make them

obtained for him the title of Philosopher Young.
His accurate knowledge of the localities of Paris,
acquired by studying the map, was remarkable.
He quitted this sublunary sphere, many years ago,
but his widow and her sister, whose lives have been
devoted to good works, still pursue the occupation
at an advanced age. The widow though childless,
has been a mother to many orphans, and her fire-
side has rarely, if ever been without such an object
of her benevolence. The father of these ladies
was a steward to General Washington for many
years, and their early life was spent on the Mount
Vernon estate. They are probably the only survivors of those who lived there cotemporaneously
with that great and good man. I trust they will
pardon this intrusion on their privacy, but such
examples should be commemorated that they may
be imitated. Mrs. Y. saw, in 1860, Rossiter's
picture of Washington at home, and declared the
likeness to be excellent.

The ascent of Church Hill in old times, and
even lately, could be attained by carriages on only
one route—the road from Main street directly to
the church-yard—and even this was "a hard road
to travel," especially by funeral processions. The
first time that I ascended it was on the solemn
occasion of a funeral pageant, a few days after the
death of Washington, when with other lads I followed at the close. Small as the population of

the city then was, I doubt if a funeral procession of greater length has extended along the street than on that occasion, except at the funeral of Washington's friend and biographer, Judge Marshall, many years after.

CHAPTER IX.

THE MAYOR.

AMBITION prevails in every sphere, and although it may have no room " to expand itself," will seek to be the centre of a circle even of very limited circumference. Aspirants for city honors, though then devoid of emolument, were as ambitious in former days as they are in the present. Among them was a worthy Irish blacksmith, who by dint of perseverance attained to the mayoralty, and his administration deserves to be recorded by the pen of a Knickerbocker. He was of the genuine Irish-Bull breed, but his attainments in public speaking fell far short of some modern city orators, of the Malaprop and Ramsbottom school, in amusing his hearers.

Butler's description of *his* hero, would apply to

ours, for Mayor M. was also captain of militia;
he was

> " Chief of domestic knights and errant,
>   Either for chartel or for warrant;
>   Great on the bench, great in the saddle,
>   That could as well bind o'er as swaddle;
>   Mighty he was in both of these,
>   And styl'd of war as well as peace.
>   But here our authors make a doubt,
>   Whether he were more wise or stout;
>   Some hold the one and some the other.
>   But howsoe'er they make a pother,
>   The diff'rence was so small, his brain
>   Outweighed his rage but half a grain;
>   Which made some take him for a tool
>   That knaves do work with, call'd a fool.

He was a strict constructionist; and on one
occasion when applied to by an old woman for a
search warrant to recover a turkey stolen from
her, he referred to the magistrate's book of forms,
in which he could find no mention of turkeys; but
there was a form of a warrant to search for a
stolen cow. After stating to the old lady the legal
difficulty, he reflected a while and thus overcame
it : " I will give you a warrant for a cow, and if in
searching for a cow you find the turkey, you may
take possession and bring it and the thief before
me." Could Sancho Panza have been more judicious ?

The worthy dignitary, by various similar exer-

cises of his judicial functions, retained and increased his popularity, not only by administering
justice, but by furnishing amusement to his constituents.

I can call to mind a practical joke played on
him by a facetious member of the municipality,
who asserted as a curious fact, that a bottle could
not be broken in an empty bag. The Mayor
expressed his disbelief; and after an argument, in
which various reasons were assigned, pro and con,
the result was a bet of a bowl of punch capacious
enough for all the members of the Common Council, the Mayor being the champion of fracture. A
fat Dutch humorist, who lived at the corner opposite to the market, (where boots, shoes, bread and
Brandreth's pills, have of late years shod, fed and
physicked the market folks,) agreed to furnish the
implements wherewith to decide the wager.

A large corner-stone, planted to protect the
sidewalk from cart-wheels, was selected as the
antagonist to the bottle. The winning parties,
(those who were to quaff the punch,) assembled,
and a crowd of curious philosophers surrounded
them.

Mr. Darmsdadt produced the bag and the bottle,
turned the sack inside out and blew into the bottle,
to show that all was fair. The bottle was then
bagged, and the mouth of the bag was securely
tied. The Mayor seized the sack with both hands,

13

just below the ligature, and swung it as he had formerly swung a sledge-hammer. He then brought it down with all his might upon the stone. The glass rattled and the Mayor exclaimed, " VICTORY !" but the judges were desired to open the bag, when, lo and behold ! it was found *not empty ;* and his honor had to stand the punch and the laugh.

In old times the municipality, consisting of Mayor, Aldermen and Common Council, met as one body, and there being no City Hall for their sessions, they convened in an apartment rented for that purpose, in the square south-west of the market bridge, and commanding a view of Manchester on the opposite side of the river.

On one warm summer day the city fathers had met in council, and their labors for the public weal had rendered them drouthy. In those primitive days the practice adopted in New York of eating, drinking and smoking at the expense of many thousands to their constituents, had not been thought of by our unpaid commonalty ; and in order to assuage their thirst with some pleasant beverage, Michael Ryan, one of the members (an author whose works are extinct), proposed a wager for a flowing bowl, and in deference to the Mayor he offered to make it with him. The Mayor replied, that Mr. Ryan had already played him one trick, and he should not catch him again.

"But," said Ryan, "if you are sure of winning this time, you'll take me up—and so to give you a chance, I will bet you that I can prove from your own admission, you are on the other side of the river." "I'll take that bet," said his honor. The wag, pointing to Manchester, asked if that was not one side of the river. "Certainly," replied the mayor. "And is not Richmond on the other side?" "Yes." "Are you not in Richmond, and consequently on the other side?" The Mayor was stumped, and ordered the beverage, but swore he would never make another bet. "I'll take you a dozen of porter on that," said Ryan. "Done!" cried the excited Mayor, and no sooner said than *done* he was.

Joseph Darmsdadt, one of the actors in the scene, was as well known for many years as the market square on which he lived. He was, as his name imports, a Hessian, and came to this country as a sutler, with the troops that were sold by their prince, at so much per head, to fight the battles of despotism. It was, no doubt, a fortunate arrangement for those of the mercenary troops who, like Mr. Darmsdadt, escaping the perils of war and the clutches of their prince, obtained freedom in the land they were sent to enslave.

Our Hessian citizen established himself in Richmond, not long after he had renounced his foreign allegiance. He was a shrewd man, and the valley

beyond the Blue Ridge being settled by Germans,
his knowledge of the language enabled him to
attract the custom of the farmers, who drove their
wagons to Richmond, laden with the products of
the dairy, the mill, the forest and the chase.

The social disposition of Mr. Darmsdadt brought
him into society, even the best. His own enter-
tainments were given daily. Almost all our citizens, in those days, went early to market, to furnish their larders ; and Mr. D. would have a large
coffee-pot before his fire-place, of the contents of
which, prepared by himself, many of his friends,
judges, lawyers, doctors and merchants, partook,
whenever they were so inclined—particularly on
wet or cold mornings ; and here the chit-chat of
the day was first heard, and much news was circulated from this social coffee-house. Its proprietor
retained it and its customers some thirty or forty
years, until his death. In his will, written by himself and spelled as he pronounced, he left $5500
to charitable objects, including female friends who
were in indigent circumstances, regretting he could
not leave more in consequence of the depreciation
of property in 1818. The rest of his estate he
bequeathed to German relatives.

To recur to the subject of this chapter—the
Worshipful Mayor—his first administration was
marked by a distinguished honor, which he seems

to have borne well, as the following record will
show, and it merits preservation :

NOVEMBER 20th, 1784.—Last Sunday, in the afternoon,
came to this city, his Excellency General George Washington,
Esq. The next day was ushered in with the discharge of
thirteen cannon, when every countenance showed the most
heart-felt gladness on seeing our illustrious and beloved
General in the Capital of the State, and in the bosom of
peace. In the evening, the city was illuminated and every
demonstration of joy was shown on the pleasing occasion.

On Thursday, the merchants of this city gave an elegant
dinner to his Excellency, General Washington ; the same day,
came from Boston, the Marquis de la Fayette, accompanied
with Captain Granshaw, of the navy of his most Christian
Majesty, and the Chevalier Caruman.

The two Houses of Assembly appointed committees to wait
upon his Excellency and the Marquis de la Fayette, who seve-
rally addressed them.

Last night, the corporation of this city gave an elegant ball
in honor to our illustrious and much beloved visitor, General
Washington.

On Monday, the corporation of this city waited on his Excellency, and presented him with the following address :

" *To* GEORGE WASHINGTON, *Esq., late Commander-in-Chief of the
American Army :*

" SIR—Actuated by every sentiment which can inspire a
grateful people, the Mayor, Recorder, Aldermen and Common
Councilmen of the city of Richmond, embrace this long wished
for opportunity of congratulating you on your return to the
bosom of peace and retirement in your native country, after so
many years honorably spent amidst the toils and turmoils of
war, which, through the smiles of Heaven on your exertions,
has been productive of liberty, glory and independence to our
extensive empire.

"On seeing you, sir, in this city, we feel all that men can feel, who are indebted to you for every social enjoyment, and who are deeply impressed with a conviction that, if the late illustrious leader of the armies of America, had not only possessed, but exercised every talent and every virtue, which can dignify the hero and the patriot, we might not at this day have dared to speak the language of free-born citizens, nor would we have seen commerce and navigation, with their fruitful train, liberated from their shackles, inviting the inhabitants of distant nations to seek an asylum and residence among us.

"When in the review of a few years, we behold you, not only forming soldiers, but also teaching to conquer; when we contemplate that prudence, courage, and magnanimity which, surmounting every difficulty, regardless of every danger, and contemning every reward, excites not only the veneration of your country, but even commanded the admiration and applause of your enemies, and spread the fame of America to the remotest corner of the world, giving her rank and consequence among the kingdoms of the earth; and when we think what we might have been if Washington had not existed, our hearts expand with emotion too strong for utterance; and we can only pray that the Supreme Giver of all victory may crown you with his choicest blessings here, and never-failing glory hereafter.

"Signed by order and on behalf of the Common Hall.

"ROBERT MITCHELL, Mayor."

"*To the Worshipful the Mayor, Recorder, Aldermen, and Common Council of the City of Richmond:*

"GENTLEMEN—I derive great honor from your congratulatory address, the language of which is too flattering not to have excited my utmost gratitude.

"To the smiles of Heaven, to a virtuous and gallant army, and to the exertions of my fellow-citizens of the Union, (not to superior talents of mine) are to be ascribed the blessings of that liberty, independence, and peace, of which we are now in the enjoyment.

" Whilst these are afforded us, and whilst the advantages of
commerce are not only offered, but are soliciting our accept-
ance, it must be our own fault, indeed if we do not make them
productive of a rich and plenteous harvest, and of that
national honor and glory which should be characteristic of a
rising empire.

" That this growing city may enjoy the benefits which are
to be derived from them in the fullest extent—that it may
improve such of the advantages as bountiful nature has
bestowed, and that it may soon be ranked among the first in
the Union for population, commerce, and wealth, is my sincere
and fervent wish.

"GEORGE WASHINGTON."

CHAPTER X.

THE HAY-SCALE WAR.

SCARCELY any country or any community, however peaceably disposed and however well governed, can be always free from domestic feuds and
internal commotions.

In the beginning of the present century, a dangerous feud arose in the city of Richmond, which
threatened dismemberment or civil commotion,
or as one of our most distinguished poets expresses
it in prose, " Where a difficulty in the parish
seemed to announce the end of the world ! " The
origin of the controversy was no less important

than the locating the first *hay-scale* erected in the
city. As such a machine was considered beyond
the skill of any American mechanic to construct,
it was ordered from England, and on its arrival, the
question arose, what part of the city should be
honored by its erection therein?

Each claimed the preference, and three parties
were formed—the *Creeks* on the east, the *Shockoes*
on the north, and an intermediate one, which I
shall call the *Carians*. The discussions in and
out of the Council waxed warmer at each renewal,
until at last, as a rhymester of the day described it,

> " The contest high and higher rose,
> Until from words they got to blows,
> As arguments of greatest stress
> That either party could express."

The newspapers were resorted to, and squibs and
even epigrams, or attempts at them, were penned
on the occasion. Such was the excitement that
one party, fearing a defeat, and preferring, like
the Czar, destruction to disgrace, threatened to
throw the scales into the river.

At length the James River Company fortunately threw a sop to this Cerberus, by offering a
piece of ground for the erection of the scales on
Cary street near the Basin, then nearly completed, and also offered to bear a part of the
expense, on condition that the Company might
have the use of the scales, when not otherwise

employed. Not the first time that the scales of justice were influenced by interested motives.

The Creek nation and the Shockoes had to succumb, and the city was saved. The flow of ink ceased, and that of blood was averted.

The scales yet retain their position, and the only objection to it was discovered too late—to wit, that the ascent to the platform, and the restricted limits of approach to it were such, that wagons laden with hay found great difficulty in reaching it, and it fell into disuse.

The defeated nations obtained their triumphs in turn. Each was honored with an independent hay-scale, and the Carians retain the empty honor of an empty platform.

How many wars originate from causes almost as puerile, and terminate in as little benefit to the victor and as little injury to the vanquished!

CHAPTER XI.

TWO PARSONS AND NE'ER A CHURCH.

"Behold, how good and how pleasant it is for brethren to dwell
together in unity!"

It is a remarkable fact that Richmond was without a church of any denomination in the early part of the present century, and previously, except the venerable old *parish church of St. John's*, on Church Hill, where religious service was performed before the Revolution, and where the first burst of political regeneration was uttered by Patrick Henry, in the emphatic words, " GIVE ME LIBERTY OR GIVE ME DEATH !"—and almost at the moment that I write the words (August, 1855), there is being elevated on the Capitol Square the splendid statue of that orator, by Crawford, represented in the very act of uttering words even more memorable, as being the grand outburst of the spirit of Liberty, personified by Henry at the age of 29, when after the passage of the stamp act, he electrified the House of Burgesses in 1765, with the grand peroration, " Cæsar had his Brutus, Charles his Cromwell, and George the Third"—the cry of

"Treason! Treason!" interrupted him for an instant—and he added—"may profit by their example—if this be treason, make the most of it." Such an occasion justified the impassioned representation of the orator by the sculptor—a work destined, if others were wanting, to immortalize both.

The use of the old church by the apostles of liberty was not considered a desecration, except by those who advocated a union of Church and State, and adored monarchy in the infallible person of George III. The liberty invoked here was besought with the aid and blessing of Heaven, and it was granted and has been perpetuated. How different was the spurious imitation in France, where religion was abolished and infidelity proclaimed; where a sort of heathen worship was adopted, by personifying Liberty as a goddess, who proved her title by permitting to her worshippers all sorts of freedom—a Liberty that did not survive the courtezan who personated her.

The only other building erected for religious worship, at the time first adverted to, was the Quaker Meeting-house, yet standing on Cary and Nineteenth streets, but in rather a dilapidated condition;* the number of members of that society,

---

* A few days after the the publication of the 1st edition of this book, the Spirit or the book moved some liberal Friends to repair the house and also the wall around the burial ground and grass plat, which was gradually falling into the street.

once large, being much diminished. Some thirty odd years ago there was a great exodus of them from Southampton and other counties, to the West. They carried to Ohio the art of curing bacon—but I have wandered from my text.*

Other religious denominations had occasional places of worship only, for occasional preachers— mere barns, where no regular weekly service was performed.

But this lack of churches in Richmond gave rise to a beautiful illustration of Christian love and union.

The population of Church Hill was then very sparse, consisting of only a few families, and the distance to the old church, from that part of the city where it was comparatively dense, was too great for worshippers to attend, especially in the condition of the unpaved streets in those days. The hall of the House of Delegates was the only apartment in the city sufficiently spacious for a

---

* Such was the spirit of intolerance in Virginia in former days, that, in 1663, a fine of five thousand pounds of tobacco was incurred by any ship-master who should bring Quakers to reside in the Colony, and the same fine by any person who should entertain a Quaker in or near his house to preach or teach. It is the more remarkable that the number of Quakers in Virginia should have become so large, but persecution acts perhaps like the pressure on a spring, and increases the re-action.

The Colony of North Carolina offered an asylum to the Quakers and other dissenters expelled from Virginia.

place of worship, and to this purpose it was devoted on the Sabbath.

But there were two ministers of different denominations, with each a congregation, and only
one hall for worship. Parson Buchanan was an
Episcopalian, Parson Blair a Presbyterian. Which
one should claim the pulpit ? He who had the
largest congregation, or he who had most influence
with the Executive and Legislature?   The two
parsons did not test the question.   The fraternal
appellation which each gave to the other was based.
on real brotherly love.

On each alternate Sunday, the one and the other
occupied the movable pulpit, which disappeared on
week days, and such was the spirit of tolerance and
liberality which the example of the pastors had
inspired in their congregations, that the same individuals formed a large portion of the worshippers
on every Sabbath.

These two clergymen were beloved throughout
the community for their many virtues. They were
not ascetics, but liked to see their flocks gay and
happy, and to promote and to partake of such feelings within proper bounds. Each possessed a fund
of wit, and was liberal in expending it. The
humorous poetical sallies of each, usually addressed
to the other, caused many a smile to be wreathed.
But I have something to record of these clerical
14

brethren which shows their characters in a more beautiful light.

Mr. Buchanan was a bachelor, and by the death of a brother inherited a competency. Mr. Blair was a married man, dependent on his parishioners and on his school for the support of a large family. Probably by some logical argument, on a witty basis, Mr. Buchanan proved that Mr. Blair was entitled to all the clerical fees of both. If not logically, he carried his point practically, and no Episcopal couple were married, nor an Episcopal child christened, that the fee, if any was forthcoming, did not help to expand the slim purse of the Presbyterian brother.

On one occasion, Mr. Buchanan played a joke on Mr. Blair, in this wise: A gentleman had engaged Mr. Buchanan to perform the marriage service in the country, some twenty or thirty miles distant, but omitted to provide a conveyance for him. At the appointed time Mr. Buchanan hired a carriage for two days, made the outward journey, and made the twain one—partook of the wedding supper, and no doubt enlivened it. On the next day, as he gave the couple his parting benediction, the bridegroom slipped into his hand a rather heavy rouleau.

The kind-hearted parson inwardly chuckled at the handsome fee he had earned for his brother.

He was anxious to unroll the paper, expecting to
find ten half joes enveloped, but he restrained his
impatience until out of sight of the wedding folks;
then, to his surprise and disappointment, he discovered ten half dollars! Vexation could not long
retain its place with him, and soon gave way to the
opposite feeling. He determined, if he could not
put a fee *into* Mr. Blair's pocket, he would get
some fun *out of* him. So, on his return home, he
drew out a regular account thus:

The Rev. J. D. BLAIR,
            To the Rev. J. BUCHANAN.

To hire of a carriage two days, at $5, - - - -	$10
To horse-feed and other expenses to and fro, - -	3
	—$13
By wedding fee received from Mr. ——, - - -	5
Balance due to J. Buchanan, - - - -	$8

The memory of these good men is enshrined in
the hearts of their survivors.

A contemporary of these Reverend gentlemen
was the Abbé Dubois, a Catholic Priest of talent
and distinction, and, like them, free from intolerance, so that they enjoyed each other's society.
The Abbé escaped from France during the reign of
terror, and came to Richmond at the close of the
last or early in the present century. He obtained
permission to perform the services of his church in
the court-room of the Capitol—the present Senate
Chamber—on the opposite side of the hall to that

in which his Episcopal and Presbyterian friends officiated.

The Abbé taught a French class in Harris's school, and also gave lessons to a select few at his own residence, in the small wooden-house which is supplanted by the new Custom-house and Post-office. When the Abbé left Richmond, a farewell supper was given to him by a brother teacher, Mr. Dunn, at which his clerical friends were among the guests. He closed his career, years afterwards, as Catholic Bishop of New York. One of his pupils, now almost an octogenarian, to whom I am indebted for this, speaks of him as a learned, accomplished and amiable man.

The humble residence of Mr. Blair yet stands at the north-west corner of Leigh and Seventh. The not less simple one of Mr. Buchanan, at the north-east end of Mayo's Bridge, has disappeared.

Since those primitive times, I have seen many churches built, and many of them converted into tobacco factories, bakeries, concert halls, dwellings, &c., but only to be substituted by larger and better edifices, and now Richmond contains as many and as handsome places of worship as any city of its size.

Within the last two or three years, in walking round little more than a square (now sub-divided), one would pass these various places of worship—a Campbellite (Disciples), a Baptist, an Episcopalian, an African Baptist, an Unitarian, a Methodist Episcopal, and a Presbyterian church, and a Synagogue.

It may be interesting, for future reference, to enumerate the places of worship in Richmond, and their pastors at the present time—May, 1860.

EPISCOPAL.—*St. John's.*—Grace and 25th street, Church Hill, Rev. J. T. Points, pastor.

Monumental.—Broad, below 12th, Rev. Geo. Woodbridge, D. D.

St. James.—Marshall and 5th, Rev. Joshua Peterkin, pastor.

St. Paul's.—Corner of Grace and 9th, Rev. Charles Minnegerode, D. D.

Grace.—Corner Main and Foushee, Rev. F. Baker.

BAPTIST.—*First.*—Broad and 12th, Rev. J. L. Burrows, D. D.

Second.—Corner Main and 6th, Rev. L. W. Seeley.

Grace Street.—Grace and Foushee, Rev. J. B. Jeter, D. D.

Leigh Street.—Leigh and 25th, Church Hill, Rev. E. J. Willis.

Oregon.—Oregon Hill.

First African.—Broad and College, Rev. Robert Ryland.

Second African.—Byrd, between 1st and 2d.

Third African.—Leigh, near Brook avenue.

METHODIST EPISCOPAL.—*Trinity.*—Franklin, east of 14th street. Rev. J. D. Blackwell; about to be transferred to corner of Broad and 20th.

Centenary.—Grace, near 5th, Rev. W. H. Wheelwright.

Broad Street.—Broad and 10th, Rev. Jas. A. Duncan, pastor.

Clay Street.—Clay and Adams, Rev. J. J. Waggener.

Union Station.—24th street, Union Hill, Rev. W. W. Bennett.

Oregon Chapel.—Oregon Hill.

Wesley Chapel.—17th, near Venable, Rev. Mr. Bellman.

Sidney Chapel.—Sidney, Rev. J. M. Saunders.

Rockett's Chapel.—Rockett's, Rev. Mr. Bellman.

African Methodist.—3d, between Leigh and Jackson, Rev. G. W. Nolley.

PRESBYTERIAN.—*First.*—Capitol and 10th, Rev. T. V. Moore,
D. D.

Second.—5th, near Main, Rev. M. D. Hoge, D. D.

United.—Corner Franklin and 8th, Rev. C. H. Read, D. D.

Third.—Corner Broad and 25th, Rev. Mr. Mitchell.

Duval Chapel.—Corner Duval and Adams, Rev. J. J. Mc-
Mahon.

ROMAN CATHOLIC.—*St. Peter's Cathedral.*—Corner Grace and
8th, Right Rev. John McGill, assisted by Rev. J. Teeling,
D. D., and Rev. J. Brady.

St. Mary's.—(German.)—Marshall, near 4th, Rev. Jos. Polk.

New.—Not consecrated, Church Hill.

HEBREW SYNAGOGUES.—*Kaal Kadosh Beth Shalome.*—(Holy
house of Peace.)—Mayo street, Mr. Geo. Jacobs reader.

Kaal Kadosh Beth Ahiba (Holy house of Love).—(German.)
11th, near Marshall, Rev. M. J. Michelbacher minister.

SOCIETY OF FRIENDS.—Corner Cary and 19th.

DISCIPLES.—*Sycamore Church.*—11th, near Marshall, Rev. W.
J. Pettigrew.

UNIVERSALIST.—Mayo street, Rev. Mr. Shrigley.

GERMAN LUTHERAN.—5th, above Jackson, Rev. Mr. Hoyer.

EVANGELICAL LUTHERAN.—*Bethlehem.*—Between Clay and Leigh,
Rev. Mr. Gross.

☞ This chapter commenced with "ne'er a church," it con-
cludes with nearly forty.

CHAPTER XII.

CEMETERIES.

"There the wicked cease from troubling, and the weary are at rest."

THE old church-yard of St. John's has been fully tenanted for a number of years, and its tombstones are memorials of many worthies, whose names might else have passed from the present generation. After an absence of some fifteen or twenty years, I re-visited it, and obtained the melancholy recognition of the names of more of my old friends and acquaintances, inscribed on the tombstones, than I found on the door-plates and sign-boards of the living generation. It recalled "the memory of past joys, pleasant but mournful to the soul."

This sacred spot has not been exempt from the barbarous desecration of the idle and worthless. The perpetration of such sacrilegious mischief is one of the most disgraceful traits of the basest characters. Tombs have been mutilated, if not destroyed, but many of them have mouldered or toppled over from neglect. One of the oldest, however, dated 1751, almost coeval with the church, remains unimpaired, except being cracked by the fall of a tree, and its preservation is attended with some mystery. It covers the remains of the Rev. Mr. Rose, the worthy grandsire of a worthy grand-daughter, the wife and widow of Gov. Pleasants, and who has recently followed them to the tomb.

This ancient cemetery has been much neglected of late years, and looks as though the present generation had other occupation than to think of the past, but the mysterious preservation of the tomb of Mr. Rose, shows that there was a remnant of "Old Mortality" that loved his memory. His tombstone was repaired from the effects of time and of the elements, at regular intervals and by unseen hands, until within the last few years, when probably a tombstone covers those kind hands. In my boyhood, the Sexton of this old and only cemetery, was a woman, Mrs. Bowers by name, and well stricken in years. Her sons were her assistants. She was a Meg Merrilies in bone and muscle, and several times have I seen her, waist or shoulder deep in the earth, apparelled in loose trousers. As she was *out of bloom,* her motive for wearing the garment could not be impeached— as she was a widow, her husband could not complain of the usurpation, and she was one of the few instances of the justifiable assumption of them.

A second general cemetery called Shockoe Hill, near the Poor-house, has been filled and extended, and a third, "the Hollywood," is now being tenanted; and it is, or will be, the most beautiful Necropolis anywhere to be found. Nature has done her part in hills, valleys, rivulets, and woods, and Art has embellished, without rendering formal, the beauties of Nature. The landscape embraces every variety—forest and placid stream, hills crowned with woods, or with steeples, shaded valleys and blazing furnaces, bridges, on which railroad vehicles are moving sixty feet in the air, and, almost beneath your feet, boats gliding on the graceful curve of a broad canal. In the distance, vast flour-mills and factories, and beyond them the vessels to be laden with their products; the perspective closing with cultivated fields, whose grain serves partly to supply those mills.

May the spirits of those whose mortal remains repose in this earthly resting-place, look down on it from a heavenly one!

[P. S.—The Oakwood Cemetery, at the eastern end of the city, is now receiving its first unconscious tenants—1858.

A Roman Catholic Cemetery has recently been established near the city, on the Mechanicsville road.

The Hebrew burial ground adjoins that of Shockoe Hill, mentioned above.]

CHAPTER XIII.

CITIZENS OF YORE.

"Honor and shame from no condition rise;
Act well your part, there all the honor lies."

Mr. Rose, the jailor, and others whom I will introduce, illustrated the truth of these lines. He flourished at the close of the last and early in the
present century. In his full suit of black, including
shorts and hose, which well suited his tall and dignified figure, one would rather suppose that he had
charge of a church than of a jail. He was a
worthy and kind-hearted gentleman, whose society
and that of his family was as highly prized as if
he was master of a palace instead of a prison.

His house, which stood on the present open
space in front of the County Court-house (which
occupies the site of the old jail), was not attractive
externally, and the stronghold in the rear of it,
called by its occupants *Rose's Brig*, had still less
outward charms, and certainly none within ; but it,
like the dwelling, had many visitors, though not
voluntary ones. Their condition, however, was rendered as comfortable as was compatible with the
duty of their custodian.

Rose's Brig (erroneously called *Jug* in the 1st edition) obtained its name thus : A sailor, who was imprisoned there, said to Mr. Rose that he could paint pictures, and if he had the canvas and other materials, he would paint one for Mr. R.   The sailor's offer was accepted, and the picture of a brig in full sail was gradually developed on the canvas, tacked to the wall.

One morning, when Mr. Rose called to see the imprisoned artist, he was not visible, and on raising the canvas, which was partly untacked, a port hole in the wall was disclosed, out of which the sailor had discharged himself, and the name of the vessel was transferred to the prison.

I have introduced the worthy Mr. Rose, as the precursor of his son-in-law, under whose rod and ferule I advanced in Dilworth as far as words of two syllables, and I now beg leave to introduce His Honor, the Most Worshipful ****** * ***** ************, a very long name for a very short man ; but though short in stature, Mr. **** ********* was not a man to be overlooked. He came from some unpronounceable place in Wales, and had served on board a British man-of-war at the seige of Gibraltar by Spain.   That was the only datum by which to calculate his age, which he never disclosed, and time did not betray it ; a score of years scarcely made any impression on his appearance, and gray hairs *could not* betray him, for no locks of any color decorated his expansive bald pate. Tired of naval gunnery in the Old World, he sought " to teach the young idea how to shoot" in the New. What vicissitudes intervened between his avocations as powder-monkey and pedagogue, I cannot say, but in the latter he served many years, acquiring in it both cash and credit. He descended from this magisterial bench, to ascend a more lofty one, but of this presently. He changed, but did not abandon his literary occupations. Instead of *using* school books, he *vended* them ; nor did he contract his sphere within the bounds of spelling books and arithmetics. Literature in general, music and book-binding came within his scope. City honors awaited him ; and, by gradual advances, he attained to the office of Mayor, which he filled with much dignity. He also became Grand Secretary of the Grand Lodge of Virginia. Mr. ************ was a patron of the fine arts, and more especially of music. He was one of the founders of the *Musical Society* that held its regular concerts at *Tanbark Hall;* and on these occasions, it may be truly said,

" With nose and chin he figured in ;"

for those features were in him exceedingly prominent, and as, like most short men, he held his head exceedingly high, he could not be otherwise than conspicuous among the harmonious band, as was his bass-viol, even taller than himself. This society contained several other members in strong contrast to each other, whose faces and figures, and ecstatic gestures, would have furnished a group worthy of the pencil of Hogarth.

Mr. ************ was a good and charitable, though not a pious man. Of his deficiency in the latter respect I would hesitate to speak, had he not given the cue, by telling a story on himself. Horsemanship was not his forte, nor could he be expected to excel in that amongst his other accomplishments. Very short legs, a seafaring life, and that of a dominie, were not favorable to the acquirement of equestrian skill. On one occasion, when in the saddle, his steed got the whip-hand of him ; and, fearing a fatal result, he attempted to offer up a prayer, but the only one he could recollect was the first he had learned ; and he poured forth—

"Now I lay me down to sleep."

Mr. ************ (I love to behold the *constellation* of his name, which I do not breathe, tho' it sleeps not in the shade) retained on the bench of justice the magisterial air he had acquired at the tutor's desk, and in every situation preserved his dignity, whether at the festive board, the whist table, or the music stand. He literally *shone* in every station that he occupied ; his capacious bald head reflecting the light in all directions, like a

15

halo. He died, full of years and full of honors, in the year 1837. His last good work was to influence the establishment of the first Savings Bank in Richmond.

Mr. *************'s book store was in the only wooden building now remaining of the olden time, already described, on the south side of West Main street; it stands at the corner of Fourteenth, or *Pearl* street. (*Mock Pearl.* I dislike these borrowed names, that impress one with the insignificance of the object, compared with its patronyme. Astor House, for instance—dimensions, 20 by 36— and Wall street. Bah!) In connection with Mr. *************'s book store, I am reminded of an humbler, but, in one sense of the word, a much *greater* personage, whose station was under His Honor, the Mayor, though not an official one.

Fat Nancy, the apple-woman, *filled* the cellar door under his Worship's shop window. There she displayed all fruits in their season; the black Pomona of the street, of which she had the monopoly, except so far as her claim was disputed (I should say, infringed upon) by a peripatetic vender, Bob Hummins by name; but as Bob had only one arm, he did not venture to dispute Nancy's supremacy, and kept out of reach of her tongue. If scolding could have *tried down* Nancy's fat, the school-boys would have reduced her to a shadow; for, as some three hundred or more pounds of flesh obstructed her locomotion, the boys stole her apples without fear of arrest (unless by the Mayor, and it was beneath his dignity to interpose) and thus they kept Nancy's scolding faculties in constant exercise.*

Another resident of the same square passes before my mind's eye. Previous to the Corsican invasion of confectioners, the dispensers of sugar plums had appeared but singly, and in the days I write of, the incumbent was a Frenchman, who bore the euphonious and sylvan name of Aubin de la Foret. Instead of the brilliant shops and saloons which now tempt not only the children, but their parents, with ices, jellies, fruits, and all sorts of bonbons and cordials, Laforet exhibited, among various less refined comestibles (not meaning that his candies were highly refined), a dozen jars of confectionery, and these did not require very frequent replenishing. Temptation has, of late years, caused many a sweet tooth to be cut, and, perhaps, to be extracted. Few

---

* It is urged that I did injustice to one of my most conspicuous personages, and to the rising generation, by suppressing his name in the first edition. There is no good reason for concealing it, for the possessor was not ashamed of it, nor of any thing attached to it.

I will now, therefore, let the *stars* pale before the bright name of William Henry Fitzwhyllson. We may thus confer mutual honor. *I* seek to immortalize *his* name, which will immortalize *my* book, and we may shine together like Gemini the second!

could compete with the Forrester for the palm of
ugliness. To look at him and at his sign, you
would be apt to think it a misnomer—so little were
the man and the name adapted to each other. His
nose would have been very prominent, but that it
was turned hard-a-starboard, which probably saved
it from running afoul of other objects. His legs
were mismatched, one being exceedingly bowed,
which gave him a lee lurch in walking. His eyes
stood so prominently out of his head that one
might suppose he could see in all directions at
once, and his complexion vied in hue and wrinkles
with his own dried figs. But, with all this lack of
" personal pulchritude," (as Mr. Rootes termed
beauty,) Mr. Laforest, as he was usually called,
was a worthy, honest and industrious man, and his
children inherited, with his good name, something
better than his figure and his features.

Among the singular characters of by-gone days,
the tall, stiff and formal figure of Mons. Joseph
Bonnardel rises before my mind's eye. This old
gent'eman (I cannot say citizen) was of the
"ancièn regime" of France, and when that was
upset he could no longer remain. The court costume which he wore, and probably the only kind
he possessed, indicated that he had known better
days.

His ante-revolutionary suits were of costly materials, and of the fashion of the times of Louis

XVI. His dress was a stiff stock of silk or cambric, fastened behind with a large buckle set in paste or other brilliant imitation of precious stones; this shone conspicuously above the vest and coat, the collars of which were extremely low, and this stock was on extra occasions ornamented in front with lace falls. His vest, of figured brocade, was extremely ample, with flaps to the pockets, and extended below his hips, garnished with many buttons in the centre of each of which glistened a brilliant of properly adapted hue. His coat, on some occasions of purple, or of snuff-colored silk velvet, and on others of a lighter silken material, was of grand proportions, the large buttons decorated like those of the vest, and with pockets of huge dimensions. His small clothes were of black satin, with elaborate knee buckles, his hose of silk, and his shoes stout, with high vamps and large buckles. He wore his hair, which was black silvered with gray, combed back from his forehead and temples (like the ladies of to-day), and gathered behind in a clubbed queue. His highly decorated gold snuff-box and cane were passports of gentility, as well as certificates of date.

Mr. Bonnardel's appearance (Frenchman though he was) was that of an animated automaton; every movement was as stiff and angular as if operated by machinery, and his manner of speaking was as slow and formal as were his motions and figure—

for the gearing that worked all this machine was of tardy movement; misfortune had probably injured its springs. The old gentleman, for gentleman he was, was very poor, and supported himself by giving private lessons in French, at a time when scholars were few. He lived in a small wooden house, one story and an attic, with a peculiar looking porch in front, yet standing on Grace street west of Fourth, with tall stumps of mulberry trees in front.* In this house he lived, "solitary and alone," for many years, with no domestic help, and but few domestic comforts—but his apartment was neat and clean, though little encumbered with furniture. Mr. B. preserved every article of his wardrobe, however much worn, which he had brought from la belle France. Paper boxes contained stockings innumerable, much dilapidated, which, perhaps, he intended to re-establish on a new footing; others with various garments and various articles edible or useless, and each carefully labeled—on one was seen "Bas de soie sans pieds."

The poor old man felt sometimes the cravings of hunger, which, perhaps, he had not means to appease, for he was too proud to ask assistance, even if he required it, and his appetite was of

---

* Demolished in 1859, as are most of the old buildings noted in 1856.

the insatiable kind. When by chance dinner was announced at the house where he was giving a lesson and he was invited to a seat at the table, the stowage he made would indicate that he was laying in provisions for an East India voyage.

Mr. Bonnardel was afflicted—I ought to say blessed—with an idiosyncracy which age did not abate. He was not only very susceptible of the tender passion himself, but he imagined, and was rendered happy in the idea, that every handsome pupil, who was old enough to discern his merits, was in love with him; and his greatest concern was, lest his devotion to any one of his admirers should break the hearts of the others. The old man rather lived to love, than loved to live.

Some of my grandma readers, nay, even some of the most youthful great-grandmas, may have been pupils of Mr. Bonnardel, and may remember his gallantry, though they have outlived the tender passion he inspired.

Let no one misconceive me so much as to think that I have introduced this old gentleman or others as subjects of ridicule. I can sympathize with a worthy man, however impoverished he may be, and whatever may be his innocent peculiarities. Dotage itself should be respected, when preceded by a life of utility and integrity.

With so successful an example before me as Hone's Table-Book, I may venture to introduce a few more of the individuals, not of every day life, interspersed among our population in the olden time.

In my boyhood one of the most conspicuous, and in one sense of the word, the *greatest* man of his day, was *Major Willis*, (more properly *Maximus*), but commonly called Jack Willis, an enlarged edition of Falstaff, whose belt would have fallen far short of encircling Willis. He was not only a Falstaff in the flesh, but also in the spirit, like him witty and living by his wits. We do not reckon flesh by the stone as in England, or I might say fat Jack would have counterpoised forty stone. His tailor used to hand him one end of the measuring tape and revolve around him with the other, till he had accomplished his circumference. Had Major Willis lived to a fat old age, he might, like Falstaff, have had a prince for his crony and rollicking companion; nay more, the prince might have called him "Nuncle," for prince Achille Murat, son of the king of Naples, married Willis's niece, a lady of great beauty; but Willis did not live to see the marriage, nor did Achille, to see the restoration of the Napoleon dynasty in the person of his cousin.

Achille's brother, Joachim, also married an American lady, and they are now (1856) flourishing in Paris as members of the Imperial family; some fifteen years ago, his glorious republican wife toiled, woman-like, to support her *ci-devant* princely husband in inglorious idleness, in the vicinity of his royal uncle Joseph, *ci-devant* king of Spain, at his seat (not throne) on the Delaware. A niece of the writer was a pupil in the boarding-school of that lady at Bordentown, New Jersey. Such are the vicissitudes of fortune !

But dazzled by regal splendor, I have lost sight of "my fat friend," as Beau Brummel called George IV. I can, however, only record, that after a short life and a merry one, he died at his lodgings—not at the Boar's head—but at the Eagle, and the undertaker had to call in the carpenter and mason to take out the door frame, before he could take out the great mass of mortality, he had undertaken to inter.

And now for a contrast to Jack Willis, which I present in the person of a little weazel of a man, who would weigh about as much as one of Jack's calves, and its stocking would be large enough for Jemmy's jacket. This diminutive specimen of humanity named Jemmy Elliot, supported himself on lizards ! Frequently have I seen him take them in his mouth, not cooked as the large species called Guana, are in the West Indies, but alive and *quick!*

To prevent any ill effect on my reader's stomach, let me add that Jemmy did not bite them like radishes, nor swallow them whole; but on opening his lantern-jaws, the lively lizard would peep out, look around, then run about his face and neck, and hide in his bosom. Jemmy would catch a fly and give it as a reward. He carried many of these familiar spirits in a little box, and would exhibit them and their training, which embraced various tricks, in number and variety according to the number of "half bits" contributed to the entertainment. Jemmy lived but did not fatten on his lizards. His life was as inoffensive as theirs, and he was probably metamorphosed into one at his death. They seemed to delight to play about his grave, especially on those nights when it was illuminated by fire-flies.

Amongst those whose appearance, not for beauty or grace, was apt to attract attention in by-gone days, was *Friend Maddux*, a tall, raw-boned Quaker, who adhered strictly to the costume of his society. Friend Maddux was full six feet in stature, and his long strides and rapid gait might have indicated that he inherited the boots of Jack the giant-killer—he strode about four feet at each step, and slung his body and arms with a vim to keep pace with his legs. His occupation was that of collector of accounts, and his approach was a terror to bad pay-masters. He was very plain-spoken, and slow to accept excuses; but although a severe dun, he must have been a kind-hearted man, as the following incident will show.

He had occasion to call on Mrs. Green, once a beautiful actress, whose " occupation was gone." Her only child, a daughter in the bloom of youth, was burned at the theatre, from which the mother escaped through a door behind the scenes, while the daughter was with some friends in one of the boxes. Mrs. Green rushed forth in the attire of the Bleeding Nun, (the character she was personating,) to seek for her daughter in the houses where she visited, those of respectable citizens; her frantic appearance exceeding any tragic acting—she flew from house to house, but, alas! in vain.

Her husband, a favorite actor, had become dissipated and left her destitute, and when friend Maddux saw her, she was living in poverty and solitude. He felt compassion for her desolate condition—a childless mother and deserted wife.

He spoke to her of religion and its consolations, and inquired if she attended church. She replied, "I do no". I have no one to go with me, and have not resolution to go alone." John's pity was excited, and he asked if she would go with him. She thanked him, but said they were not of the same creed. He replied, "I will go to thy church with thee." She assented, and he promised to call on the next Sunday. As John exacted punctuality, he also practiced it—accordingly, on the day appointed the Episcopal congregation were astonished by the entrance of the tall and ungainly Quaker, with the pale and delicate actress arrayed in weeds, leaning on his arm. Their devotion was suspended and their curiosity excited.

The next day one of them rallied John on his gallantry.

"True, friend Jane," he replied, "I carried a poor, desolate sinner to hear the word of God, but I do assure thee I saw many there who stared at *her*, that required the word as much as that poor soul did."

The name of Maddux is perpetuated, to this time at least, by being given to the hill on which he resided, overlooking the valley of Shockoe Creek, and south of Howard's Grove.

Friend Maddux was so enterprising as to publish the first Directory of Richmond, in 1819, which contained about 1100 names. With the aid of large type, an almanac and various tables, he eked out a small, thin volume. The Directory for 1859 contains the names of about 6600 persons, of whom not more than 44 are registered in that of 1819, as far as I can tell.

The office of Town Cryer once existed in Richmond, and the last incumbent, more than a half century ago, was a little, shriveled, querulous old man, of whom little remained but his voice, who bore the name of Tankard, but did not seem to rejoice in it, nor indeed in anything else, except

Crying. If the public attention was to be called to any subject—a lost or found child, a stray horse, a public meeting, or a public sale, it was announced by the cryer's bell, which rang most perseveringly throughout the (then narrow) city limits. It was taken for granted that no *vendue* could be held, even if the toddy bowl was filled, without the aid of Tankard, who most tediously and nasally cried the bids, if he heard or saw them, but as neither his ear nor his eye was very acute, he frequently scolded the bidders for not speaking out. "A nod was as good as a wink" to him—he regarded neither.

Among the singular characters who appeared in Richmond in by-gone days, was Mr. K., or any other initial you please. He resided, when at home, in a small log house in the country. His raiment on all occasions was of gray or mixed homespun cloth and home or country made. His brawny neck was unincumbered with a cravat, and his limp shirt collar was tied with a bit of tape or black ribbon. The brim of his hat exceeded in breadth by several inches that of the staunchest Quaker, and by this and his other habiliments, he was generally known or could be described to those who sought his very efficient services as a lawyer or collecting attorney. His bed was a truss of straw, and as a substitute for sheets, he slipped into a bag some two yards long and two yards wide,

16

the neck of which was drawn and tied around his
own. Bacon and hoecake were his food, and milk
or water, sometimes diluted with spirit, was his
drink.

In this manner it was his determination, as he
declared, to array the outward and to satisfy the
cravings of the inward man, until he should amass
the sum of $50,000.

After some years of assiduous toil, saving and
perhaps shaving, he emerged one day from his sack
and his homespun, like a butterfly from a chrysalis
state, in a full suit of fine broadcloth and satin,
with a shining beaver hat and a proud and gallant
bearing. He had plucked his plum and intended
to enjoy it. He visited, drank punch and mint-
julep, ate roast beef and canvas-backs, and fell in
love.

The lady of his choice amused herself by coquetting with him and keeping his hopes alive.
After prosecuting his love-suit for a longer term
than he had usually expended on a law-suit, he
determined to close the pleadings and ask for a
verdict. Greatly to his joy, and a little to his
surprise, it was given in his favor, and tenderly
parting with the mistress of his heart, he went on
his way rejoicing. But alas! how momentary and
uncertain are the visions of human bliss—fleeting
as the vision of a humming bird—and such a bird
was his Dulcinea.

Her mother had listened at the key-hole, and knowing that her daughter did not intend to accept Mr. K., she was astonished at what she heard. No sooner had he left the room than she rushed into it and exclaimed, "Why, Letitia, do you intend to marry Mr. K.?" "La, no! mama, I was only joking!" "That won't do, my dear; make haste and call him back before it is too late." The dutiful daughter raised the sash and hailed her suitor, who was walking slowly and indulging a day dream of future bliss. He heard her charming voice, which had charmed him unwisely but too well, and retraced his steps to enjoy more of its melody.

How suddenly, alas! were his hopes dispelled. No verdict of a jury against a rich client and a fat contingent fee, when he felt sure of a favorable one, ever astonished and disappointed him more than the reversal of decision he then heard, in the few words, "Mr. K., I was only joking."

One so long accustomed as he had been to the glorious uncertainty of the law, and to making a prompt rejoinder to adverse counsel, could not be easily taken aback or at a loss for a reply. Bowing most profoundly, he merely said, "So was I, Miss Letitia," and again went on his way—not rejoicing, but repining at his non-suit. He never appealed, nor did he commence a new suit in the court of Cupid. But like his prototype, the but-

terfly, he did not very long survive his change of
raiment. The Flush times then prevailed, and
"our flower was in flushing when blighting was
nearest." He did not however "die all for love."

CHAPTER XIV.

OLD FASHIONS.

The fashion of gentlemen's garments some fifty
odd years ago, bore a strong contrast to the present, especially at the upper and at the nether
ends. The throat was sweltered in as many yards
of muslin, as would at the present day suffice for
the lowest flounce of a lady's skirt, which if it were
permissible to handle, I would not merely guess to
to be about ten yards in circumference, but drop-
ping that forbidden subject to take up the almost
interminable one of the gentleman's neck gear,
let me attempt to describe the process by which
the exquisite of that day contrived to invest himself, like a silk worm, in tho circumvolutions of
his cravat. If he enjoyed the services of a valet,
he held one end of the long and thin texture; and
his attendant taking the other, walked round him
until both ends met, when they were tied in a large

bow, and perhaps a small beau was tied therein.
If he had to rely on his own resources, the plan
was, to attach one end of the cravat to the bedpost,
walk off to its full length, if the room permitted,
and then revolve on his own periphery, till he was
wound up like the main spring of a watch, or
an Egyptian mummy, and when the envelopement
was complete, the chin could be drawn within it,
like the head of a terrapin into its shell.

Those who could afford neither the valet, nor so
extensive an investment of muslin, resorted to a
substitute for its bulk, in what was called a pud-
ding, or to speak more intelligibly (since a some
what similar appendage has been adopted by the
gentler sex, and been promoted under a more
respected name to a different, if not a higher
station) a pad, which formed the foundation on
which the cravat was built. As at the present
day, as was whispered to me by a lady, who wished
to exonerate herself from the suspicion of extravagance, the *foundation* of her splendid dress
was mere canvass, and only the superstructure or
flounces which entirely concealed it, were of the
costly material—reversing the figure of a cloud
with a silver lining. Here, again, have I trodden
on forbidden ground—indeed, apart from all figure
of speech, it requires great caution to approach
a lady at the present day, without treading on her
skirts.

The very stiff collar of a dress coat was made to sit as high as the ears, and to stand off several inches from the back of the head, which, otherwise, could not be turned. I saw a clumsy waiter at a dinner party, attempt to place two small dishes of custard on the table, and while he reached over a gentleman's shoulder with one dish in his right hand, his unconscious left poured the contents of the other, into the space between the collar and the neck—the custard flowing down that channel, without soiling the coat externally.

[One word respecting the Paris fashion of ladies in 1802, which I find thus condensed; "nearly in the style of Eve—bosom prodigally displayed, petticoat festooned up rather higher than the ankles."]

Buck-skin breeches and fair-top boots, were the fashionable apparel for the nether man, except at parties and balls. The perfection of both consisted in the tightness of the fit. Artisans in buck-skin were entirely distinct from tailors, they assimilated to glovers.

On one Sunday morning, seated in an upper room, I happened to overlook an apartment opposite, in which the maker was endeavoring to invest his customer in a pair of new buck-skins. The operator was a stout man, and his patient a small one, whose legs were inserted into the garment, and the maker was in the act of thrusting his limbs home, as a sailor would say. He seized the waistband, and shook the tenant of the breeches into them, raising him from the floor at each effort, until the bare-skin and buck-skin were in such close contact, that I cannot imagine how a separation was afterwards effected. *That* was a perfect fit.

A humorous old gentleman used to tell how he went a-courting in a new pair of buck-skins. It was in the country, and in November, that he mounted his horse and his new breeches.

Before he reached the residence of his dulcinea it began to rain, the wet buckskin stretched so as to permit easy movement, and in this condition he dismounted, but at each step, as the leather rubbed in contact, it sounded p-i-s-h, p-i-s-h, and to this music he entered the parlor, where the ladies were seated around a cheerful fire. They could not suppress a smile at the tones of the leather, and the Major, for my hero was a Major, felt the perspiration oozing out in spite of the cold. As he stood before the fire making his obeisance and compliments to the ladies as deliberately and as gracefully as cir-cumstances permitted, he suddenly found himself enveloped in a cloud. He looked round for the cause, and to his dismay and confusion discovered it to be the combined effects of heat and moisture on his breeches. He could not stand the smiles which the ladies in vain endeavored to conceal, and as the fog increased in density every moment, the

Major, like a skillful soldier, retreated under cover of it. He called for his horse, made an apology to his host of sudden indisposition, or something else, and, taking leave, attempted to mount, but his buckskins, tho' expanded by the wet, had so contracted by the heat that he could not raise his foot to the stirrup. Uncavalierly as it was, he ordered the groom to lead the horse where there was vantage ground for mounting, and here, after two or three desperate efforts, he at length attained the saddle, but, in doing so, he found, to the annihilation of his vanity and of his hopes, that his buckskins had proved false, and had ripped from stem to stern, and, casting his eyes round to see if he was observed, he detected the ladies at the window in convulsions of laughter at his discomfiture.

The Major died a bachelor. A jovial man he was, who could set the table in a roar, with this among other side-splitting tales, which he told and acted with the skill of a Matthews. My attempt at the recital, compared to his, is as tame and flat as the champagne of Johnny King, who decanted his the day before the feast.

The hero of this true story was for many years Sergeant-at-Arms of the House of Delegates, and his successor was the celebrated Peter Francisco, the gigantic warrior, whose feats of strength were almost incredible to those who had never seen the astonishing development of his muscles.

One of his successors of late years could almost have walked between his colossal legs without stooping.

One solitary specimen of the fashion of those early years of the century (fair top boots, corduroy shorts, very long waisted and broad tailed coat, hair in a queue) may yet (1856) be seen in our streets occasionally, in the tall figure of Mr. D. B., who greets his old acquaintances as if time had increased his kind feelings toward them.*

CHAPTER XV.

QUACKERY AND CREDULITY.

At the close of the last century, a notable and successful instance of quackery occurred, in the introduction of "*Perkins's Metallic Tractors*," as they were called by an ingenious (not ingenuous) adventurer from the land of steady habits, so mis-called. Fluent of speech, not deficient in address and appearance, and still less in confidence, Mr., or Dr., Perkins traveled through the U. States,

---

* This last specimen of the fashion of the last age, died in Nov. 1858. The lapse of a few years makes this volume a record of mortality.

carrying healing on his wings, or rather on his points, and he afterwards extended his philanthropic journey to Europe. Such influence did he acquire, that a "Perkinean Institution" was formed in London, and many sage publications, no doubt, were issued by it.

Perkins's instruments consisted of two pieces of cunie-formed metal, about four inches long, flat on one side and rounded on the others, so that when the flat sides were placed together they formed a a figure like a marling-spike. By a scientific application of these points to the skin, alternately or otherwise, drawn in a certain direction with various other mystical manipulations, the Professor professed to cure rheumatism, gout, tooth-ache, head-ache, and, in short, all the ills that flesh is heir to.

The virtue of the instruments, as he stated, consisted in the peculiar mixture of certain metals, and the (Galvanic) effect they produced, which he illustrated in the sensation created by zinc and silver applied to the tongue. But the great virtue of the tractors was the transformation of the brass of the vendor into pure silver. He stated that a certain peculiar mode of manipulation, which he explained, was required for their efficacy, but, in fact, it was nothing more than drawing the points over the skin of the parts affected, or, in still plainer terms, scratching with them. Either the excitement created on the surface of the skin, or on the imagination of the patient, operated, in many instances, favorably for Perkins, and, of course, the cures recorded were numerous and astonishing—not so the failures. Many persons bought a case of the tractors for $20 (which cost as many cents), expecting, through their use, to dispense with doctors and drugs, and also to dispense relief to all the rheumatic old women of both sexes in their neighborhood.

I have seen the arm and shoulder of a rheumatic negro scratched until the skin looked almost white, and he would move the joint, which he had not done before, and declared "the rheumatis was gone." Whether the doctor administered metal in any other form to the patient, neither of them mentioned.

After awhile some incredulous or inquisitive persons began to make experiments (in violation of the patent) with tractors made by themselves, and calculated to detract from those of Perkins, and one went so far as to make a pair of wood, and paint them of the right color. On credulous and nervous patients, these were found as efficacious as the genuine, and, like the rod of the Magi of old, they also wrought miracles.

A Hudibrastic poem of considerable length, with notes, like the tail of a kite, much longer than the body, was written by a satirical genius named Fes-

senden, called "Terrible Tractoration." Perkins
was soon forgotten, and so was the poem. But he
was succeeded by many quacks, and Fessenden by
many rhymesters.

CHAPTER XXI.

MINERAL WATERS.

A week rarely elapses now-a-days without the
announcement of some "*useful and valuable discovery.*" Schemers are on the look out for minerals, fluid or solid, to purify the system or to
replenish the purse, and numerous dupes have they
found. Many years ago, when a mineral mania
prevailed, a Dutchman discovered on his farm what
he thought was an indigo mine, and announced it
in Richmond. The golden era has recurred in
Virginia several times, but was usually of short
duration, long enough, however to transfer the gold
of the dupes from their pockets into those of the
projectors.

My tale, however, and a true one, has nothing
to do with schemes or plots. Early in this century a great Hygeian discovery was made in Richmond. An inebriate who was so prudent as to

walk off and wash off the effects of his evening potations at an early hour the next morning, resorted for the purpose to a secluded spot in the valley: when questioned for the motive of his matutinal stroll, he replied that he found great benefit from the use of a mineral spring to which he resorted. Others tried it, and perceived that its taste and color differed from pure water, and that its effects were beneficial. The report of its virtues spread around, and several invalids resorted to the yellow fountain each summer morning at sunrise. Its good effects were felt or imagined, the number of visitors increased, and instead of two or three, they soon numbered two or three score. The virtues of the water were evident to those who were, or to those who were not invalids, so long as it was drank in moderation and at an early hour; for the sun dispelled its virtues, and as he rose, they fell. If he were always to shine he might disclose the lack of virtue in other objects of unsuspected purity.

Young ladies resorted to the spring, which they found to deepen the hue of the roses on their cheeks, and young gentlemen went to fill the glasses and admire the roses.

Saratoga in those days possessed rather a glorious than an aqueous celebrity in Virginia; and although our own Warm, and Hot and Sulphur springs had attained some celebrity, the attain-

17

ment to them by invalids was attended with much
labor and fatigue; so that our newly discovered
domestic fountain possessed great advantages so
long as faith in its virtues remained unshaken,
and this was as long as those virtues possessed
the magic of mystery. But some prying chem-
ist—I will not suspect that he was a physician
who was deprived by the waters of some of his
patients—made an analysis of them, and detected
a minute portion of ignoble iron. Many of its
former votaries deserted it, but those whose faith
was *of* iron and *in* iron continued their sunrise
potations, and to derive the benefit which faith
and early rising deserved.

Query: Would patent panaceas stand the test
of an exposure of their ingredients, which might
disclose little else than an ordinary prescription?
Even bread pills and aq: font: would lose their
efficacy if not prepared according to ℞.

Our diseases are now much more refined than
formerly. Dyspepsia and neuralgia were sour
stomach or pain in the head, or stitches elsewhere,
which had not aspired to the refinement of Greek
appellations. It is no doubt some comfort to be
thus classically affected, as a lady who complained
of *the* chronic seemed to think it genteel. Another
lady remarked, that when she was a girl people
had backbones and fits, but now they had spines
and spasms.

In the Flush times, which were not confined to
Richmond, a similar Hygeian discovery to that
just mentioned was made at Lynchburg. I have
no illiberal feeling toward Yankees, nor toward any
nation or section; but my truthful history does
not permit me to deviate from facts, unless I do so
under false impressions. I must therefore state,
that in the very height of the Flush that dazzled
and deceived the speculative town of Lynchburg,
an adventurous Yankee purchased a piece of ground
adjoining the town, which was soon to embrace and
enrich it, as he guessed : but the limbs began to
retract and lose their strength, the appetite failed,
and the Yankee feared he would be left a poor
outsider. However, he determined not to submit
without an effort. He dug a well on the premises, and it yielded a strong mineral water, similar,
as some thought, to one or another of the celebrated springs in the mountain region. Invalids
resorted to it in the early mornings, for it was
open at certain hours only, and they derived benefit. Its celebrity rapidly increased, and its visitors
became numerous. Even the faculty recommended
the use of the waters, especially to patients whose
diseases were imaginary. It was suggested, perhaps by a friend of the fortunate owner, that a
regular watering-place should be established for
the benefit of invalids, and for the prosperity of
the town. The proprietor agreed to accept for the

property a good profit on his outlay ; the bargain
was closed and he went on his way rejoicing.

After the lapse of some little time, the waters
were thought to decline in strength, which was at
first attributed to an excess of rain; but as they did
not strengthen with drought, it was deemed best to
have the well cleansed and examined. The process was commenced, and to the dismay of the
owners, when they reached the bottom of the well,
where truth should reside, they found bags of brim-
stone, rusty nails, &c.; the saline and other solu-
ble ingredients had disappeared.

The fair historian of Lynchburg has, I find,
recordedthis affair in a much more graphic style.

CHAPTER XVII.

DISTINGUISHED VISITORS.

" *The Invisible Lady*" visited Richmond before
Tom Moore addressed her, under the name of Tom
Little, about the year 1809. She had many admirers, and, coquette-like, made a kind response to
all, but no other was so gallant and poetical as Little
Moore, who was then as great a coquette as she—
courting in sweet odes all the Caras and Coras,

Neas and Noras he met with.   His fanciful lines to
the lady above mentioned, commencing—

> " They try to persuade me, my dear little sprite,
> That you are not the daughter of ether and light,
> Nor have any concern with the fanciful forms
> That dance upon rainbows or ride upon storms ;"

are no doubt familiar to all my readers.

Caressing and caressed, Moore spent some days
in Richmond, singing sweetly his own songs, and
penning some sweet lines to eyes and lips and hair ;
among others, to a charming lady who I hope may
read these, albeit thro' spectacles.

The reign of the Invisible Lady, like that of
other coquettes, was short and brilliant, and soon
forgotten ; but the most remarkable part of her
history was, that she relapsed into silence after
passing her teens.

About the same period, some other meteors appeared in our firmament, that bid fair afterwards
to become fixed stars, but did not.   Jerome Bona-
parte, with his Baltimore bride, a descendant of
" Old Mortality," immortalized by Walter Scott,
arrived in Richmond with his bride in Nov. 1804.
He was accompanied by Col. Reubel, not " Gen.
Reubel, that demon of Hell," of whom " the anti-
Jacobin " sung, but one of the same family, and no
demon, and *he* also found a beautiful bride in Baltimore—Miss Pascault, if I remember rightly.   Je-

rome had sailed for France in a French frigate, but put back into the Chesapeake,—ominous to his young bride,—for, Napoleon-like, and, by his orders, he repudiated her (reluctantly it was said), and, in 1806 or '7, married a princess and became a king—pro tem. In March, 1856, at the point of death, as was supposed, he was attended in Paris by his Paterson son and grand-son.

CHAPTER XVIII.

PLACES OF AMUSEMENT.

The very first dramatic performance in Richmond was, as I have heard, in a wooden house, large in that day, which stood in the rear of the old jail (Rose's Brig), and which, if I mistake not, was demolished only a few years ago; but let that pass, and we will take a look at the first regular theatre opened in the city, to reach which we must travel through an old and interesting record. If the reader finds it dull, he can skip over a few pages, but mayhap fare no better. If he reads it, he will be rewarded for his pains.

The writer is indebted to a gentleman of literary taste and research for the use of an exceedingly rare little volume (in French), entitled, "Memoir

and Prospectus concerning the Academy of Fine
Arts of the United States of America, established
at Richmond, the Capital of Virginia, by the
Chevalier *Quesnay de Beaurepaire*, Founder and
President.

"*Monumentum œre Perennius.*"

Paris, printed by Cailleau, Printer to the Richmond
Academy, 1788."

It opens with a letter from M. Quesnay, to the
Royal Academy of Sciences of Paris, which is followed by an extract from the Register of the Academy, dated March 14, 1788—here translated :

"The Committee appointed by the Academy have examined
the scheme presented by the Chevalier Quesnay de Beaurepaire,
for the establishment of an Academy of Arts and Sciences at
Richmond, the Capital of Virginia, in America, situated 75
leagues from Philadelphia, and 35 from the ocean.

" The author having served ten years in British America, and
traveled through all parts of the country, has been enabled to
observe the need of instruction, and has conceived a plan for
relieving this necessity, with the additional advantage of increasing, under circumstances so interesting as the birth of the
republic, the relations between it and France, and of uniting it
with his country by new ties of gratitude, of conformity of
tastes, and of a more intimate connection between the individuals of the two nations.

"He chose Richmond as the spot, where he had most friends,
and from his own resources, together with a liberal subscription
of nearly 60,000 francs, he succeeded in procuring a superb
situation, and in having erected on it an edifice destined to become the centre of the new Academy.

" A number of citizens zealous for the public good, fathers anxious for the education of their children, and officers attached to the government listened eagerly to his plans, and hastened to share the honor of the establishment by contributing to it their talents, their influence and their wealth; and on the 24th June, 1786, the corner-stone of the walls of the Academy was laid with great solemnity, as described in the ' Virginia Gazette,' now before you.

" The next step is to procure for this institution tutors, models for the arts, scientific instruments, &c., for which purpose M. Quesnay has come to Europe. He has consulted with great masters in all departments, has collected materials, and he hopes, on his return to Virginia, to open schools in which may be taught Medicine, Astronomy, Natural History, Chemistry, Mineralogy, Painting, Sculpture, Architecture Civil and Military, and the Foreign Languages.

" The advantages of such a scheme are obvious. We have already received from America various trees and shrubs which may be cultivated in Europe on spots hitherto regarded as barren, and which may become valuable ; but, as yet, we are only acquainted with her sea-board and the margins of her rivers, and it is desirable for the advancement of Botany and Mineralogy, that a more intimate intercourse should be estab_ lished. * * * * The means of instruction in America, in all branches, are rare and difficult, but the enterprise of M. Quesnay will add to them, and it appears to us that much may be hoped from it.

" We shall not enter into the examination of the economical and pecuniary plans which he proposes for the support of the establishment, this is out of our province, nor is it in the memoir which he presents for the suffrage of the Academy; but his plan for the advancement of science in America, for the enlightenment and development of its vast republics, must meet with the approbation of the Academy, which cannot fail to applaud the zeal of M. le Chevalier Quesnay, to give him their encouragement, and to desire success to his establishment.

" Done at Paris, in the Assembly of the Royal Academy of Sciences, March 14th, 1788—DE LA LANDE, THOUIN, TENON, LAVOISIER.

"A true copy,   *Le Marquis de* CONDORCET."

(Here follows the memorial on which the preceding was founded :)

" MEMORIAL and Prospectus of the Academy of Arts and Sciences of the United States of America, established at Richmond, read before the Royal Academy of Sciences at Paris, 5 March, 1788.

" At the time that the Cavalry of the King's Guard, to which I belonged, was disbanded, and when the convulsions of civil war were agitating a portion of the New World, attracted by the brilliant hope of distinguishing myself in arms, I went to America and served in Virginia (I can say with honor) in the rank of Captain, during the years 1777 and 1778.

" But the loss of my accoutrements, and also of all my letters of recommendation, which latter were mislaid in the office of the then Governor of Virginia, Mr. P. Henry, in whose care I had left them, finally a long and severe illness and a want of pecuniary resources at so great a distance from home, forced me to abandon the profession of arms and to seek some other means of supporting a name which, unattended with fortune, was the only patrimony I inherited from my grandfather, Dr. Quesnay, first consulting physician to the King, a man eminent for his talents, his universal information, and his public spirit.

" I had occasion during the war, and afterwards, to traverse a large portion of the American States. My acquirements in the fine arts, induced me to suppose that if this republic had no cause to envy Europe on the score of Science, yet the Fine Arts are so little known that, even with moderate talents, I might become useful in that department.

"I sought at first to arouse and excite the taste of the people by giving private lessons. I soon had many pupils, and conceived the idea of founding an academy."

M. Quesnay then speaks of his efforts in the principal cities of the Union to excite an interest in his project, with which was connected the formation of similar establishments in them; gives the reasons already quoted for selecting Richmond as the great central establishment, having spent in Virginia the early portion of his sojourn in the United States, and having there many and good friends, and then adds: "Finally, on the 24th June, 1786, after years of perseverance, I had the satisfaction to witness the imposing ceremonies with which the laying of the corner-stone of the Academy was honored."

Two silver plates were deposited in the corner-stone. On one was an inscription in Latin, on the other in French. The Latin translated reads thus:

"In the year of our Lord, 1786, the 10th of the Republic, viii Calends of July, PATRICK HENRY *being Governor of Virginia,* the plan of an Academy projected by ALEXANDER MARIA QUESNAY, and assisted by the liberality of many meritorious citizens is at length consummated. This corner-stone was laid, JOHN HARVIE *being Mayor of the city.*"

The inscription on the other plate contains the following:

"Corner-stone of an Academy in the city of Richmond. ALEXANDER MARIA QUESNAY, President, laid by the officers and brethren of Lodge No. 13, on the festival of St. John the Baptist, in the year of Light 5786, and of the Vulgar Era 1786. JOHN GROVES, *Master;* JAMES MERCER, *Grand Master;* EDMUND RANDOLPH, *Past Grand Master.*"

M. Quesnay inserts the following Letter of Introduction to Dr. Franklin, from his daughter, Mrs. Bache:

PHILADELPHIA, 27th February, 1783.

MY DEAR AND HONORED FATHER: With this letter you will receive a scheme for a French Academy which it is desirable to establish here. It is a very extensive plan, which will do honor to the gentleman who has conceived it, as well as to America. If it can be executed, it will in no wise interfere with the plans of the Colleges, and will be devoted only to completing the education of young men after having graduated. Those who are already under M. Quesnay's instruction have made great progress.

He regards you as the father of sciences in this country, and highly appreciates the advice and instruction you have never failed to give to those whose talents deserve encouragement. Money is the thing that is required, but the brother of M. Quesnay, who has charge of this, will inform you how your assistance can be most useful.

I can well conceive how much you must be occupied at this important crisis, but as a mother, who desires to give her children a useful and polite education and who will be proud to have them formed in her own country, and under her own eyes, I beg you to give to M. Quesnay all the assistance which may be in your power. I have written to you by another opportunity, and will only add the love and respect of all the family.

I remain your affectionate daughter,

SARAH BACHE.

To give some idea of the welcome which the author and his enterprise received in the different States he visited, he gives the names of the persons who have rendered their aid, and who have testified the greatest friendship for him:

In Gloucester county, Virginia, after he was obliged to leave the army, Sir John Peyton, touched with his destitute condition, kindly invited him to his house and insisted on his remain‐ ing there while he was awaiting assistance from his own country and restoration of health. For nearly two years, he bestowed on him every mark of kindness, and treated him as his own son. During the whole time of his residence in Virginia, the house of this excellent and kind man, and those of all his connections, appeared to M. Quesnay to be places of refuge for distressed and unfortunate strangers. The names mentioned (but he sometimes mistakes them) are Thacher Washington, Throgmorton, Jno. Dixon, Tabb, Bolling, Sam. Washington, Jno. Page of Rosewell, (Lieutenant Governor, and the foremost man to promote his object;) Whiting, Perin, Rev. Mr. Fontaine, Willis, Hubard, Nuttall; who, with one accord, he says, "acted towards the author with that delicacy which, knowing how to respect misfortune, adds inestimable value to all benefits." In addition to the names above recited, M. Quesnay enumerates, among his patrons, the following gentlemen, with special thanks appended to several of them for their great kindness: In Richmond, John Harvie, esq., Mayor of the city and Register of the Land Office, Col. Thomas Randolph of Tuckahoe, Edm'd Randolph, Governor of the State, Patrick Henry, late Governor, Col. Cary, Speaker of the Senate, Col. Matthews and Dr. James McClurg, Councillors of State, Mr. Ambler, Treasurer, Col. Robert Goode, Dr. Wm. Foushee, Messrs. Wm. Pennock, Rob't Mitchell, Gabriel Galt, J. Buchanan, Robert Boyd and Marshall magistrates; also, Messrs. McKean, John Barret, Wm. Lewis, Taylor, Sims, Nelson, Skipwith, Dan'l Hylton, Jas. Hayes, Wm. Mayo, Daniel Vandewall, Samuel McCraw, John Dixon, Thos. M. Deane, John Pryor, Nicolson, Francis James, Moses Austin, Edward Voss, James Warrington, Carter, Watkins, John Kerr, Henry Banks, Richard Southgate, Abraham Lot, Jos. Higbee, Rev. J. Buchanan, Dr. Turpin, J. Groves, Pleas't Younghusband, R. Adams, Griffin, and many others of all conditions, in town and country. In Petersburg, Mrs. Bolling and her two sons,

Dr. Shore, Mayor of the town, Cols. Banister and Davis, Dr. Walker, Dr. Jones, Major Gibbon, Mr. Gordon, &c. In Norfolk, Col. Parker. In Williamsburg, Rev. Mr. Madison, President of the College, John and Thomas Carter, Gen. Gibson. At Alexandria, Col. Semmes, Gen. Roberdeau, Mr. Hunt, &c. Then follow Baltimore and the Northern cities.

Among the names now recorded in history may be recognised in Philadelphia, the successive Governors Reed, Moore and Dickinson, Mrs. Bache, Messrs. Willing, Shippin, Rob't Morris, Lawrence, Francis, Benezet, Bingham, Rittenhouse, Penrose, Peale, Humphries, Gens. Wayne, Wilkinson, Stuart, and many others of high respectability.

In New Jersey, M. Coxe, Lieut. Governor, the families of De Hart, Barnet, Ogden, and especially Mr. Mathias Higgins, who accompanied the author during two years as secretary and friend. In New York, Gov. G. Clinton, Mayor Duane, Baron Steuben, Gen. Van Cortland, Col. Bland, Dr. Cochran, and the families of Livingston, Hoffman, Hallett, Pintard, Seaton, White, Niven, Ludlow, Ogden, Vandyke, Israel, &c.; to these may be added the Chevalier de la Luzerne and M. de Marbois.

The author then says this detail will prove that he has obtained the support of a large proportion of the distinguished men of the country, persons through whom a nation should be judged. He would be gratified if he could aid in removing the unfavorable impressions that some persons have received and expressed of this fine country, in consequence of not having resided there long enough to be able to distinguish the new comers and the foreign adventurers from the native citizens.

He remarks, in another place, that many persons who have left their own country for misconduct, offer themselves in this as masters of Languages, of Music, Dancing, Painting, &c., and go from town to town, remaining long at none, because their pupils learn nothing, but these impostors make a great deal of money, such is the generosity of the Americans; but they have to repent of the confidence reposed in such masters, and these adventurers create a bad opinion of the French in general.

18

"Among the many instances which he might cite of the native goodness of these brave and honorable people, of the hospitality exercised among them in the most paternal manner, of their generous and grateful sentiments, the author cannot refrain from mentioning one circumstance which occurred in Williamsburg, in the month of December, 1786, attested by a multitude of witnesses, and which he received from the lips of the Consul."

A Frenchman, one of those refugees who are a disgrace to their nation, was guilty of crimes deserving the severest punishment. M. Oster, in his capacity of Consul, demanded the execution of the sentence in the name of the French nation. The gratitude of the inhabitants overruled the sentence. They were content with banishing the offender, and in their enthusiasm they exclaimed—"No! a Frenchman shall never suffer a disgraceful death here. Go and receive elsewhere the punishment you deserve."

This long document will conclude with the names of subscribers to the Academy which have not been previously given. The shares were 1200 francs each ($240) and sub-divisions of halves and quarter shares. These names are introduced because some of the descendants may be gratified to recognize them after so long an interval, as I do many in memory.

Gabriel Galt, Serafina Formicula, William Lewis, Francis Goode, Turner Southall, Robert Greenhow,, Stephen Tankard, N. Wilkinson, Francis Graves, John Stockdell, Robert Bolling, Samson Matthews, Barnett Price, Dabney Miller, John Gunn, Mrs. S. Nevens, William Duval, Archibald Cary, William Lyne, Thomas Rosser, Henry Randolph, Robt. Boyd, George Pickett, Arch'd McRobert, David Lambert, Francis Dandridge, Cohen

& Isaacs, Robert Goode, Richard Morris, Benjamin Lewis, Alexander Montgomery, John Stewart, William Burton, John Kerr, Richard Gernon, William Haslet, Thomas McCreery, John McKeand, Gilbert Hay, Robert McLaughlin, Chiswel, Barrett, Thomas Richard, Reuben Coutts, Samuel Trower, Thomas M. Deane, Richard Bowler, John May, Ant'y Geohegan, Jesse Roper, Bickerton Webb, Henry Dixon, Foster Webb, John Gibson, Daniel Truehart, Peter Tinsley, William Booker, William Coulter, David Humpheys, Curtis Haynes, N. Raguet. Smith Blakey, Samuel Couch, Isaac Younghusband, Erasmus Gill, H. Giraud, John Burton, Thomas Gordon, William Davis, James Brownley, R. Armistead.

The site chosen by M. Quesnay and on which he erected his Academy, is the square on which the Monumental Church and the Medical College now stand, the grounds extending from those lower points up Broad and Marshall to 12th street. The Academy stood nearly on the spot where the Carleton house stands.

The worthy Chevalier was far ahead of the times—more than seventy years—as the absence of such an establishment at this day proves. His meritorious enterprise failed, but how, or under what circumstances, is not now to be discovered, unless among court records. The extensive square, with the Academy-building on it, became the property of West and Bignal, or some other English actors, who managed the theatres in all the Southern States. They converted the Academy into one, and here the tragic and the comic muses first excited the tears and smiles—in an edifice devoted to them—of a Richmond audience.*

But greater actors performed, and a more glorious work was rehearsed and brought out, in that theatre, than in any other, either in this country or in Europe.

Therein assembled, in 1788, the *Convention* of sages, patriots, and statesmen, who ratified the *Constitution of the United States*, as framed in Philadelphia.

Could such a constellation of talent, of wisdom, of pure patriotism, be formed in our political firmament at the present day, under similar circumstances? From the two subsequent efforts, I fear the reply must be in the negative.

To prove that this is not mere hyperbole, I will introduce the testimony of Mr. Wirt, who, in his Life of Patrick Henry, thus eloquently describes this assemblage :

"The Convention had been attended, from its commencement, by a vast concourse of citizens of all ages and conditions. The interest so universally felt in the question itself, and not less the transcendent talents which were engaged in its discussion, presented such attractions as could not be resisted. Industry deserted its pursuits, and even dissipation gave up its objects, for the superior enjoyments which were presented by the hall of the Convention. Not only the people

---

* In 1752 Hallam introduced Theatrical performances in Williamsburg—probably the first in America.

of the town and neighborhood, but gentlemen from every
quarter of the State, were seen thronging to the metropolis,
and speeding their eager way to the building in which the
Convention held its meetings.

"Day after day, from morning till night, the galleries were
filled with an anxious crowd, who forgot the inconvenience of
their situation in the excess of their enjoyment; and far from
giving any interruption to the course of the debate, increased
its interest and solemnity by their silence and attention. No
bustle, no motion, no sound was heard among them, save only
a slight movement when some new speaker arose, whom they
were all eager to see as well as to hear, or when some master-
stroke of eloquence shot thrilling along their nerves, and
extorted an involuntary and inarticulate murmur. Day after
day was this banquet of the mind and of the heart spread
before them, with a delicacy and variety which could never
cloy. There every taste might find its peculiar gratification:
the man of wit, the man of feeling, the critic, the philosopher,
the historian, the metaphysician, the lover of logic, the admirer
of rhetoric,—every man who had an eye for the beauty of
action, or an ear for the harmony of sound, or a soul for the
charms of poetic fancy—in short, every one who could see, or
hear, or feel, or understand, might find, in the wanton profusion and prodigality of that Attic feast, some delicacy adapted
to his peculiar taste. Every mode of attack and of defence, of
which the human mind is capable, in decorous debate—every
species of weapon and armor, offensive and defensive, that
could be used with advantage, from the Roman javelin to the
Parthian arrow, from the cloud of Æneas to the shield of
Achilles—all that could be accomplished by human strength,
and almost more than human activity, was seen exhibited on
that floor."

The dramatis personæ of this grand performance
embraced, among many others, James Madison,

John Marshall, James Monroe, Edmund Pendleton, George Wythe, George Nicholas, Edmund
Randolph, George Mason, Grayson, Innis, Lee,
and last, not least, Patrick Henry. It were useless to name more in such a brilliant constellation.

What a perilous descent have I now to make,
from this theatre of glorious scenes and splendid
actors, to the common-place subjects of my narrative!

I will here close the chapter, to break the fall
and lessen the contrast.

CHAPTER XIX.

PLACES OF AMUSEMENT.

(Continued.)

At the corner of the Academic Square, where
now stands the handsome mansion of Mr. Allen,
was erected a Market House—the then New
Market—but it did not thrive. It was occupied
by live cattle and goats, instead of beef and mut-
ton. Hens, chickens and ducks volunteered their
presence, without the fear of spit or frying-pan,
and even laid their eggs in remote and dark
corners, not likely to be visited by any other cus-

tomers than prying school-boys or vagrant children. A few vegetables also volunteered their verdure; such as dandelions—an excellent salad—butter-cups, with roots more pungent than red pepper, chick-weed for bird fanciers, and thistles—but not a good substitute for artichokes.

I don't assert that the fox made his hole and the wren built its nest in the market-house, but it is true that Fox & Wren occupied it and built coaches there. The Wrens now nestle elsewhere, cherished and cherishing—of the Foxes only one remains in quiet retirement.

The Academic, Forensic, *Dramatic Theatre* maintained its latter character and was thought to maintain it well for several years, but it met the fate of almost all similar edifices—conflagra-tion, but without other disaster. The Market-house, guiltless of blood and slaughter, was demolished many years later.

Theatrical performances were afterwards held (in 1802,) in the upper part of the old Market-house, on Main and Seventeenth streets, recently demolished and rebuilt; and after that, in Quar-rier's Coach-shop on Cary and Seventh streets, where Thomas' large Tobacco-factory stood, and was burned in 1851.

Temporary theatres now again gave place to a regular one. A large brick edifice was erected in the rear of the Old Academy or Theatre Square.

That, alas! was the scene of the most horrid
disaster that ever overwhelmed our city, where
seventy-two persons perished in the flames on
the fatal 26th of December, 1811, where the
Monumental Church now stands, and its portico covers the tomb and the ashes of most of the victims.

The writer, with some friends, reached Richmond that evening from a Christmas jaunt in the
country, and went with them to the Theatre—but
it was so crowded that they could not obtain
admission. A very few hours after, he was
aroused by the cry of fire, and hastening to the
spot, the first object he encountered on an open
space, was a lady lying on the grass apparently
in a swoon. He attempted to raise her, but she
was dead. He afterwards learned that she had
leaped from a window, but before she could be
removed from beneath it, was crushed by those
who sought to escape by following her. The next
object that thrilled him was a gentleman so dread-
fully excoriated, that death mercifully put an end
to his tortures in a few hours—but it were cruel
to rehearse the many individual instances of intense suffering by the victims, and of the scarcely
less intense agony of their relatives and friends.

On the ensuing morning, the mangled, burnt
and undistinguishable remains of many of the
victims were taken from the ruins and interred
on the spot, where their names are recorded on

the monument already mentioned, and the ground was consecrated to the erection of a church.

It is due to an humble but worthy man, to record the services rendered by him during the progress of this dreadful calamity. Gilbert Hunt, a negro blacksmith, possessed naturally a powerful frame, and by wielding the sledge-hammer, his muscles had become almost as strong and as tough as the iron he worked. Gilbert was aroused and besought by Mrs. George Mayo to go to the rescue of her daughter. He was soon at the theatre. Within its walls, then filled with smoke and flame, was Dr. James D. McCaw, a man who might have been chosen by a sculptor for a model of Hercules. The Doctor had reached a window and broken out the sash, when he and Gilbert recognized each other. He called to Gilbert to stand below and catch those he dropped out. He then seized on the woman nearest to him, and lowering her from the window as far as he could reach, he let her fall. She was caught in Gilbert's arms and conveyed by others to a place of safety. One after another the brave and indefatigable Doctor passed to his comrade below, and thus ten or twelve ladies were saved. The last one providentially was the Doctor's own sister, whose proportions were a feminine epitome of the Doctor himself. Gilbert caught her and broke her fall, but he says he fell with her, both unhurt.

The Doctor having rescued all within his reach, now sought to save himself. The wall was already tottering. He attempted to leap or drop from the window, but his strong leather gaiter, an article of sportsman's apparel which he always wore, caught in a hinge or some other iron projection, and he was thus suspended in a most horrid and painful position; he fell at last, but to be lame for life. The muscles and sinews were stretched and torn and lacerated, and his back was seared by the flames, the marks of which he carried to his grave.

The Doctor directed Gilbert to drag him across the street, and place him with his back against the wall of the Baptist Church; then to get two palings from a fence opposite. With these for splints and handkerchiefs for bandages, the limb was bound. Gilbert then went in search of a conveyance to carry the Doctor home. His removal from beneath the wall of the theatre had scarcely been effected, before it fell on the spot where he had fallen!

After a long period of suffering, he was able to resume practice; and his profession has been adopted by son and grandson, perpetuating the good name of Doctor McCaw, which its founder had worthily established.

Gilbert, then a slave, afterwards obtained his freedom—I wish I could add, at the hands of a grateful community; but it was by his own industry.

His philanthropy and efficiency in rescuing his fellow-creatures from the flames, were exhibited on another occasion. When the Penitentiary was burned, some years later, the only outlet was cut off by the flames, and the only means of rescue for the prisoners was by opening a new one, through one of the grated windows; no ladder was at hand to reach it. Gilbert placed himself under the window, and Captain Freeman, an active and efficient fireman, mounted on Gilbert's shoulders, and thus elevated and supported, the Captain cut out the brick work in which the grate was inserted, and through the breach thus formed, some of the prisoners were rescued; but the same operation had to be repeated at the second and third stories, and the enterprising pair contrived to reach them by the means now brought for their aid, and succeeded in making other breaches. Just as the flames reached them, the last of the convicts was rescued.

Gilbert went to Liberia in its early settlement, when, like all young colonies, it was subject to many hardships and privations. He preferred ease and comfort, and returned to Richmond, where he resumed his work at the anvil, which poverty rendered it necessary still to prosecute.

After the dreadful catastrophe at the theatre, a

cessation of theatrical amusements ensued for several years; but such was the change and the accession of population during the period, that, whilst the church was under construction, another theatre, the present one, on Broad and Seventh, was commenced and completed not very long after the church was consecrated.

Dancing, and gaiety of every kind, was suspended for a long while; but about the time that the present Theatre was established, there was erected in the rear of it, on Grace street, by Mons. Bossieux, a large wooden building (where a circus had previously stood), which he dignified with the name of *Terpsichore Hall*, and there the rising generation, to whom the disaster was almost tradition, were taught "the poetry of motion;" but before the succeeding one had acquired the graces from Mons. B., who had no rival, his hall was destroyed by fire, and the ground is now covered with workshops.   •

A much frequented place of amusement, in old times, was the *Haymarket Garden*, or better known as *Prior's*, on the grounds now occupied by the Richmond and Petersburg Railroad Depot and workshops, a tobacco warehouse, the paper-mill, and some machine shops. It was quite a capacious inclosure, with a graduated lawn in front of the large mansion, which, with its extended wings and pinions, divided the lawn from the garden in the rear. A succession of grassy or flowery slopes and terraces extended down to the river, or rather to Ross's canal (now Haxall's), and the upper portion of the garden commanded a fine view of the river, the islands, and of the country beyond.

Here fireworks delighted the spectators, and equestrians and rope-dancers astonished them. Here ice-creams and cakes were eaten, but very little liquor drunk—the beverages being chiefly lemonade and porteree. Thus the grounds were generally quiet and orderly.

The then elevated ground between the basin and the garden, was occupied by a few residents, and formed a sort of distinct village, called Haymarket. These existed before the basin was navigated, and in its early days.

A more entire transformation cannot well be imagined, than from the quiet and rural aspect of that day, to the throng of travel, the roaring and whistling of steam, and the rumbling of water-wheels and machinery of the present. *Trent's Bridge*, built on the rocks in the falls, only two or three feet above the water, is now supplanted by the railroad bridge, some sixty feet high.

A more ancient and less frequented place of resort for recreation, was the *French Garden*, beyond the Ravine (now being filled up), between Clay and Leigh, and 7th and 10th streets.

Some refugees from the horrors and massacre of
19

St. Domingo, found their way to Richmond. One
of them built a tall thin house, like himself, and,
with his co-exiles, laid out a garden in this then remote suburb. A small tract of land was purchased
by Didier Colin, from Dr. Turpin, which obtained
the name of the French Garden, and the district
still retains it, though now laid out in streets and
built on where the surface is not too precipitous.
Here lemonade, fruits, &c., were served to visitors,
and here the worthy man, who had been reduced
from wealth and comfort to comparative poverty
and to exile, spent his remaining days. On the
spot where his house stood, may be traced a portion of the foundation. Some of his surviving
partners in misfortune, thinking that he had, for
fear of another disaster, buried his money, dug up
his flower roots, his strawberries, and other fruits,
in their fruitless search for the hidden treasure.

Mitchell's Spring, to the east of Academy Hill,
and north-east of the Poor-house, was another
place of resort for recreation, but many years the
junior of Haymarket. It was "a spot of great
capabilities," but not very much improved, and,
like its founder, soon fell into the sere and yellow
leaf, though its spring continued to send forth a
copious supply of excellent water. This beverage,
however, was not a sufficient temptation to attract
visitors, when furnished only in its elementary
state.

I have mentioned *Academy Hill*, but I doubt if any of my readers ever heard of it before. It is north of the valley, in rear of the Poor-house, and the foundation of the Academy was laid long before that of the Poor-house; but it never rose above the basement, for which neglect I know not who is to blame. The window frames were stolen out of the brick work, as were the coins from the corner-stone. Thorns and thistles grow where bays and laurels should have flourished; sheep and calves graze where youths should have sought the flowers of literature and the fruits of knowledge.

Goddin's Spring, at Bacon Quarter Branch, was, in old times, a place of resort for amusement, as was the tavern for "Entertainment of Man and Horse." Shovel-board and other innocent games were played at the cool and shaded spring. The tavern was preferred by some of the western members of the Legislature, on the score of economy, to those nearer the Capitol, and it was said some of them would save and make during the session, enough to buy a negro boy to carry home with him "en croupe," as he made the journey on horseback. One member who served for a number of years, thus increased his black family as fast as his wife did the white.

Jackson's Garden was a pleasant place of resort some forty years ago, and was tastefully embel-

lished on public occasions. It was situated on
Leigh street, extending from Second some distance
west, in a portion of the city now designated in
the map as "Jackson's addition." The proprietor
occupied a station in the First Auditor's office,
now filled by his son, with a fair prospect of a
lineal succession.

This completes the list of places of amusement,
except one public garden in the rear of Galt's
City Tavern. Such places of resort have ceased
to exist for many years, but the Germans recently
established a "Volk's Garten." They are a joy-
ous race.

CHAPTER XX.

PHYSICIANS.

IN the year 1800 the population of Richmond
was 5,300, embracing almost an equal number of
white and black, and there were some ten or twelve
physicians. The number in 1856 may exceed a
hundred, to minister to about forty thousand in the
city and suburbs.*

---

* Some persons now (1860) estimate 50,000—the census will
presently decide.

Of the ancient stock, Dr. Leiper was perhaps, next to Dr. McClurg (already respectfully noticed), entitled to precedency ; his brother, Thos. Leiper, was the great tobacconist, once Mayor of Philadelphia. The Doctor's residence was on Franklin street, and his office adjoined it at the corner of Eighteenth. In that office, W. H. Harrison, afterwards President of the United States, began the study of medicine. Dr. Leiper's dwelling, a wooden building, is still extant; the basement converted into shops and the upper part into a tavern for market folks.

Dr. Foushee resided on Main above Fourteenth street ; his house was afterwards purchased and occupied by the United States' Bank, and on its demise was bought and demolished by Mr. Hubbard, to make room for his extensive shoe-store. Dr. Foushee was a gentleman of fine personal appearance and deportment, and a favorite physician with the ladies, who said his visits were restoratives without the aid of medicine, so bland and kind were his manners and conversation. This calm and sunshine which distinguished his medical character, could be changed to storm and thunder in his political one. His house contained some rare attractions, which caused it to be a favorite resort for the beaux, who called it the home of the Graces. They were soon dispersed, however, and each embellished a home of her own. Mr. Carter, of Westover, Mr. Ritchie, of the Enquirer, Col. Parker (of the now forgotten Miranda expedition) and his brother, carried off these prizes.

In the accomplished wife of the son and successor of Mr. Ritchie, we now recognize a lady, who under a former name acquired histrionic and literary celebrity, and yet continues to add to the latter, and to perform many good works which are not published.

The writer of these pages, inspired by the grace and beauty of the paragon of these sisters, perpetrated in his youth the following lines, of which, if she saw them, she knew not their source:

> When the Supreme Creative Power
> Decided on thy natal hour,
> Prepared to form thy beauteous face,
> Thy limbs to mould and give them grace,
> And to complete his work, impart
> Within that breast a kindred heart,
> He from the angels round his throne
> Chose those whose beauties brightest shone,
> And cull'd from each, with skill divine,
> Some perfect part and made it thine.
> * * * * *
> But merciful to man, on thee
> Bestow'd not immortality!

Dr. Foushee filled many stations. He was Mayor of the City, President of the James River

Company, and was appointed to the station of Postmaster after the death of Col. Vandewall. I do not use the word *office*, as neither of them occupied it *in propria personæ*. During his incumbency the post-office was burnt, and I happened to have the key of an unoccupied store not far from it. With the aid of other firemen and citizens, the contents of the office were safely removed to the store, and on meeting the Doctor early on the next morning, I had the satisfaction to assure him that all was safe and to show him where his office was.

When the Doctor was supposed to be on his death-bed, a rumor of his actual death was circulated, and one of his political friends posted off to Washington in hot haste to seek consolation for his loss in succession to his office. The prospect of it served to dry the tears of this disinterested friend, and when he thought, "good, easy man, full surely, his *appointment* was a ripening!" with what varied emotions was he affected on his return to Richmond to find the Doctor alive and convalescent!"

Foushee's garden, at the north-western boundary of the city, was quite an extensive and well cultivated possession. It now forms several squares, and Foushee street passes through it.

At the corner of Broad and Tenth streets, opposite the First Presbyterian Church, resided Dr.

Currie,* a strong contrast to the gentle, kind and graceful physician last mentioned, but he had an extensive practice and accumulated a large fortune, which the other did not, because, like many other physicians, he was more attentive to his practice than to his fees, and earned many which were not worth attention.

Dr. Cringan, who resided in the wooden dwelling on Eighth street, in the rear of the United Presbyterian Church, was much esteemed, and in professional deportment held a middle station between the two I have mentioned. His student, Dr. John Adams, became his partner in medical practice.

I remember no other cotemporaries of the oldest physicians I have introduced. Doctors Lyons, Greenhow, Watson, Nelson, Clarke, Trent and Bohannan, succeeded them, and Doctors Chamberlayne, Cullen and Warner, bright names in the faculty, were of still later date, though their cotemporaries for many years. I may have omitted many names of more or less celebrity in years long past, as well as more recent; but if I were to attempt an enumeration of those of later date, I might, if memory served, enlist as many as I allot to the city at the opening of this chapter.

---

* His house was taken down in 1859 to be supplanted by a Methodist church.

I will therefore discharge the physicians and turn to their subalterns, the *apothecaries*, though in old times each doctor was his own pharmaceutist, keeping medicines in his office, which his students—if he had any—would prepare according to his prescriptions—if they understood them.

There could not be employment for many apothecaries when physicians made up a large portion of their own prescriptions; but they obtained their medicines from these druggists. About the year 1800, there were but three—if I am correct—occupying the two corners and the centre of the square on Main between Thirteenth and Fourteenth streets. The shop of the brothers Ternan (Irishmen) was at the lower corner, in a part of the same wooden house already twice mentioned as yet standing there. A visit to their shop might have rendered an emetic superfluous, so begrimed with dirt was it and its attendants; but they made a fortune. Crawford's, at the upper corner where the cannon stands erect, was quite a contrast in point of neatness; but he was less popular, though also from the Emerald Isle, and did not reap so rich a harvest. Duval, the sire and grandsire of apothecaries, occupied the central shop, and was among the first to prepare nostrums in the shape of anti-bilious pills, in opposition to Dr. Church. He also established a pottery and a manufactory of tiles for roofing, but with all his enterprise and industry, I doubt if his dirty rivals did not make the most money.

The *Medical College* is of modern date, having been established in 1837, by the united influences and exertions of Doctors Chamberlayne, Cullen, Warner, Maupin and Bohannan. The Union Hotel was converted into a medical school and hospital. Limbs, instead of cutting capers, were cut in pieces in the ball room—potions were mixed instead of punch—poultices supplanted puddings, and Seidlitz water, champagne. Now, the former order of things is reinstated at the Hotel, and young doctors are diplomatized and patients are physicked in the Egyptian edifice on the old Academy or Theatre Square—so frequently mentioned in these pages.

The Medical College erected there has acquired stability and celebrity under a succession of competent Professors. In 1860, about 200 medical students seceded in a body from the Northern Colleges, in consequence of the John Brown raid at Harper's Ferry, and the excitement created by his admirers, the abolitionists. Thereupon the Virginia Legislature granted $30,000 for the extension of the College and Hospital.

CHAPTER XXI.

NEWSPAPERS AND PRINTERS.

THE oldest newspaper in Richmond in my young days was "*The Virginia Gazette*," Federal in politics, published semi-weekly by Augustine Davis, editor and printer. In the former capacity the implement he chiefly used was the scissors, and he resorted to the pen on indispensable occasions only, as in his hands it was a dull one compared with the other. The Gazette was little more than half the size of the present "Dispatch," but did not contain half as much in matter, and was not more than one-fourth of the broad sheet of the "Richmond Whig" or "Enquirer."

Mr. Davis was Postmaster in those days when the northern mail arrived thrice a week, and was five or six days coming from New York, and he performed in person the duties of the office. The news from Europe was seldom less than five or six weeks old, and occasionally ten. Under such circumstances, the accumulation of news when it came had to be compressed in small space. "Correspondence," foreign or domestic, was not even *imagined*, and I suspect that term might justly be applied to much that appears now-a-days, and has so imposing an aspect, especially under the foreign head, emanating from the garret of "a penny-a-liner," and hashed up from a mass of European papers, or prompted by some stock-jobbers or brokers.

Mr. Davis's Gazette was Federal in politics, and being for many years without any professional editor, rendered no service to the party it professed to espouse. Its Republican opponents sometimes cunningly used it as a tool for their own purposes. Mr. Jones of the "Examiner," and some of his co-laborers, would occasionally send Mr. Davis anonymous articles in reply to their own in the "Examiner," the drift of which would escape Mr. D.'s acumen, and he would publish them, whilst the authors would laugh at the success of their trick, and reply to and expose the weakness of the article they had palmed on their adversary.

The old saying that "a lie in a newspaper is good for two paragraphs," assertion and contradiction, did not hold good usually in Mr. Davis's time. There could generally be enough of "authentic intelligence" collected in three days to fill his short columns, without having recourse to any thing but plain matters of fact, as was the case with newspapers generally; rendering manufactured news a dull and unprofitable commodity; so that there were few workmen in that line, and no reporters to exercise their wit on drunken vagrants or quarrelsome couples.* As to false reports, the long interval between the publication of two papers, like hot weather in a fish market, caused the article to spoil before it could be used. Mr. Davis's office was in the same basement, corner of Main and Eleventh, whence " The Enquirer" is now issued.† In the adjoining tenements, also his property, was " the Queen's palace," after the removal from that on Cary street, which the reader will find noted in the history of her reign.

The political or politic toleration declared in Mr.

---

* It is much to be deplored that many editors at the present day, instead of endeavoring to form or to reform, and to refine the taste of their readers, are too apt to pander to the grossness of the least intelligent of them, and in many instances to render their sheets unfit for the perusal of a family circle. Editors who have wives and children should blush to publish what cannot with propriety be read in their own families. Crimes of the most disgusting character are detailed with a minuteness which is not bestowed on worthy and generous actions. " Let this be reformed altogether."

Perhaps this abuse of the public press is an evil inseparable from it, for as long ago as 1802, Chancellor Wythe remarked, that " the occupation of newspaper editors had become lower than that of scavengers; the former brought filth into our streets, the latter cleansed them." This is extracted from a Richmond paper, which was not obnoxious to the charge.

† In 1860, instead of the cellar on 11th, the " Enquirer', emanates from an attic on 12th street. Whether the change is merely local, its numerous readers can judge.

Jefferson's inaugural message, "We are all Republicans, we are all Federalists," was not exercised in Mr. Davis's case, and he ceased to be Postmaster. His successor made it a *sinecure* office, by placing it under the charge of Mr. Davis's eldest son. This proscription excited the ire of the editor, and he changed the title of his paper to that of "Patriot," a title that disappointed politicians are apt to assume. He employed a pungent and spicy editor named Prentiss, but, if I remember rightly, his paragraphs were too highly seasoned for the taste of his readers.

A contemporary paper, but the junior to the Gazette, was " *The Virginia Argus*," Democratic (then styled Republican) in politics, and published by Sam'l Pleasants, also semi-weekly. Mr. Pleasants was, like his rival, more expert in wielding the scissors than the pen. The two editors did not draw their weapons on each other sanguinarily, though espousing opposite parties, and seldom came in collision in their editorials, unless when represented by champions under their masks, and as the editor of the "Argus" was a Quaker, there was no danger of a duel, or of a resort to the peace-maker "*if*" to avert one. The eyes of "Argus" began to wax dim, when they were suddenly brightened, and he was rendered wide awake by a good genius * who,

---

* The Spy was discovered to be William Wirt.

under the mask of "*A British Spy*," furnished, in 1803, a series of letters which not only kept open the eyes of "Argus," but also those of his readers. They furnished much to interest and amuse the public, and brought a great increase to the subscription list of the paper; but with the departure of the Spy, departed many of the subscribers, and after the war excitement was over, the "Argus" closed its eyes. Its old antagonist, under its patriotic appellation, was extant in 1818 and later.

While these two non-combatants were pursuing their quiet course, there was a furious Republican champion in the field. "*The Examiner*," edited by Meriwether Jones, who was an editor, not a printer, and in consideration of this qualification and disqualification, he was elected printer to the Commonwealth. It might be curious to see some of the typographical work which was executed in his office for the public. Much of it, however, was underlet to practical printers.

There was a celebrated and notorious hack-writer in Richmond in those days—James Thompson Callender, a well educated Scotchman, an able writer and a great sot. He was employed by the editor of the Examiner in promoting the election of Mr. Jefferson to the Presidency, and good service he performed—his potations stimulated his pen, and drunk or sober, his paragraphs were ably written. Democracy was in the ascendant, and

Mr. Jefferson was elected. Callender thought his services might claim a reward, as he saw rewards conferred upon less able partizans. His claim, very properly, was not admitted, and like many other unrewarded partizans, he changed his politics. Just about this time, a practical printer named Pace, who could compose types much better than he could paragraphs, attempted to establish a paper called " *The Recorder*." It was dying of inanition in its cradle, when Callender offered to save its life and make a giant of it. He became the anti-administration combatant, and opened his batteries on Mr. Jefferson in a series of the most furious and Billingsgate articles against him and his principles, moral and political. Callender had been imprisoned for libel during Adams's administration, from whence he was released by the clemency of Mr. Jefferson. He now got back again into his " old quarters in the Richmond jail," (whence he dated his writings,) for a libel on Mr. Hay, district attorney, appointed by Mr. Jefferson.

Callender's pen was at the service of whoever would pay for it, and he was employed by some of the members of the legislature to write circulars for them to their constituents at the close of the sessions. As the fee for such a composition was equal to several days' pay, two or more members from counties remote from each other would club together for a circular, chock full of democracy, manufactured by a Scotchman for the nonce. One of them would obtain it and place it in the printer's hands, with instructions to adapt the captions and signatures to suit the several members who clubbed their money instead of their wits.

On one occasion the boys in the printing office, who folded and directed the circulars, were so mischievous as to direct them indiscriminately. Thus some of the letters signed by an eastern member would be sent to a western constituent, and vice-versa, tending to show a remarkable coincidence in the sentiments and language of different individuals. One of these boys was afterwards Capt. J. B. Nicolson, of the navy, and the writer admits that he was the instigator, and though not one of the devils, aided and abetted them.

Poor Callender, a martyr to both democracy and federalism, and also to liquor, died a whiskey and watery death. He had one day imbibed too much whiskey before taking his daily bath in the river, and was drowned.

Another hack-writer came to Richmond about 1803 or '4—John Wood, a Scotchman also, and of the most forbidding aspect; but he did not exercise his venal pen here; his occupation was that of teacher and surveyor, and he assisted Bishop Madison in constructing a map of Virginia. He had previously acquired notoriety by writing a distorted "History of John Adams's administration," about the period of its close in 1801, to suit some party purpose, which did not suit Aaron Burr, who contrived to suppress the book, (but it leaked out,) and employed Wood to write a distorted biography of himself, (Burr,) which he also found it politic to suppress—it was supposed that this second thought arose from a scheme he had in view of ingratiating himself with the Federal party. Wood, soon after his arrival, went to Kentucky, set his venal pen to work on a paper called "The Western World," but he was accompanied from Richmond by a young man named Street, who was to be the fighting editor, for Wood was a great coward, and although an atheist, was afraid of ghosts. His employers soon ceased their pecuniary contributions, and Wood left the *beaten* path of venality and returned to Richmond to resume that of instruction. Among other things, he published a theory of the tides, based on the principle of the change in the volocity of a cart wheel in its rotary and progressive motion.

A cotemporary and strenuous opponent in politics to "The Examiner," was "*The Virginia Federalist,*" published by Stewart and Rind, and ably edited. The talent it displayed induced some party leaders to cause a change in its place of publication to Washington city, where it appeared under the title of *The Washington Federalist.*

On the death of Meriwether Jones, his brother

Skelton, of duelling notoriety,* edited the Examiner, but the pecuniary affairs of the establishment had always been embarrassed—subscriptions to newspapers are, notoriously, difficult to collect, and the publication ceased. But the *Enquirer*, like a Phœnix, arose from its ashes in 1804, and under the judicious and energetic management of Thomas Ritchie, aided by many able contributors, "The Enquirer" acquired a greater circulation and influence than any of its predecessors. Looking at the signatures of its numerous correspondents, one might suppose that all the sages and patriots of Greece and Rome had arisen from their tombs to enlighten the existing generation. If spiritual manifestations had favored that generation, as it curses this, the communications and revelations might thus have been accounted for ; but, in many instances, they would have proved, that intellect is not progressive in a future state, and that the future state is a democratic one. Such was the success of the Enquirer, that Mr. Ritchie found it expedient to attach to it a sort of tender, as a vehicle for city advertisements, and he purchased " *The Compiler*," which had been commenced by Leroy Anderson and W. C. Shields.

To counteract the influence of the Enquirer,

---

* In those days " Coffee and Pistols for two" were almost as much in requisition in Virginia as in Ireland.

there was brought out, in 1824, a powerful opponent, in " *The Whig*," edited by John Hampden
Pleasants. These two papers have been political
opponents for many years, and would I could add
the antagonism had been political only.

It is deeply to be regretted that our newspapers
should be so frequently disgraced by personalities,
which have no connection with the subject under
discussion, and which tend to show a lack of sound
argument, and certainly of good manners. What
have become of the rules adopted by a Convention
of Editors some years ago ? Like the proceedings
of most conventions, they were forgotten after the
farewell feast had been eaten, and the fraternal
sentiments then expressed, evaporated with the
fumes of the wine in which they were drunk. We
see no personal abuse of each other by European
editors.

Many ephemeral papers have appeared, like
meteors, and some of them may " have shed a bale-
ful influence." Among the number that sought to
enlighten the people, were two " Standards" that
struck their colors ; a " Shield " that cease to protect ; a " Star" that was extinguished ; a " Phœnix"
from whose ashes no other was hatched ; a " Spirit
of '76 " that vanished ; a " Jeffersonian" that was
probably a misnomer, and sundry " Times;" whether
dull, or brisk, or hard, they did not become old.

PERIODICALS.

The first and grandest attempt to establish a literary periodical in Richmond, was by L. H. Girardin, a learned and scientific French gentleman, who was at one time the principal of a female school. He issued, in March 1805, the prospectus of a monthly magazine in quarto, entitled "*Amoenitates* " *Graphicæ*, or instructive and amusing collection " of Views, Animals, Plants, Flowers, Minerals, " Antiquities, Customs, and other interesting ob- "jects. Selected and engraved from drawings " after nature, with descriptive and explanatory "sketches in English and French. The text, by " L. H. Girardin, Professor of Modern Languages, " History and Geography in William & Mary Col- " lege. The engravings by Frederick Bosler."

There's a title page for you! and like some empty pretenders, it could not support its title. The first number contained six fine plates, colored, price $2—each succeeding number $1 ; but no 2d number succeeded, and all that breath was expended in vain.

The next attempt was made about 1807 or '8, by Seaton Grantland, who published a thin but neat monthly, called *The Gleaner* ; but there were no rich fields to glean from then. Literature was cultivated, but not authorship. Even English Magazines and Reviews had not then acquired celebrity by paying for talent, except the Edinburgh, the great pioneer, then but recently established. The "Gleaner" did not get through its teens when Mr. G., who was both editor and printer and quite a young man, very judiciously transferred himself and his types to Georgia, where he became printer to the State, a member of Congress, and, what was better, acquired a large fortune.

In 1809, the community was waited on by "*The Visitor*," who called once a fortnight, in a rather brownish garb, but composed of pretty good materials, and in a square form; in other words, invested in a dingy quarto sheet. As Mr. Girardin's grand project had failed, he felt a sympathy for this modest one, and contributed to its pages, in which appeared what he had probably composed for his own still-born bantling, a long Latin poem, entitled "Monomachia—sive Duello."

The publishers of the "Visitor" were Lynch, a practical printer, an Irishman of diminutive size, and Southgate, a musician, an Irishman of very large size, who filled many of the pages in musical type. The Rev. Mr. Blair, Mr. Munford, and others, kindly furnished contributions. But, of course, the circulation of such a paper was very limited, and, after a few efforts and throbs, it ceased with its second volume, no successor appearing to claim the barren realm for many years.

The *Southern Literary Messenger* originated

from a remarkable combination in one individual of enterprise, industry and perseverance; one who could contribute little else than mechanical skill to such a periodical as he succeeded in establishing more to his honor than his profit. Thomas W. White commenced the publication in 1834, at a time when even our large cities sustained very few such enterprises. A local sale of 5,000 copies was more probable and feasible in New York or Philadelphia, than one of 250 in Richmond. Mr. White used every effort to obtain contributions from the best sources, and was even importunate in his applications to the comparatively few writers who at that time had attained to celebrity, and who would bestow any of their talent on what might be considered fugitive literature.

A short time after its commencement, he obtained the services of Edgar A. Poe as editor, which were continued for eighteen months—an unusually long period for that erratic genius to devote to one occupation. His successor, for a still shorter period, was H. T. Tuckerman; then it passed into the hands (editorially) of James E. Heath, who wrote for it and selected the material. The Rev. E. H. Chapin rendered the same service at a subsequent period. None of these gentlemen were ever known to the public in the capacity of editor; Mr. White's name remaining on the cover as editor and proprietor. After Mr. White's death, the magazine

was bought by B. B. Minor, who conducted it for
four years, when he was succeeded by John R.
Thompson. The contributors to the "Messenger"
have been very numerous, and represent all parts
of the country and all classes of cultivated mind.
The list embraces many of the most distinguished
names in American literature : Edgar A. Poe, H.
W. Longfellow, Mrs. Lydia H. Sigourney, William
Gilmore Simms, Amelia B. Welby, Richard Henry
Wilde, Philip Pendleton Cooke, H. T. Tuckerman,
Louisa J. McCord, Alexander B. Meek, Donald G.
Mitchell, Paul H. Hayne, Caroline H. Glover, Jno.
Esten Cooke, Geo. D. Prentice, &c., &c. Besides
these professional writers, a very large number of
persons, eminent in other walks of life, have contributed to its pages papers of remarkable ability
and cleverness, either with the view of influencing
the public mind or *pour s'amuser*. Professor Dew's
strong arguments on the slavery question, Lieut.
Maury's " Scraps from the Lucky Bag," the elegant
essays of the Tuckers, (Henry St. George and Bev-
erly, both eminent as jurists, and George Tucker,
the biographer of Jefferson and historian of the U.
States,) the notes of travel of Dr. Ruschenberger of
the Navy and of P. St. George Cooke of the Army,
all attracted great attention to the " Messenger "
as they appeared. The " Reveries of a Bachelor,"
by Ik Marvel, and Joseph G. Baldwin's inimitable
" Flush Times of Alabama and Mississippi " were

originally published in the "Messenger" during Mr. Thompson's editorial management of it. But the most popular story ever brought out in its pages was "Judith Bensaddi," by Dr. Henry Ruffner, latterly and widely known as the author of the "Ruffner Pamphlet," first published in 1847, and afterwards reprinted in consequence of a loud popular demand in 1859.

For the credit of Virginia, and as furnishing a respectable vehicle for the literary productions of her men and women of talent and genius, and also information and amusement to her reading public, it is to be hoped that the "Messenger" will not only be supported, but receive a largely increased patronage. It has striven against adversity, and deserves to taste the sweets of prosperity.

PRINTERS.

The oldest printer whose name I can recall, was Dixon, who came from Williamsburg when its glory departed; after him, T. Nicholson, the very beau ideal of an old bachelor, if *beau* and *ideal* can be thus applied. The work of printing the first volume of Call's Reports occupied his energies for about twelve months. He was Librarian to the Society formed some sixty years ago, and woe to the member who retained a book beyond the limited time! Under his care the library was well sus-

21

tained. The site of his Printing Office and of the Library, is now occupied by Goddin's Hall.

One of his apprentices, or journeymen, is now the oldest of the craft in Richmond, and the oldest citizen of Richmond birth. The venerable Mr. Warrock, at the age of eighty-three, still handles the composing-stick, and continues to publish his Almanac,* which has recorded half as many years as himself.

Though somewhat damaged by time, his *case* has no bad type, and, after the impressions of so many years, his *form* is still capable of work.

[Mr. Warrock died March 7th, 1858, aged 84 years and 4 months.]

---

* Apropos to Almanacs; it is a curious fact that, in the commencement of this century, "Bannaker's Almanac" was annually issued and was calculated by Benjamin Bannaker, a black man, who resided in Maryland, and whose name has been rendered conspicuous in the records of the Maryland Historical Society by Mr. Latrobe and Mr. Norris.

CHAPTER XXII.

PUBLICANS AND PATRIOTS.

DR. JOHNSON says, "who drives fat oxen should himself be fat." In Richmond it was proved that he who served the beef should acquire the obesity.

The hosts of our taverns, in old times, were a jolly looking set. The oldest in my day were old Burgess and his wife, round and rosy, of that ancientest of inns, " *The Bird in Hand,*" at the foot of Church Hill. Then came in succession locally, Raphael, of the *City Tavern,* fat and lazy. These hosts were not distinguished by military titles, as were most of their local superiors. Major Bowler has already been described. Caspar Fleisher and his wife were host and hostess of the *Rising Sun*—as round and as red as he, when seen through a fog—against the effect of which Caspar furnished an antidote. *His* sun rose and shone for many years near the old Capitol, and on the spot now occupied by stores on Fourteenth street, north side of Exchange alley.

The rotundity of Caspar and his wife gave warranty that their table was well served and

their beer not small, for beer was a general and
genteel beverage in those days, although *lager* had
not raised it head, if it has any. *   At that time
very good beer was made by Hay & Forrester, at
their brewery on Canal and Fourth streets. We
were independent of the North for all our beverages.   Our French brandy and Jamaica rum were
not distilled in New York, nor our champagne (if
we had any) bottled in New Jersey.

Col. Radford of the *Eagle*, was of grand dimensions, as was his house in those days, and of
great resort.   Esme Smock afterwards became
landlord of the Eagle.   I mention him because
the name is now obsolete here, as applied either to
men or things.

Crouch's *Virginia Inn*, on the ascent of Gov-

---

* P. S. 1860.—*Lager has* raised its head and a strong one
it is, as are those of its countrymen. Lager has gone ahead of
all other beverages. The number of "Saloons" that bear its
name, is scarcely exceeded by that of clothing-shops, kept also
by Germans. They are a valuable acquisition to our city, in
many useful trades. They are also our gayest citizens, and
enjoy their hours of relaxation. They have their Musical and
Turner's Societies, their private theatres, their "Volks Garten,"
and support two or three newspapers, and though last, not
least, Churches of different denominations.

This is a new and pleasant phase in the aspect of our city.
More German names than any other appear over the doors in
some parts of it, and to judge by the conversation heard in the
streets, one might be at a loss to know whether German or
English is the language of the country.

ernor street, had nothing to distinguish it that I remember, except the difficulty of getting to it, and the small inducement to do so. Where now stands the *Exchange*, or a very small portion of it, stood *Major Davis's Tavern*, itself of very small pretensions, but its host of very great—never less than a scarlet vest, cocked hat and other externals to correspond, and a very martial air, even when not on parade. A tough pull was it, in wet weather, to attain to the Major's house, the locality of which was chosen in respect to *Byrd's Ware-house*, a tobacco inspection opposite, which may be said to have gone to h—l, or h—l to it—according to a modern application of that word, unfit for ears polite—considering how a portion of the site is now occupied. Major Davis's tavern, was invaded and demolished by Byrd's Ware-house, which, from some motive, politic or otherwise, changed sides, and took possession of the whole of the present Exchange premises, but in a few years came to a conclusion.

Col. Goodall, of the *Indian Queen*, was a man of commanding mien, rotund and rosy, as if he enjoyed the good things he dispensed to his guests.

The Queen, like all her race, was deposed, and her effigy which was arrayed in furs and feathers, was supplanted by a martial figure of *Washington* on horseback, sword in hand. His "*monument*" was substituted for himself in designating the old tavern, and even this did not prove "durable as brass," but subsided into the unaspiring cognomen of "*Central.*" But the Colonel deserves to be mentioned in a different character than as host of the *Indian Queen,* under whose plumes he nestled.

When Governor Dunmore, like a thief in the night, took a quantity of powder secretly from the magazine at Williamsburg, in 1775, Patrick Henry was elected to the command of the *first company of volunteers* that took up arms against royal authority, or encroachment, in any State south of Massachusetts, and immediately after the affair at Lexington and Concord. The volunteers of Hanover dared to offer resistance to their King, the Elector of Hanover. Of this band of patriots, Patrick Henry was Captain, Samuel Meredith Lieutenant, and *Parke Goodall* Ensign; and he was detached, with sixteen men, to demand of Richard Corbin, the king's Receiver-General, the sum of three hundred and thirty pounds, in payment for the stolen powder, or in case of refusal to take him prisoner. Mr. Corbin was not at home, but Dunmore found it prudent to order him to pay the money. This was the first overt act of *rebellion* in Virginia against royal authority, and Colonel Goodall deserves to be remembered for his participation in it.

The *Union Tavern,* (previously Mrs. Gilbert's Coffee-house,) was kept in 1802, by Wm. Booker, whose threshing machines, (for wheat, not for guests,) were probably the first ever made in Virginia. His successor, as a host, was Jas. H. Lynch. The tavern, which, though of moderate dimensions, assumed the *Globe* for its sign, was when in a state of dissolution, removed to the suburbs, to make room for the grand store of Kent Paine & Co., as already mentioned.

The *Swan Tavern* was kept by Major Moss, who probably also served in the Revolutionary war. He exhibited good breeding, good feeding, and good fellowship in his full figure and face. His house might have been called the Lincoln's Inn or Doctor's Commons of Richmond, for there assembled, in term time, the non-resident judges and lawyers; and though of unpretending exterior, the Swan was the tavern of highest repute for good fare, good wine, and good company. Here centred "the logic and the wisdom, and the wit," nor was "the loud laugh" wanting. It has lost its name and fame, and few of its professional guests survive.

An occasional appendage to the Swan was a house nearly opposite to it, at the corner of Broad and Ninth streets, where a large China store now stands. In that house Aaron Burr was kept prisoner during his trial for treason, the Federal Court having no prison under its control. His first place of imprisonment was the common jail,

but his counsel stated to the Judge that there
was no privacy there to allow of free conference,
and he was removed to the Penitentiary, where
pleasant apartments were assigned him—if apartments in a prison can be called pleasant—and from
thence, when his trial came on, he was incarcerated
in the house above mentioned, being near the Court
room. He was the first of modern filibusters, and
had not his plans been thwarted, might have become
the Napoleon of the West, the scourge of Louisiana, the liberator of Mexico, with a host of
adherents who, fortunately for themselves, had not
become so far implicated in his plots as to be
arraigned at the bar.

The occasion of his trial brought to Richmond
many distinguished men, as counsel, witnesses, &c.,
some of whom would have held a very different
position, had Burr's plans proved successful.
Among the number was the purblind but accomplished Mr. Blannerhasset, and Dr. Erick Bolman,
who was devoted to the ladies, and paid his addresses to all who gave him an opportunity. He
had distinguished himself previously by an attempt
in concert with Mr. Huger, of South Carolina, to
rescue Lafayette from the Castle of Olmutz.
Gen. Jackson was one of the witnesses, with whose
tall, lank figure was contrasted the short, fat and
pompous one of Gen. Wilkinson. The concourse
that assembled in Richmond, serious as the occa-

sion was to the parties accused or suspected, made
it a gay time, and those parties, except the principal, generally partook of the gaiety.

CHAPTER XXIII.

RACES AND BALLS.

IN old times in Virginia, *horse-racing* was the
sport of gentlemen. Many wealthy planters had
their stud of horses of the best stock, as well as
of the most useful, and bred them for the turf, the
saddle, the harness, and the plough. There was
no *West* then, as now, to supply them, and mules
were scarcely known. One gentleman who had
seen their value elsewhere, for the purpose of
introducing them, brought two or three jacks to
Richmond, but in vain. He turned them out on
the common, and the school boys derived great
sport from riding them. Washington Irving has
introduced a gentleman in one of his sketches,
under the name of Ralph Ringwood, who I must
also introduce here as one of the school-boys. To
make sure of a holiday ride, he caught one of the
donkeys over night, and stabled him in his father's
smoke-house. At an early hour in the morning,
the household was alarmed by a most unearthly,

but not a heavenly noise. The house-keeper
thought her bacon had gone to the devil or the
devil had got into it. The young scamp had to
allay the demon by producing the key and releas-
ing the donkey. Irving gives a richer, and of
course an amusing version of the story, showing
that the adventure with the donkey tended to make
Mr. Duval Governor of Florida.

Gentlemen of town and country formed the
Jockey Clubs, which held the Spring and Fall
races at Richmond and Petersburg, and perhaps
elsewhere. They and their friends came to town
in their coaches and four, in their phaetons, char-
iots and gigs, bringing their wives and daughters;
a very convenient time for obtaining the Spring
and Fall fashions. The race-field presented a
brilliant display of equipages, filled with the reigning belles and their predecessors. Many were the
pairs of gloves lost and won between them and
their beaux. Nothing could appear more animated
than such an assemblage of beauty and fashion.
The equestrians, on fine blooded horses, riding
from coach to coach, or during the heat of the
race, going at high speed, to obtain a commanding
view of the contest. The race week was a perfect
carnival. The streets were thronged with equipages, and the shops with customers. Not only
taverns and boarding-houses were filled, but private families opened their hospitable doors to their

country friends. Among the amusements of the week was the *Race Ball*, which (as well as the regular dancing assemblies of the winter) was held in the large ball-room of the Eagle. Boots and pants in those days were proscribed. Etiquette required shorts and silks, and pumps with buckles, and powdered hair. The ball was opened by one of the managers and the lady he thought proper to distinguish, with a *minuet de la Cour*, putting the grace and elegance of the couple to a severe ordeal.

Such bowing and courtseying, tiptoeing and tipfingering, backing and filling, advancing and retreating, attracting and repelling, all in the figures of Z or X, to a tune which would have served for a dead march! A long silken train following the lady, like a sunset shadow; and the gentleman holding a cocked hat under his arm, or in his hand, until at last the lady permitted the gentleman at full arms-length, to hand her, by the very tips of her fingers, to a seat, when, with a most profound bow, he retreated backward to seek one for himself.

Then commenced the reel, like a storm after a calm—all life and animation. No solemn walking of the figure to a measured step—but pigeon-wings fluttered, and all sorts of capers were cut to the music of Si. Gilliat's fiddle, and the flute or clario-net of his blacker comrade, London Brigs.

Contra dances followed, and sometimes a congo, or a hornpipe; and when "the music grew fast and furious," and the most stately of the company had retired, a jig would wind up the evening, which, by-the-by, commenced about eight o'clock.

The waltz and the polka were as great strangers to the ball-room floor, as were champagne and Perigord pies to the supper-table.

> No hands were then "promiscuously applied
> Around the waist or down the glowing side."

The sports of the turf have so degenerated of late years, that few ladies of the present generation ever saw a race. The field is now chiefly in possession of a class, termed in softened phrase, "sporting characters," in the same way that negro-traders are called "speculators." Exclusive of the racing, the field presents a scene of the lowest gambling and dissipation; but there is now a prospect of the sport being more respectably patronized and conducted.

CHAPTER XXIV.

SOCIETIES.

THE worthies of Richmond, of the last century, formed among themselves three associations, for very different purposes—charitable, literary and social—in which order I shall introduce them.

THE AMICABLE SOCIETY was instituted in 1788, with the benevolent object of relieving strangers and wayfarers in distress, for whom the law makes no provision.

The first officers elected by the Society were Anthony Single-ton, president; Alexander Montgomery, vice-president; Alexander Buchanan, treasurer; and Charles Hopkins, secretary. Their successors were, in the presidency, in 1794, Andrew Ronald, and in 1800 the Rev. John Buchanan, who retained the office for a great number of years; in the vice-presidency, in 1791 John Henry, in 1792 John Groves, in 1807 John Richards; and as treasurer William Berkeley in 1801, John Foster in 1807, and subsequently Edmund W. Rootes until his death.

It may be curious, if not gratifying, to the few survivors and to the numerous descendants of the early members of the Society, to inscribe their names on these pages. The following is an extract

22

from the records of the Amicable Society, kept in
clerkly style :

"A company of gentlemen having met at the Richmond
Coffee-house, on Saturday, 13th December, 1788, viz: Alex.
Montgomery, John Groves, George Wier, Charles Hopkins,
John Graham, and Alexander Buchanan, they resolved to form
themselves into a society, by the name of the *Amicable Society
of Richmond*, on the principles and for the purposes expressed
in the Rules which were then considered and adopted; at
the same time, the following gentlemen were considered as
members :

"James Montgomery, Anthony Singleton, George Pickett,
Andrew Ronald, Philip Southall, John Cunliffe, and Joseph
Higbee.

"The same evening officers were appointed, to remain in
office till the next annual meeting:

"Anthony Singleton, president; Alex'r Montgomery, vice-
president; Charles Hopkins, secretary; Alex'r Buchanan,
treasurer.

"On the 20th December, 1788, the following new members
were admitted:

"Arthur Stewart, Thomas Keene, Richard Hartshorne, John
Marshall, William Wiseham, William Shermer, Joseph Lakel,
and William Fenwick."

On the 7th February, 1789, the accession of new members
was, William Mitchell, Jos. Dalzel, John Cringan, John
Buchanan, John Harvey, James Kemp and Joseph Darmstadt.

At a meeting on the 2d May, 1789, the following entry is
made on the record of the Society: "It having appeared,
by advertisement, that a surplus of a fund arising from a
ball on General Washington's birthnight was to be given to
this Society, Mr. Alexander Montgomery, as a manager of
that ball, paid this evening, to the treasurer, the said surplus,
amounting to twenty pounds, sixteen shillings and sixpence."

At this meeting, the following new members were admitted:

Thomas Mann Randolph, Geo. Nicolson and James Brown; and on the 7th November, 1789, Jas. Strange, of Manchester, and Alex. Youille—at which time a vote of thanks was given to Alex. Donald for a donation of five pounds.

The new members in 1790 were Robert Gamble and John Ker. The Legislature of 1790–'91 authorized a lottery, to raise one thousand pounds for the benefit of the Society. In 1791, Andrew Leiper, George Gray, James Knox and Charles Hay, were added to the members, and also Abraham Lott, Hugh J. Crawford, John Henry, Thomas Rutherfoord, Wm. Hay, Wm. Foushee, Wm. Mewburn, Wm. Heth, Jas. Innis, Patrick Hart, John H. Briggs and John Satchell; subsequently, John Hopkins, John Banks, Alex. Quarrier and Thos. Gilliatt were admitted, and a rule adopted that the Society should be limited to sixty resident members. The admission of members subsequently, were, in 1793, John Richard; in 1797, Charles Copland and Jos. Anthony; in 1798, Wm. Berkeley and John Foster; in 1804, Wilson Allen; in 1809, John G. Smith and M. W. Hancock. In 1811 a revival occurred, and twenty-one members were added, namely: W. H. Fitzwhyllsonn, J. G. Gamble, R. Gamble, John Adams, J. Brockenbrough, A. Pollok, C. J. Macmurdo, Thos. Taylor, Samuel Myers, Jos. Marx, Jas. Gibbon, Wm. Hay, Jr., James McClurg, E. J. Haven, W. N. Morris, Robert Johnston, E. W. Rootes, C. B. Page, J. Wickham, M. B. Poitiaux and Robt. Gordon.

In 1812, Jas. Brown, Jr., and Dr. J. D. McCaw.

In 1813, Robt. Greenhow and S. Pleasants; 1815, W. Lambert; 1816, Wm. Finney; 1822, Rev. J. H. Rice and T. H. Bradley. In 1825, a second revival brought a large accession of members, namely: S. Jacobs, B. Brand, A. Otis, C. J. Nicholas, W. Bibber, L. J. Salignac, R. G. Scott, G. C. Pickett, G. H. Backus, J. Bronaugh, J. Goddin, J. McKildoe, W. H. Hubbard, J. H. Eustace, T. Brockenbrough, W. Galt, Jr., Jaq. Taylor, Dr. T. Nelson, D. Warwick, J. Rawlings, T. Ritchie, J. Hall, Dr. J. Trent, W. Gilliatt, R. Gwathmey, T. Gwathmey,

J. Bosher, W. Munford, J. Ambler, J. Parkhill, W. F. Micou,
W. W. Henning, R. Wortham, N. Sheppard, W. Brockenbrough,
D. J. Burr, M. Walthall and T. Diddep.

Having extended the record through the period
of two generations, I will leave the last thirty
years untold. Of all those named, I can count
up but thirteen survivors.

The funds of the Society accumulated, and the
surplus of interest on its investments was regularly re-invested.

In 1841, when the stock held by the Society
was about $9,000, it made a donation of more than
one-half to the *Female Humane Association* of
Richmond, in fifty shares of bank stock, in aid
of the large bequest made by the benevolent
Edmund Walls, a native of Ireland, and for many
years Inspector of Flour in Richmond, who left the
great bulk of his fortune to erect a building for
that charity, which has been faithfully applied.

On the formation of the *Male Orphan Asylum*,
the Amicable Society made a donation to it of
$1,000—in 1851.

The Society still exists in a small number of
members, and it is to be hoped that it will acquire
additional and active ones, whose exertions may
invigorate and perpetuate it.*

---

* It is gratifying to state that since the preceding was
written, this research has recalled the attention of a
public spirited gentleman to the long dormant Amicable So-

As an institution of our forefathers, it should be honored and cherished for their sakes; and as a charitable one, for our own and our successors. It should be deemed a perpetual legacy, from generation to generation.

The LIBRARY SOCIETY under the management of its founders, who embraced most of the persons constituting the Amicable Society and in general the principal citizens, was as well conducted as such establishments usually are, and under the custody of Thomas Nicolson, Librarian, the books were well cared for, and the circulation of them was extensive. To what its failure is to be ascribed, I know not, unless it was an undue influence obtained by some lady novel readers, who induced their friends of the directory to fill the shelves with " Minerva Library " novels, a notorious London mint for the issue of trash, such as is now hawked about our streets at twenty-five cents, for as much worthless matter as then cost two or three dollars.

After an existence of twenty years or more, the

---

ciety. At his instance, a new accession of members is obtained. Some funds have been invested and some have been applied to the relief of the distressed during this, the severest winter (1855–6) known for many years. Snow has mantled the earth for six weeks, and the rivers in Virginia were closed to navigation during the months of January and February, with ice more than a foot in thickness.

early teens of which were vigorous and useful, the library gradually declined; the books were distributed among the members, and the society ceased to exist.

An interval of seven years ensued, of literary darkness, so far as a public Library was necessary to diffuse light, and then a successor to the old institution was created, and would I could add, a thriving one, and that its readers were as numerous as the number and character of its volumes should invite. It requires a considerable accession of members to keep its shelves furnished with the valuable and the good current literature of the day. For the credit of the city, it is to be desired that all who can enjoy such literature, should make the small contribution required to entitle them to membership, and to sustain so useful an establishment. It would be a reflection on the intellectual character of the city to say, that it cannot support a Library, nor even a Reading Room. The city appropriates an apartment in the Athæneum, with light and one hundred and fifty dollars annually, to the use of the Library, on condition that every visitor may there have gratuitous access to the books. *

---

* In a paroxysm of municipal frugality the Athæneum and the fine lot of land attached to it were sold—the lot fronts on Marshall street and extended from Tenth to Eleventh. The building has been demolished and dwellings are erected on the

I will now introduce the Quoit Club, or as it is called, THE BARBACUE CLUB,

"Who mixed reason with pleasure, and
Wisdom with mirth."

This club was formed some sixty years ago, and met on Saturdays during the genial season, at *Buchanan's Spring*, under the oaks of original growth, with no other shelter than the shade they afforded, and an open shed, to protect the dinner table. Quoits was the game, and toddy, punch and mint julep the beverages, to wash down a plain substantial dinner, without wines or dessert.

Among the most skillful in throwing the Discus as he was in discussion, was Judge Marshall, even in advanced years, and it delighted his competitors as much as himself, to see him "ring the meg." The brother Parsons, Buchanan and Blair, were honorary members of the club, and the latter, though apparently of fragile form, was a practical member with the quoits, and both of them with the jests and good humor that prevailed.

---

grounds. Soon afterwards in a fit of prodigality, La Fayette Hall fronting the Capitol Square on Tenth, with grounds extending back to Ninth street, was given as a donation, to the Mechanics Association. An injudicious location for their object and a loss to the city, which cannot be replaced in point of locality, for the use of the fire, water and gas departments. These are not the only instances of injudicious management of city property, in the last few years. (1859.)

A list of the members of this club, would comprise many of the most worthy citizens of their day—but are not their names written in the book of the Amicable Society? I will record here, only Jasper Crouch, their mulatto cook, and who officiated at all public dinners; he acquired the gout in this congenial occupation, and also the rotundity of an alderman and fell a victim to the good things of this life. A similar club was formed many years after, and met at *Clarke's Spring*—near the Hollywood Cemetery—not then established. The two clubs were not rivals, but on the contrary, so cordial an understanding existed between them, that their meetings became alternate at each other's fountains.

I should not omit to mention, that if any bets were made at the meetings of the club, they were forfeited to it, and as such a case occurred now and then, when an interesting game was in progress, these forfeits served to furnish some extra viands for the feast, all which were provided by a committee of caterers, who also acted as masters of ceremony to strangers, etc.; the members serving in rotation.

The exercise and recreation, bodily and mental, at the close of the week's labors, were most grateful and invigorating, and the social intercourse was promotive of good fellowship. Respectable strangers, and more especially foreigners who were invited to the *barbacue*, as the feast was called, could there see Liberty, Equality and Fraternity, without licentiousness, presumption or demagogueism, and pure Republicanism, represented by some of the distinguished men, who aided in forming the Republic.

The trees still furnish their shade, and the spring its cool stream, and some of the descendants of those that first assembled there, even of the second and third generation, yet partake of them, and pitch their quoits, or crack their jokes there.

The mention of Clarke's Spring, (connected with the Clubs) reminds me of a gentleman connected with Col. Clarke. Major Clarke established a cannon foundry and boring mill on the river, some miles above Richmond, and induced the Federal Government to establish an Arsenal on the land adjoining, which obtained the appropriate name of Bellona Arsenal—and which, like the Navy Yard at-Memphis, was most inappropriately located.

The unhealthiness of the spot caused the Arsenal to be abandoned, and the Government permitted a gentleman to substitute silk worms for soldiers, and to try whether cocoons could be substituted for cannons. This was about the time that the Morus Multicaulis fever raged so extensively, and to many, so fatally. The Mulberry slips were planted, and the eggs of the silk worms set for hatching—but unfortunately, the praise-worthy effort, though promising well at first, proved abortive, and the worthy projector had, like his predecessor, to abandon the establishment, and after remaining vacant for several years, it was sold in 1856, including all the extensive buildings, for a few hundred dollars, having cost more than as many thousands—no unusual case where public interests are involved.

CHAPTER XXV.

EVENING PASTIMES.

"See how the world its veterans rewards,
A youth of folly, an old age of cards."

IN the first decade of the present century, a resource for winter evening's pastime was found, by many of the ton-ish ladies, in a game of *Loo*. Its attractions were such that few evenings of the week passed without an assemblage at the rooms of one or other of the sporting circle. After discussing a dish of tea (*dish* was then the word), and another of scandal perhaps, the card-table was introduced and a circle formed around it.

In this enchanted and enchanting circle gentlemen were admitted, and he who played the most
careless and hazardous game was sure to be the
most welcome, provided luck did not run too
strongly in his favor ; but, on these occasions, the
gentleman who accompanied their ladies usually
amused themselves with a quiet rubber of Whist.
Quiet was a term not applicable to the ladies' table,
except during the intense excitement created by a
large sum on it. The original stake was small, but,
by the forfeits of losers and contributions of dealers, the money in "*the pool*" would sometimes
accumulate to a score or two of dollars, and even
to three or four score, but this latter rarely occurred.

As the contents of the pool increased, so did the
excitement and anxiety of the players (I won't say
gamblers). Many a charming face would lose its
sweetness, many a rosy cheek its hue ; many a
bright eye would almost be dimmed by a rising
tear, and many an apparently smooth and gentle
temper would betray the indications of an approach-
ing storm. Gentle accents would be changed to
loud tones, and endearing epithets to harsh and
insulting ones ; but as duels are the exclusive privilege of gentlemen, or of those claiming that title,
no other weapons than those they most exercise
and can best wield, were resorted to by the ladies,
except now and then in a very extreme case, when
a curl might get deranged, or a cap be torn,—

but on such occasions the cause of irritation was extreme, such as the accusation of concealing a card, or other foul play.

The practice (of playing I mean, not of fighting) had attained to an extreme height; domestic and maternal duties were neglected, and some purses much lightened, when a true Knight came to the rescue of the enchanted fair ones. Under the assumed name of *Hickory Cornhill,* he entered the lists against the demon Loo, for the relief of the distressed dames and damsels who were suffering under his enchantments.

At the very first charge he disarmed the demon, but did not utterly destroy him. His abettors, who assumed the titles of Kings and Queens, and others who appeared in their true characters as Knaves, dared not show their faces publicly. They, and a few of their spell-bound victims, continued for a short time to hold their revels in a sneaking way; but the latter gradually became ashamed of themselves and of each other, and were ultimately reclaimed. The former ceased to persecute the fair sex, but found plenty of adherents among the other.

When Hickory Cornhill's vizor was removed, it disclosed the features of George Tucker, and his squire was E. W. Rootes.

I will add, in seriousness, that the disaster at the theatre gave a better tone to society and a death-blow to female gambling and, perhaps, to some of its votaries. May it never revive! A specimen or two of Hickory's onslaught will show something of the fashions and pastimes of his day, and the similarity in some respects, and the contrast in others, with those of the present:

> "And first, all the morning, the debates I attend,
> Of the folks who our laws come to make and to mend;
> Where sometimes I hear much fine declamation
> 'Bout judges and bridges, the banks and the nation;
> But last night my amusement was somewhat more new,
> Being asked to a party of ladies at *Loo.*
> Oh! then, my dear friends, what splendor was seen,
> Each dame that was there was arrayed like a queen;
> The camel, the ostrich, the tortoise, the bear
> And the kid, might have found each his spoils on the fair.
> Though their dresses were made of the finest of stuff,
> It must be confessed they were *scanty* enough;
> Yet naught that this scant may their husbands avail,
> What they save from the body they waste in the tail.
> When they sit, they so tighten their clothes, that you can
> See a lady has legs just the same as a man;
> Then stretched on the floor were their trains all so nice—
> They brought to my mind Æsop's council of mice.
> Ere tea was serv'd up they were prim as you please,
> But when cards were produced, all was freedom and ease.
> Mrs. Winloo, our hostess, each lady entreated
> To set the example—'I pray, ma'am, be seated'—
> "After you, Mrs. Clutch'—'Well' if you insist.'
> ' Tom Shuffle, sit down, *you* prefer *Loo* to Whist.'
> Around the green board now they eagerly fix,
> Two beaux and four ladies composing the six.
>
>   *   *   *   *   *   *
>
> ' Well, Mr. Shuffle, you are dealer—begin.'

23

'Is that the trump-card ?   then I cannot *stand.*'
'And I must throw up.'   ' Let me look at your *hand.*'
*   *   *   *   *   *
'Oh, there's Mrs. Craven, she threw up the *knave !* '
'I know I did, madam, I don't play to save.'
*   *   *   *   *   *
And thus they went on—*checking, stumping* and *fleeting,*
And much other jargon that's not worth repeating—
Till at length it struck twelve, and the *winners* propose
That the *Loo* which was up then the session should close.
On a little more play tho' the *losers* were bent,
They could not withhold their reluctant assent.
Mrs. Craven, who long since a word had not spoke,
Who scarce gave a smile to the sly equivoque,
But like an old mouser sat watching her prey,
Now uttered the ominous sound of ' I play !'
And swept the grand *Loo,* thus proving the rule,
That the still sow will ever swill most from the pool.
Though much had been lost, yet now they had done,
The deuce of them all would confess she had won.
But soon I discovered it plain could be seen
In each lady's face what her fortune had been."

" January, 1806."

The reformation in female society of the vice of gaming, tended no doubt to diminish it in the male ranks also, and to confine it in some degree to the frequenters of the Tiger's den, or to a portion of those who enact laws against it, and themselves test the futility of their own enactments.

But there was another vice very prevalent among gentlemen of the past generation, which is greatly diminished, has gradually abated, and is now scarcely heard in refined or respectable society.

Formerly almost every sentence was rounded off with the (now disgusting) expletive of an oath, uttered unconsciously. D—d was the term by which to express admiration of a good fellow or detestation of a rascal. Souls were pawned to establish the truth of an assertion, or it was vouched for by a violation of the Third Commandment.

This practice no longer exists among gentlemen, at least to any extent, nor amongst refined ones at all. When heard now, as I regret to say it frequently is in the streets, or in bar rooms, it is ascribed to the lack of good breeding or of good sense, or to sottish vulgarity.

CHAPTER XXVI.

A MEDLEY.

AMONG the enterprising men in Richmond toward the close of the last century was *Moses Austin*, who afterwards emigrated to the West, and who deserves to be called *the founder of Texas*. By his influence and unwearied exertions, sanctioned by the Spanish government, he infused so large a portion of bold and enterprising citizens of the United States into the mixed population of that then Spanish colony, as to establish ultimately an ascendancy, which redeemed Texas from Mexican degradation, and has rendered her one of the most thriving States in the Union.

Moses Austin founded in Richmond a shot and pewter button factory (not a tower) on the lot where the gas house now stands,* on Cary street, and he built, of Philadelphia brick and wood-work and marble, the once fine house, now Lisle's corner, formerly Gamble's, on Main and Fourteenth streets, the most imposing structure of its day. In its elaborate cornice *the martens* used to build their nests, and when the young could take wing, the number of old and new broods was so great that their noise drowned all competition. The nuisance could not be abated by any other mode than by covering the cornice with canvas, which now disfigures it.† From this nursery, or colony, the martens adjourned to the Capitol,

---

* Demolished, to be succeeded by a "Sewing machine manufactory," which I hope will be permanent and successful.

† Some familiar spirit that haunts "Lisle's row," must have peered over my shoulder, or over that of the compositor, when its domicile was thus spoken of, and must have whispered to its owner the warning given by Burns to his "brither Scots:"

> "If there's a hole in a' ye'er coats,
>   I rede you tent it;
> A Chiel's amang ye taking notes,
>   An' faith, he'el prent it,"

for on the day this book (1st edition) was announced, the ragged canvas was torn from the cornice, and a new coat of paint put on the whole edifice, restoring its pristine gentility.

where a general congress from all the surrounding
country was annually held for about a week or
more previous to their exodus to a warmer climate
or to winter quarters. On the day previous to
their departure they assembled in myriads, and on
the next day they had vanished invisibly and in-
audibly. Fortunately their sessions preceded those
of the "unplumed bipeds" (as some wise man
calls his brethren), who deliberated in the halls
below—some of whom probably feathered their
nests and others were plucked.

Fortunately, I say, the martens adjourned before
the law-makers assembled, for voluble and loud as
the latter sometimes are, the martens would have
silenced them. But it is remarkable that with
all their noise, the martens were never "out of
order." Their sessions and adjournments were
conducted with the utmost regularity, and their
commonwealth seemed to be governed by consti-
tutional principles, which were neither changed
nor violated. Their example would be no ignoble
one to others, whose sessions are held in the same
building.

What has become of the martens? have they
changed their seat of government? It is several
years since they assembled in Richmond, and few
are to be seen in the city or its vicinity. I hope
they will revisit us, for though not musical, they
are examples of industry and parental love, and

moreover, a colony of them would be more efficient in ridding the trees of insects than all the beltings and washes that have been tried. Birds would be more numerous, but that boys amuse themselves with throwing stones in the Capitol square, to the annoyance of pedestrians as well as of birds. If the latter were unmolested, and even fed at certain seasons, their music would add to the charms of the grounds, and their appetites would diminish the number of caterpillars that destroy the foliage.

In Philadelphia, the innocent denizens of the woods are considered denizens of the city, and are so entirely unmolested in the public squares, as to lose their natural timidity. They are so accustomed to receiving food from children and other visitors, that the squirrels will approach and in beseeching attitude beg for nuts and fruit, in the unmistakeable though silent language of nature.

The Armory was erected soon after the adoption of the celebrated "Resolutions of 1798–'99," when the apprehended encroachments of the Federal Government on "State Rights and Strict Construction," induced Virginia to prepare for the worst.

At this establishment the manufacture of arms and artillery, from pistols to thirty-two pounders, was carried on for several years. This has ceased

long ago, and some of the buildings are now used
as an arsenal and barracks, but portions of those
in which the water-power was employed, are adapted to the peaceful occupation of grinding grain.
[P. S. 1860. Since the murderous and treason-
able attempt by fanatics, at Harper's Ferry, it is
proposed to resume the manufacture of arms at
this establishment, and to introduce all the recent
improvements in effecting it.]

The large and ugly block of brick buildings
erected by Col. Harvie, on Cary street, near the
head of the basin, has now anything but a literary
aspect, but it was once *Haller's Academy*, and the
first portion of the block was doubled in size to
accommodate that extensive establishment. Haller
was a Swiss or German adventurer, who with little
learning, had address and impudence enough to
impose on the community; but he also had judgment enough to enable him to select good teachers;
among those, good or bad, of his or of his successor, Girardin, was Mons. Fremont, the father of
Col. Fremont, of Pacific and warlike celebrity.
But for the sake of all parties concerned, we will
let this subject drop.

DENTISTRY AND ARCHITECTURE.

Now-a-days the profession of dentistry gives
lucrative employment in our city to a score of

practitioners. In the days of my boyhood, only one *Tooth-drawer*, who probably never heard the word dentist, did all the work and all the mischief in the dental line.

Peter Hawkins was a tall, raw-boned, very black negro, who rode a raw-boned, black horse, for his practice was too extensive to be managed on foot, and he carried all his instruments, consisting of two or three pullikins, in his pocket. His dexterity was such, that he has been known to be stopped in the street by one of his distressed brethren, (for he was of the church,) and to relieve him of the offending tooth, gratuitously, without dismounting from his horse. His strength of wrist was such, that he would almost infallibly extract, or break a tooth, whether the right or the wrong one. I speak from sad experience, for he extracted two for me, a sound and an aching one, with one wrench of his instrument.

On Sundays he mounted the pulpit instead of black bare-bones, and as a preacher he drew the fangs of Satan with his spiritual pullikins, almost as skillfully as he did the teeth of his brother sinners on week days, with his metallic ones.

Peter's surgical, but not his clerical mantle, fell on his son, who depletes the veins and pockets of his patients, and when he has exhausted the latter, the former are respited. The doctor dismisses himself, and as likely as not, carries the malady with him.

Opposite to the residence of "Peter Hawkins, Tooth-Drawer," on Brook Avenue, stood, or tried to stand, a most singular specimen of architecture, without form, but not void. It was a hovel built by its sable occupant, of brick-bats and mud, and as the ground on which it stood formed a trapezium, he adapted his edifice to it. Square and plumb and level had nothing to do with the lines of its walls. The materials were gathered from the ruins of old buildings, or the refuse of new ones, and as they were gathered, the structure progressed. The timbers were all sorts of drift and refuse wood, and the partitions were adapted to them. The roof was of boards, or slates or slabs, which ever came to hand, and the chimneys were topped with headless barrels. A portion of the scrambling walls would fall, while another portion was being erected, and thus the industrious architect and sole workman and tenant, found incessant occupation for a score or more of years, and probably till his death; for his ruins (as they appeared to be when standing) have fallen to the ground.

Many nondescript specimens of architecture existed, and some still exist in our city. It is only of late years that edifices to which the term architecture can be applied, have been erected, with a few exceptions—but the fantastic style still occasionally intrudes.

CHAPTER XXVII.

THE SHARP-SHINS AND SHIN-PLASTER CURRENCY.

In the beginning of the present century, and for some years of the last, after State and Continental paper money had disappeared from circulation, under a depreciation so ridiculous, as to render a dollar's worth more than one's pockets would contain, there existed in Virginia and in some other States, a currency, that from its triangular shape and acute angles, was called sharp-shins.

In those days a bank note was a rare, though not a despised currency. Virginia, under the guidance of her Revolutionary Apostles, held banks in abhorrence, and having seen that baseless paper-money was a base currency, she would tolerate no other than gold and silver. As Alexandria was about to leave the pale of the Old Dominion, she yielded to her urgent entreaties, and granted to her a taste of the forbidden fruit, which so far from causing her downfall, tended greatly to her prosperity ; but as there may be too much of a good thing, she was afterwards ruined, or nearly so, by the introduction of six or eight unchartered banks.

It was some convenience to merchants travelling north to obtain money in a more portable form than gold and silver, especially as the modes of conveyance were either by a stage-wagon, twice or thrice a week, or on horse-back with saddle-bags, or in a stick-chair, (now a sulky,) or in a coasting schooner. Few merchants however then visited northern cities to obtain supplies of goods. The English, Scotch and Irish merchants or agents established here, imported from London, Bristol, Glasgow, Liverpool and Dublin, where their principals resided, every sort of goods, and all articles from a nail to a clock, and in those days a clock was *something* to have. I do not include West India products; these were obtained at Norfolk, then one of the largest markets in the Union for the importation of rum, sugar, coffee, molasses, &c. The few store-keepers (as they were called) who bought their goods at the North were looked upon as little above the grade of pedlers.

The Bank of Alexandria, that of Baltimore, the old "Bank of North America," (the patriarch of American banks, and a worthy exemplar for them,) the first "Bank of the United States," and two or three New York banks, furnished all the bank notes which then circulated in our towns, and they were readily taken by the merchants;

but the whole amount was small. The modern contrivance of forcing bank notes into circulation as far as possible from their place of redemption, had not then been adopted.

I have deviated somewhat from my subject, and after a few more prefatory remarks will enter upon it.

The great mass of the currency was Spanish dollars, some ugly French crowns, little or no English silver, but a large quantity of gold, in Spanish, Portuguese, French and English coins; also a portion of *Cob* gold and silver in irregular uncoined pieces, with some unintelligible figures and letters stamped on them, to denote perhaps the weight, fineness, and assayer's initials. All gold coins passed by weight, and as the several nations had different standards of fineness, those of each had to be weighed separately, and the value to be calculated by printed tables. To effect this, each merchant and trader was provided with the requisite apparatus of scales, weights and tables of rates; indeed many persons carried a case of pocket scales, &c., and it was also necessary to have some skill in discriminating between genuine and base coin, as many counterfeits were made.

It was usually no small trouble to receive and pay a few thousand dollars, and in my boyhood, I have frequently staggered along the street with

my arm bruised under the weight of a heavy bag
of dollars, which I hugged most hatefully. Then
came the counting and re-counting and exam-
ining for counterfeits, and weighing and calcu-
lating the value of various pieces of gold. Money
was really a misery—at least to me—for no
more stuck to my fingers than I could wash off
after counting.

I well remember the day when relief came.
When the Bank of Virginia was opened for deposits, in the basement of the Capitol in 1804, and
I followed a stout negro wheeling $10,000 to the
vaults.

And now for the Sharp-shins, which did not cut
their way later than about 1802 or 1803. The
supply of small silver coins for change, was insuffi-
cient for the traffic of the country generally, and
recourse was had to subdividing the larger ones, by
the aid of a shears, or a chisel and mallet, or even
of an axe in expert hands. A quarter of a dollar
would be radiated and subdivided into six parts, or
a pistareen into five parts, each one of which
called a "half bit," passed for three-pence; but
it was strange, that these several parts formed a
sort of Chinese puzzle, and less possible to solve,
for you could never put the five or six parts together so as fully to cover a similar coin entire.
The deficiency went for *seignorage* to the clipper,
and from him to the silver-smith. "Bits" were in

24

semi-circular form; "half bits" in quadrants. The coins that were to suffer the torture of dismemberment were, it was said, first beaten out to increased expansion, so as to be susceptible of a sort of Hibernian divisibility, into three halves, or six quarters, besides an irregular bit, which was not good money except to the coiner. The eighth of a dollar (twelve and a half cents) was expanded and cut into two bits, or sixpences. Dollars even were cut into halves and quarters in cases of emergency. It was no uncommon thing in the country, when change could not be otherwise made, to chop the dollar into parts with an axe, and thus meet the contingency.*

Purses and pockets were not proof against sharp-shins. Money is said to burn the pockets of some folks—sharp-shins cut the pockets of all—and the profit of making them induced many to engage in it. Like various other evils, it cured itself by excess.

The market became overstocked with cut money and perfect coins disappeared in the same proportion. So on one fine day, several influential citizens met and drew up an obligation, by which

---

* A jar containing $500 worth of old silver coins, including cob dollars, cut dollars and half bits, was ploughed up in Surry, in 1859.

every one who signed it, bound himself not to receive or pay a piece of cut money after a certain
day; and behold, the sharp-shins disappeared at
the appointed time, as their successors, of somewhat similar name, the small-fry currency of shin-
plasters have since vanished at two or three
successive periods; some by redemption and
some by repudiation, when the community refused to submit longer to the evil—and thus
endeth the chapter of sharp-shins, shin-plasters
and sharpers.

While on the subject of currency, it may not be
amiss to notice a species of paper money issued on
State authority soon after the Revolutionary war,
of which, that issued by North Carolina survived
all other, and was current to some extent in Petersburg and Southern Virginia, until absorbed some
thirty or forty years ago by the Bank of North
Carolina. This money was called *proc.* (*i. e.*, pro-
clamation money,) and was issued on bits of thick
paper, about the size of a playing card, and
for various sums, from sixpence up to forty shillings. It was receivable for taxes, and circulated
currently in North Carolina and on her borders, at
the rate of ten shillings to the dollar; and at that
rate the State redeemed all that appeared—a rare
instance.

As to the old continental paper money and other

paper representatives, it was no uncommon thing to find a box or drawer full of it in the garret, or some other obscure part of an old store-house, and utterly worthless.

———

CHAPTER XXVIII.

THE FLUSH TIMES IN RICHMOND.

AFTER the war of 1812–14 with Great Britain, when specie payments were suspended, or rather some time after peace was restored, but before specie payments were resumed, when bank credits were as unlimited as was the issue of irredeemable bank notes, the spirit of speculation, like the great comet that preceded it, shed its influence over the land.

I will borrow from Washington Irving his description of the speculative mania a century before :

"Every body trusts every body. A bad debt is a thing unheard of. The way to certain and sudden wealth lies plain and open, and men are tempted to dash forward boldly from the facility of borrowing. Negotiable notes interchanged between scheming individuals are liberally discounted by the banks, which become so many mints to coin promises into cash, and as the supply of promises is inexhaustible, it may readily be supposed what a vast amount of promissory capital is now in circulation.

"Every one talks in thousands; nothing is heard but gigantic operations in trade, great purchases and sales of real estate, and increased prices at every transfer. All, to be sure, as yet exists in promise, but the believer in promises calculates the aggregate as solid capital and is amazed at the amount of public wealth and the unexampled state of public prosperity.

"Now is the time for speculative and dreaming or designing men. They relate their dreams and projects to the ignorant and credulous, dazzle them with golden visions and set them crazed after shadows. The example of one stimulates another; speculation rises on speculation—bubble rises on bubble—every one helps with his breath to swell the windy superstructure, and admires and wonders at the magnitude of the inflation he has contributed to produce."

This is a true picture of the state of things in Richmond about the years 1816–17. Real estate in and around the city, soon to rival New York, rose in value (or price) from day to day. Steep hills and profound gullies were leveled or graded—on plats of surveys—and some work was commenced in reality, as scarified hill-sides attest at the present day—their green slopes changed to bare and inaccessible precipices; the debris washed by rains from the unprotected surface, serving to increase the bars and diminish the depth of water in the river.

The limits of Richmond were too contracted for

the imaginary population which was soon to over-
flow the city, and new towns or extensions of the
old were tacked on in every direction. Corn-
fields, slashes and piney thickets were laid out into
streets and squares.

City lots proper advanced in price, two, three,
five, aye, ten fold, and those in the suburban
towns, displayed on a highly colored plot—but
not so highly colored as the descriptions of those
who plotted to catch purchasers—instead of being
sold by the acre at ten to fifty dollars, were re-
tailed by the foot at ten to fifty times their former
value.

There were not days enough in the week, nor
hours enough in the day, for the rival auction sales
of *real* estate—so called. Red flags waved in
every street, or where a street was in embryo.
They flaunted in many a corn-field, where they
served as scare-crows, aided by the ringing of the
vendue bells, which resounded throughout the land,
and attracted crowds, as the dinging on a tin-pan
collects a hive of bees; but there was a larger
proportion of drones among the bipeds than among
the insects.

As buyers and sellers had not time to go to
their meals, cold meats, mint juleps, toddy and
punch were plentifully provided at the place of
sale, and these attractions drew a crowd of idlers
as well as bidders; and the former could not do

less in return for the viands, than to act as puffers ; as stool-pigeons minister to faro-banks, where they enjoy canvas-backs, oysters and champagne gratis, with the victims they entice to partake. The concourse of bidders, puffers and lookers-on formed quite an animated scene. The auctioneer in the blandest tones, assured the bidders in words the most persuasive, and with a countenance the very picture of candor, that the purchasers would double their money before they would be called on to pay more than the first or second instalment. Long credits were usually given, dividing the pay-ments into four, five or six instalments—the last extending, perhaps, to two or three years.

It may be presumed that there were by-bidders to set the ball in motion, or to give it an impulse when retarded. The excitement of bidding was also aided by the stimulating influence of the viands, and it did sometimes happen that he who drank the most liquor became the most spirited bidder. But the auctioneer kept a sharp look out for the main chance, and would knock down a *bargain* to a substantial bidder, rather than hazard obtaining a higher bid from an unsubstantial one.

Not one buyer in twenty purchased with the intention of building, or even of holding longer than till the second or third instalment should fall due, when, according to the auctioneer's *assurance*, he would double his money.

This excitement continued for many months. Sales and re-sales were made, each at an advance on the last. New enterprises were commenced by some of the most active among the speculators and whose credit was strongest. A fine hotel and a number of large stores and dwellings were erected in a part of the city that had fallen into decay—its former trade having sought another locality. Extensive glass-works were put in operation in the rear of the proprietor's large mansion, now occupied as a hospital, on the ascent of Church Hill; a sugar-house was erected on that hill; the India House* was built; a shot-tower, of which I have elsewhere spoken, raised its column near the river; the dock was projected, and the river was to be deepened, &c., &c.

But alas! the banks were required to prepare for the resumption of specie payments, and the speculators in lots were required to prepare for the payment of second or third instalments.—Presto! change! The city and suburb lots were again on the market, but the prospects had changed as much as had the aspect of the corn-fields—from waving blades and ears tipped with

---

* The India House, after being a long time in obscurity, is now (1860) one of the prominent houses on Main street. It contains a bank, insurance offices without number, lawyers, doctors, barbers, baths, &c., at high rents.

silken tassels, to dry stalks and refuse shucks. Sales were advertised, but where was the demand that was to double the cost? Alas! all were sellers or the only buyers were the original owners, who re-purchased at half-price, or less, and never got the other half; or the cool lookers-on during the excitement, who now stepped in and bought on their own terms.

The glass-works burnt out, the sugar-house melted away, the shot-tower fell, the hotel was converted into an infirmary, the ware-houses were untenanted, and the walls of the grandest are unroofed.* The banks resumed specie payments, and nine-tenths of the speculators ceased payments of any sort. The corn-fields, the slashes and pine saplings retained their sylvan aspects until within the last few years, when a real population began to appear, instead of the imaginary one anticipated nearly two generations ago, and the prophetic visions of the departed auctioneer begin to be slightly verified at the end of nearly forty years, instead of half as many months.

To obtain access to the remote regions of Leigh street, even on foot, without doubling the cape of a deep ravine, a bridge some hundred feet long and about forty feet high, was erected on the line of

---

* The walls (in rear of the Union hotel) are now leveled (1860.)

Ninth from the corner on Clay street; but the
bridge decayed before the remote regions were
inhabited by a sufficient number of persons to pay
for keeping it in repair. After thirty or more
years of non-intercourse by that route, it has just
been re-established by the construction of a causeway, wide enough for carriages. One of the new
public grounds reached by this road, if placed
under a skillful landscape gardener, is susceptible
of great improvement; nature having diversified
the surface, and given to it the command of a fine
view. Soon after our naval heroes had conferred
great glory on the nation, the taking name of
Navy Hill was given to a suburb still further
north. Another deep ravine, beyond that which
obstructed the access to Leigh street, intervened
between that street and Navy Hill, and another
bridge was proposed or commenced to reach that
Ultima Thule, by an extension of Sixth street;
but the bubble burst before the bridge was built,
and the ground has been usefully applied to the
culture of vegetables and fruit, until very recently,
when another effort is about to be made for a sub-
division of territory, and a connection with the inhabited regions is suggested by the construction of
a causeway.

One of the most eligible suitors for an union
with Richmond, or coquetting to encourage a rival
to her, was *Marion Hill*—not flesh and blood, but

field and forest. This beautiful hill, near Powhatan's old residence, was laid out as a town. A large building for an Academy was erected on its summit, and several handsome residences around, and it bade fair to reward its projectors, but the academy was destroyed by fire. At a convenient distance, and on the river below Rocketts, another town was projected, called *Port Mayo*, and a large warehouse was built there, as an example for others to follow. This was to be the commercial place, for which its situation is well adapted, and Marion Hill was to be the residence of the anticipated merchants. "Who knows what may happen a hundred years hence?"

I can call to mind an instance of the rapid depreciation of some suburban property. A bold speculator bought ten acres, about a mile beyond the city limits, west, for $10,000 ; one-tenth in cash, and nine-tenths in nine annual instalments of $1,000 each. He inclosed it with a substantial fence at a cost of several hundred dollars, and made it a good clover-field. When the first instalment fell due, the land was advertised to be sold at auction, or so much of it as would meet the payment of $1,000, and behold ! the smallest portion that the best bidder would agree to take, was nine-tenths, or nine acres, including the fence on three sides !

A worthy old gentleman told me a few years

ago, that he had just sold a large piece of land
which cost him $22,000 in the flush times, and after
thirty-seven years, although the value of property,
had again advanced, he could obtain for it only
one-sixth of the cost, not including the interest
and taxes. A stronger case occurred in the purchase of a piece of land adjoining the city at
$ 1,000 per acre and the sale of it forty years
after at $80.

The Governor's garden, on Council Chamber
hill, 293 feet on Ross street, with a depth of
120 feet, was sold by the State for $51,000. At
the expiration of thirty years, the purchaser of
one-third, and the most valuable part, sold it for
$5,000—and this is the only portion yet improved.

The rage of speculation was not entirely confined
to real, (query, unreal?) estate. It attached to
such objects as flour and tobacco. The price of
flour, which during the war had been as low as
three or four dollars, ascended at one time to fifteen or sixteen, and tobacco, from being in mercantile parlance, "*a drug*," at two to five dollars,
attained to fifteen and twenty-five, and even thirty
dollars per 100 pounds. The speculators imagined
that they had a good basis for their operations,
but it proved like the real estate mania "the baseless fabric of a vision," leaving many a wreck
behind.

After all these golden, or rather paper visions

were dissipated, when each five dollar note was supplanted by one silver dollar, those who retained any of either, resumed the old jog-trot of trade, attended to their regular business, were satisfied with moderate profits and a gradual increase of capital at the year's end.

Prosperity followed in the wake of prudence and industry. Manufactures which could not thrive under the hot-bed system, gradually grew up, but slowly against the competition of Eastern rival-ship—more economical and skillful, but afar off. The city increased slowly and gradually in popula-tion and capital, and in the course of time acquired a high character for thrift and punctuality. May she long retain it! She has perhaps in her corpo-rate capacity, launched imprudently and beyond her means, in enterprises, which although useful, should have been left to individuals or to communi-ties who were to derive the greatest portion of advantage from them. The distant farmers and land-owners who are most benefited, are generally the smallest contributors to the promotion of their own interests. They are like the waggoner who called on Hercules; they do not put their own shoulders to the wheel.

I am unable to specify the dates at which the various suburbs of Richmond were founded, but will endeavor to record the names, (some of them not very euphonious) of those which retain also " a local habitation." Others, depicted on paper in the flush times, have passed too far into oblivion to be rescued, unless some curious antiquary has retained copies of the highly colored plots and advertisements in which they were sketched and puffed.

Those now extant, embrace *Sydney*, a thriving colony, not like that in New Holland a penal one, except to purchasers in the flush times.

Union Hill has also a thriving aspect, and both are handsomely situated and respectably inhabited.

Bacon Quarter, an old suburb, owes its name to the great rebel who encamped there one hundred and eighty years ago, and it has had many unruly subjects in later times.

Shed Town is also an ancient settlement, and derives its name, as some say, from the style of its architecture, adapted to the original and gradually increasing means and requirements of its inhabitants—a prudent race. But this derivation is contested by some historical investigators, who say the true name is *Shad Town*, from the piscatory occupation of its founders, at a time when our shad fishery was much more abundant than of late years.

Butcher Town requires no explanation as to its origin. Its juvenile citizens accustomed to the sight of blood and slaughter, are a belligerent race, and if they see any young mountaineers (Hill-Cats

as they call them) descending towards their valley,
they immediately raise the war-cry and a battle is
apt to ensue, in which stones are hurled by the
combatants, until one or the other party retreats
with its wounded; or the civil authority (like
Austria & Co.) puts an end to the war.

Screamersville owes its musical name to the
sonorous voices of its inhabitants, although it must
be confessed there is a lack of harmony among
them, and once upon a time it might have been
described as a place

> " Where hungry dogs from hungry children steal,
> And pigs and chickens quarrel for a meal."

It is now, no doubt, much more refined and daily
improving.

Oregon Hill was so called, probably, from its
remote and inaccessible, though beautiful situation,
and is inhabited chiefly by a hardy and industrious
and fiery race, disciples of Vulcan.

Darby Town was founded by the Enroughtys,
and the two names being most strangely synony-
mous, they chose the shortest, though least im-
pressive. For the etymology and affinity of these
names I must refer to some curious investigator,
and my excellent friend, the Rev. T. V. M——, is
better qualified than any other person this side of
the Herald's College to solve the question. I will
not *Trench* on his privilege by attempting it. I

can only state the premises, that all who bear the
name of Enroughty, are called by and answer to
the name of Darby, even if the sheriff calls, and
I leave to my friend to draw the conclusions.

Scuffle Town I was well nigh forgetting—
whether it owes its active and sounding name to
the industrious or to the belligerent habits of its
founder ; whether they scuffled *with* each other, or
scuffled *for* a livelihood, or both, some more profound historian must decide.*

The Irish blood of the Mayos of Powhatan was
reinforced in one branch of the family by the
marriage of a daughter to Mr. Fulton, a fine specimen of his race and a man of industry and energy.
He obtained a portion of the extensive tract of
land attached to Powhatan, the residence of his
father-in-law and of his royal predecessor, and on
a beautiful elevation, in the midst of a fine grove
of native oaks, &c., he fixed his seat and called it
Mount Erin. The *Town of Fulton* is rising at
the foot of this hill, and I therefore have a right

---

* Since writing the above, the "Profound Historian" has
appeared. An antiquarian friend has traced this name to a
different and very plausible origin. The original settler kept a
tavern there, with the anciently used sign of a globe, the head ·
of the proprietor protruding at the north and his feet at the
south pole, with the legend, "Help a *scuffler* through the
world." Thus the poor fellow became immortalized by his
martyrdom in the bowels of the earth.

to introduce its founder in this out-of-the-way place.

Mechanicsville must not be omitted in recording this cluster of towns, for it retains a respectable place on the map, which cannot be said of *West-hampton* and *Bankstown*, as they are almost *terra incognita* to the present generation.

In distant connection with the flush times, and a lineal descendant of them, the *Morus Multicaulis* mania deserves to be recorded, and may be compared to the tulip mania in Holland, except that the adventurers looked to a permanently beneficial result, from the introduction of silk culture.

This species of mulberry was said to be the favorite and most productive food of the silk-worm, the rearing of which could be effected by the then unemployed labor of women and children. The papers teemed with essays on the subject. Some plants of the *morus multicaulis* were obtained by favored individuals ; these were cut into slips of a few inches long, each retaining a bud, from which a twig was produced in a few months. The demand for them was immense, and twigs were sold at three, four, five or six cents per bud. In the next season whole plantations were set out, many persons paying five hundred or a thousand dollars for cuttings. Some were offered many thousand dollars for the produce of one acre. A few cocooneries were formed, but not skillfully managed. No regular market was at hand for the cocoons that were produced, but the trial went on. I saw on one occasion a wagon load of multi-caulis plants brought all the way from Tennessee and never removed from the store where they were unladen, unless to kindle fires. The wise ones began to sell out very soon, and realized large profits. Many more sold at a later period, but the high price and great decline broke the purchasers. At last the plants were worth no-thing; they could not be given away; caterpillars and other insects would not prey on them; they would not grow up into trees, and they could not be rooted out, for they sprouted tenfold when cut down; and now after a lapse of twenty years, one of the plants may be occasionally seen in a hedge-row, and regarded as a weed.

P. S. Since the first edition of this book was published, the author has obtained re-possession of a manuscript written by him forty years ago, which contains the following curious narrative, entitled

THE SECRET INQUISITION AT WESTOVER.

" You already know that the city of Richmond and the land extending some distance above it, was laid off in lots by Col. Byrd, and that subsequently a lottery scheme was formed in which the lots constituted the prizes. A large portion of the tickets were sold—many of them to persons who set no value on the prizes, but who partook of the Colonel's hospitality, and therefore purchased tickets. But many tickets remained un-

sold. The lottery was drawn, and the possession of a prize
ticket was *prima facie* evidence of a title to the corresponding
lot. The greater number of those who drew prizes took possession of their lots, but many tickets were never produced,
and were supposed to be lost—the owners of them unknown.
The lots which fell prizes to such tickets lay many years neglected, until some persons finding the property valuable,
inclosed the derelict lots and paid the annual taxes on them.
Years passed, and no owners appeared, except occasionally,
when the resurrection of a prize ticket which had been buried
among musty papers claimed the corresponding lot. But of
late years, real estate in Richmond has attained to an immense
value, and the heirs of Byrd have been advised to claim all
that portion for which no prize ticket has been produced.
Many very valuable lots are thus situated. *Now for the
robbery.*

"Some months since (Sept., 1816), when the mansion at
Westover, on James river, the seat of the Byrd Family, was
without a solitary occupant, nor any white person on the estate,
the house was entered in the night, through a window, every
book-case, drawer and chest was opened and every bundle of
papers examined. But so far as is known or believed, not an
article, except it may be an instrument of writing, was stolen.
Not the least trace has been found of these inquisitorial visitors,
except of footsteps, which imprinted the shape of neatly made
boots.

"In the morning the servants found bundles of papers
spread open on the tables and chairs, and immediately sent for
Mr. Harrison, of Brandon, who married a Miss Byrd. He had
previously, when suits were brought for the lots, placed with
an agent in Richmond the important papers relative thereto;
and now with apprehension lest he should be assaulted on the
highway, he carried the remaining papers with him. Whether
any were stolen is not known. The whole is a singular mystery,
and rumor may have exaggerated it."

CHAPTER XXIX.

THE JAMES RIVER CANAL.

The progress of Richmond and of the James River Canal were so intimately connected that it is due to the one to notice the other. This was the first canal commenced in the United States. It was projected by the *first man* in the State, in the Union, in the Universe—by WASHINGTON—the object of whose visit to Richmond in November, 1784, when the Legislature was in session, was chiefly to promote a junction between the East and West, by connecting the waters of the James and of the Potomac rivers with those of the Ohio. On the 5th January, 1785, acts were passed for clearing and improving the navigation of the James and Potomac,* and subsequently in the session (too late for a refusal to be received,) for vesting in General Washington an interest in each company, 100 shares or $20,000 in the one, and 100 shares or £5000 sterling in the other, as donations from the State, in token of respect for his services, not only

---

* On the 5th March, 1802, the Potomac Canal was opened, and two boats laden with flour passed through the locks at the Great and Little Falls.

in suggesting these works, but also for those to his whole country." Washington, like himself and no other, respectfully declined the donations for his own emolument, but offered to hold them in trust for such public institutions as he might designate and the Legislature approve. The result was that he bequeathed the $20,000 to Liberty Hall Academy, now Washington College, in Lexington, and the £5000 towards the endowment of a College in the District of Columbia. *Wherever* WASHINGTON'S *hand was placed it conferred a blessing!* O, my countrymen! base on his *precepts* your political faith, and require your representatives to make his *example* the guide to their conduct: Let *Washington* be their standard of rectitude and patriotism!

Mothers of America! teach your children *Washington* from the pages of Marshall, of Sparks, and the yet more attractive ones of Irving, but not from those who had not the soul to appreciate him!

Can disorganizers and politicians by trade, read the Farewell Address of *Washington*, without a blush of shame?

To descend to the subject of our chapter—the James River Navigation Company was chartered with a capital of $100,000. On the 20th October, 1785, the stockholders met and elected George Washington President; John Harris, David Ross, William Cabell and Edmund Randolph, Directors.

Washington declined the active Presidency, because he could not give it his personal attention, and Mr. Randolph acted as President *pro tem*. In 1789 he was appointed Attorney General of the United States, and William Foushee was elected President, which office he retained till 1818, when he was succeeded by J. G. Gamble, whose successor was W. C. Nicholas in 1819, and in 1820 a new charter was granted, subject to the assent of the stockholders under the old one. The capital expended up to that time was $140,000, and the profits in addition increased the amount to $234,000— for the relinquishment of which and of their charter the stockholders were to receive an annuity of 15 per cent. on the capital of $140,000.

The narrative must however recede to give it continuity. On the 29th December, 1789, the members of the Legislature were invited to take a trip up the canal and through the locks. The canal was then opened from Westham to Broad Rock, a short distance above the city. In 1795 the canal was completed to the head of the Basin, and in November, 1800, the water was let into it.

The principle of rotation in office does not seem to have prevailed in those days. Perhaps the loaves were lighter or the fishes smaller than in later ones. Be, this as it may, Dr. Foushee retained the office more than a score of years. Robert Pollard filled and fulfilled the offices of

Treasurer and Secretary for thirty years, to May, 1823, and Hezekiah Mosby performed strictly and correctly the duties of toll-gatherer for thirty-seven years, terminating with 1830.

As the charter of the Company required a connection of the canal with tide-water, a contract was entered into with one Ariel Cooley, a cute, uneducated, but practical man, (at least as far as Ariel was interested) for the construction of thirteen locks between the Basin and Mayo's Bridge, for the sum of $49,000. A large excavation was required to be made along the descent of the hill, which Cooley estimated at about $9,000. He stipulated for the use of the water in the Basin, if he required it; and he did put it in requisition to some purpose. He cut a small ditch along the centre of the line which the locks were to occupy, and opened a sluice into it from the Basin. A rapid and increasing sluice it was. In some twenty-four hours the water had wrought the $9,000 worth of excavation, and the only difficulty was to prevent its "helping over much." It had wrought an opening for the upper navigation and a contrary effect on the lower one, by washing an immense quantity of earth into the river, making work for another Cooley.

The whole work was executed in the most economical and temporary manner; a few boats passed the locks, after which they became locks without keys or hinges, and the gates were never more opened. The upper chambers had to be filled with clay to prevent the escape of water from the Basin, and when the present splendid locks were constructed, which were opened in 1854, the rubble stone and some of the timber of their predecessors were removed.

The canal as originally constructed was navigated by open batteaux, carrying ten or twelve hogsheads of tobacco, and the river was rendered navigable by dams and sluices as far as Lynchburg. The continuous canal of increased capacity for boats of sixty tons, was opened to Lynchburg in 1841. It now extends sixty-five miles further to Craig's Creek nearly, and it requires a further extension of twenty-nine miles, and an expenditure of about as many hundred thousand dollars to reach Covington, its western terminus, unless it be practicable to reach the Kanawha.

The cost of the work executed has thus far been $10,437,000, and the estimate of that to be executed, is about $13,000,000.

Besides the State subscription to capital stock of $3,000,000, she has loaned $3,352,000, and guaranteed $2,260,000, and the Company is otherwise in debt, about $400,000. As this statement presents a hopeless aspect for the progress of the work, or the payment of the debt, the Legislature has granted most liberal relief, by increasing the stock of the Company to $12,400,000, taking it at par, (tho' it has but a nominal value at present) to the amount of her loans and guaranties, and also of the annuity to the old stockholders and the floating debt,

in all 74,000 shares or $7,400,000. The Company is also author-
ized to borrow at 7 per cent., $2,500,000 for completing the canal
to Covington. In addition to all this, the State agrees to place
under the exclusive control of the Kanawha Board, the sum of
$300,000 in 6 per cent. State stock, for the improvement of
the navigation of Kanawha River. May the result of all be
propitious.

It was the first canal commenced in the United
States. It is to be hoped it will not be the last
one to be finished.

CHAPTER XXX.

ROADS.

THERE has been a wonderful change in the
facilities and the mode of transportation from the
interior, during the period embraced in these
reminiscences. At the early dates referred to in
them, McAdam had not broken a stone; turnpikes
bore the highest rank in furnishing the tracks for
travel or trade, but not a *turnpike* road entered
Richmond, and the *natural* ones (so called) were
almost impassable in wet seasons and in winter,
when the farmers were most at leisure to send their
crops to market.

The *Brook Turnpike,* towards the north, was the
first one constructed; then north-westwardly the

26

Richmond Turnpike, in the line of Broad street; the *Westham*, in the direction its name indicates, and lastly, the *Mechanicsville*, north-eastwardly; but neither of these extended beyond eight or ten miles, and some of them soon acquired the name of *mud pikes*, the demand of toll being the only distinction by which to know them from county roads.

Railroads have fortunately been substituted for some of them, and the experiment of *plank roads* recently tried on others, but it is a doubtful one, for already it is proposed to substitute gravel for timber on one, while the reverse has just been adopted on another road.

The substitution of *railroads* offers an immense facility to the farmers, at the expense of the stockholders, who are receiving little or no profit on their outlay. The travelling community also derive great facilities from them, and it has increased so much, that as many cars carrying fifty passengers each are now required, as there were formerly of stage coaches carrying nine passengers each; but some of our most important railroads have only *one end* to them in a practical and profitable sense, for they do not connect with important lines of rail, west or south-west. * They are like neigh-

---

* The Virginia & Tennessee Railroad and extensions West have removed the barrier, and New Orleans is but three days from Richmond. In 1815, it was three weeks. Dividends also begin to appear.—1860.

borhood roads on an extended scale, and they must extend their arms further, to reach those ready to meet them, and then in their joint embrace they will include the regions from the Mississippi to the Chesapeake; but the log-rolling system of Virginia has diverted her energies from the completion of any one useful work, to partial operations on a great number, many of which are antagonistic, and others, if completed, would scarcely be profitable.

The travel and transportation on our railways are small, compared with those north and west of us. We have no large cities to create a great local travel, nor any connection with the Western States to furnish an extensive traffic. We waste our energies on various local improvements, instead of carrying out one or two grand extensions.

P. S. 1860.—The railways which commence at Richmond, are 1st, *the Richmond, Fredericksburg and Potomac.* 2d, *the Central,* which extends west, and will soon reach the White Sulphur Springs on its way to the Ohio, which it will not soon reach. By means of the Orange and Alexandria road, the Central connects with Lynchburg and the great West, and also with the northern cities. 3d, *the Richmond and Petersburg road,* connecting with Norfolk, and the entire south and west. 4th, *the Richmond and Danville road,* connecting by the South-side road with Lynchburg and thence to the great West, north and south. 5th, *the York River road*, now near completion—a great desideratum to the lovers of fish and oysters, and the salt-water bath.

Petersburg commenced the first great railway enterprise in Virginia, by constructing her road to the *Roanoke*, whence it now connects interminably with the south and west. 2d, *the Southside* to *Lynchburg*, thence by the Virginia and Tennessee road it has a continued line to New Orleans, the lakes and everywhere. 3d, *the Petersburg and Norfolk road*, from which latter place the traveller may go by land or water to both extremities north or south. Alexandria is extending, and Fredericksburg is commencing her roads. There are many other projects which will die in the bud or be slow to expand.

After two such dry chapters, I advise the reader to take a drink, if he is awake. If he is a stockholder, I fear he has not enjoyed the perusal of either.

CHAPTER XXXI.

THE BRIDGES AND MANCHESTER.

MAYO's bridge, at the Richmond end, and as far
as the toll-house on the island, was, I am told,
originally constructed of large logs, raft-like,
spiked to the rocks, with a rough floor laid on the
logs, and from the island to the Chesterfield side,
a bridge of boats was thrown.

The log system was soon abandoned, (I wish
the log-rolling system was,) as each freshet threatened, or effected its demolition; but the boats
floated a number of years, and were very popular
with anglers.

What with one change or another, with the
destruction or decay of one portion, while another
was being repaired or renewed, the bridge was in
the hands of workmen through two generations,
and the work was completed when the third came
in possession. On one occasion, when the floor of
the bridge had been taken up for repair, and the
large sleepers remained, the keeper of the toll-
gate on the island was aroused one dark night, and
to his astonishment, found not only a man but

also a horse waiting to pass. "For God's sake, how did you get here?" he asked. "By the bridge, to be sure; how else should I?" replied Isham Randolph. "No other man could have done it," said the toll-taker; "the floor is taken up." "Well," said Mr. R., "floor or no floor, I rode here, and now I'll pay my toll." "Pass on, Mr. Randolph; I wont take toll from a man who rides where there is no bridge." A wonderful instance of courage and steadiness on the part of the horse; as to the rider, he was fearless also, and a man of great muscular strength and power of endurance. He would occasionally take a walk from Eastern Virginia to West Tennessee, and he bore arms under Jackson in some of his Indian fights—being a man after his own heart.

Mayo's bridge had a formidable competitor in "*Coutts's Ferry*," a more ancient establishment, the proprietor of which long resisted the grant to Mayo for the erection of a bridge, on the ground that it would be a violation of his rights. Finding opposition useless, he at length withdrew it, saying: "Let him build the bridge, if he can, but he will be ruined first."

Col. Mayo was indefatigable in his efforts, but lacked the means to erect a permanent work, and moreover the science of bridge-building was not then understood or not acted on. A writer in the Southern Literary Messenger, who seems to know, states that Col. Mayo was frequently arrested and placed within the prison bounds from inability to meet his engagements; his expenditures on other objects than his bridge absorbed so large a portion of his means.

The ferry landing was on "*the Sandy Bar,*" at the end of Eighteenth street, and the ferry was kept up for many years after the bridge was constructed; indeed, it could not have been dispensed with, as the bridge was very often impassable—besides which, the charge of six and a quarter cents for each person, horse, and wheel, was so heavy, that by accepting a lower rate of toll the ferry attracted much of the travel.

At that period, the resort of shad and herrings to James river was much greater than now. Coutts had a fishery as well as a ferry, and he once crossed the river without the aid of either boat or bridge in real Triton style.

A large sturgeon caught in the seine, and hauled to the water's edge, was on the point of returning to it, when Coutts made a simultaneous leap with his captive, alighted on his back, and fixed his hands in the gills. Off they went together. The fish could not stay under water, nor could he dismount his rider, who piloted his nose towards the opposite shore. A speedy and successful voyage they made. Had Coutts been a Barnum he would have kept his sturgeon in training, and added others, so as to have formed a team; harnessed them to a car of Neptune, and rode the waves triumphant.

When Coutts was on his death bed, he received a message from an old crony who was ill also, requesting Coutts to wait a few days and they would go together. The reply was, "When Patrick Coutts is ready, he waits for no man." It became a proverb.

The progress of shad and herrings up the river has been so much intercepted by the numerous floating and other seines lower down or by some other cause, that few comparatively pass up the falls. Formerly, during the fishing season, the rocks in the falls were alive with fishermen casting their nets in the sluices, and catching the finest shad—such as had strength to stem the torrent of several miles continuance. It was a beautiful sight in May, when the vegetation on the islands had assumed its delicate green, and the flowers, shrubs and trees were in bloom, to see each rock tenanted by a fisherman.

On one occasion this scene was awfully changed. It was a beautiful May morning, and there were an unusual number of fishermen on the rocks in every part of the river above Mayo's Bridge. Suddenly, without the slightest previous indication or warning, the river rose so rapidly that all had to run for their lives. Swimming was in a very few places practicable. A great number of the men were partially immersed before they were aware of it, and their access to the shore cut off. As the water rose, the poor fellows might be seen clinging to the rocks, and presently a huge log would be borne along by the current, strike against one of them, break his hold, and perhaps a limb, and sweep him down the rapids against the rocks in his descent.· Another more expert, would be saved by seizing on the floating tree or log and descend with it to smooth water. The cries and supplications of the distressed victims were drowned by the roaring of the waters, but not disregarded. Boats and ropes were obtained, and some daring and skillful men attempted by shoving off from the shore some distance above, to float down near enough to cast a line to the fishermen—but in vain, with very few exceptions. The rapid current took possession of the boat, and all that its occupants could do was to direct its course so as not to be swamped themselves.

This awful scene lasted many hours. It was chiefly on the Manchester side, and the river bank was thronged with spectators, viewing the sufferers, without the means of rescue—but among them were agonized wives and children watching the rising and raging flood which would in a few moments overwhelm the one dearest to them.

The number known to have perished, was about

twenty. No rain in this part of the country had preceded the flood, which was caused by a most violent one some distance above, raising the streams instantly, which swept away mill-dams in their course.

Trent's bridge, erected about 1815, in the rapids, by spiking the timbers to the natural rock-work, was a short-lived structure; but it was intended by its enterprising projector merely to precede a permanent one, and he commenced quarrying granite for the purpose, but his efforts were arrested, first by lack of means, and then by death. Just above its site now looms the high *Petersburg Railroad bridge*, awful to timid passengers. A short distance above Mayo's, the *Danville Railroad bridge*, or rather bridges, span the river from island to island, by four successive leaps.

I introduce the bridges with the intention of taking my readers beyond them to the *town of Manchester*, originally designated *Rocky Ridge*, a more appropriate name, as was Bellehaven for Alexandria.* Virginia and New York have been peculiarly injudicious and deficient in taste in their nomenclature. New York was ridiculously classical; her Surveyor General made Lempriere's Clas-

---

* Alexandria and Balaclava have borne the same name, according to some etymologists of the latter, who derive it from Bella Chiava, the beautiful haven of the Genoese, as Alexandria was originally called Belle Haven.

sical Dictionary his vade mecum; and as he laid
off the western portion of the State, he labeled his
maps with the names of ancient poets, philosophers, orators, cities and countries, in the most
indiscriminate manner—bringing Syracuse, Man-
lius, Jordan, Rome, Delphi and Tully into a queer
proximity, such as their original owners never
dreamed of; and Virginia almost abjectly loyal,
must have made the Court Calendar her guide;
instead of retaining as far as practicable the Indian names, all the royal families of successive
reigns, and many of the nobility were put in
requisition, to furnish names by which to distinguish her counties, rivers and towns. *Anne* seems
to have been a great favorite, for we have Princess
Anne, Urbanna, Rivanna, Fluvanna, North Anna,
South Anna, and Rapid Ann—resigning to Maryland Queen Ann and Annapolis. Elizabeth was
not neglected, nor Charles, nor James, but their
counties were dubbed cities. Why? I should like
to know. The most glaring and unjust usurpation
of a name (and which ought even now to be restored
to its original monarch), was the depriving of Powhatan, the patron of the Virginia weed, of the
name of the river which watered his own dominions, and conferring on it that of the "learned
fool" King James, who wrote the counterblast
against tobacco.

In this tirade against the misapplication of

names, I have wandered from Manchester's rocky ridge, and will return from the digression. This town, which is now in the course of resurrection, was once a place of considerable trade. Several wealthy British commercial houses had establishments there, and imported large quantities of goods. Three tobacco inspections received five or six thousand hogsheads of tobacco; a flour mill was in operation, and Manchester felt herself a rival of Richmond. So she might have been, and a powerful one too (according to tradition), but for the selfish and narrow-minded policy of one of her richest merchants. When the James River Canal was projected, an engineer who made the survey for its connection with tide-water, reported that the best route for the terminus of the canal and for the required connection, was on the south side and through the town of Manchester, and his report was submitted to the Legislature.

A wealthy Scotch merchant believed that if the canal was brought to Manchester, it would induce many merchants to establish themselves there, and create competition for the trade, which was then in few hands. He therefore retained Patrick Henry with a large fee, to oppose the adoption of the proposed route of the canal, and if he did not show his judgment in opposing the improvement, he did in the selection of his counsel, for Henry succeeded in diverting the canal to the Richmond side, and his client lived to see the folly of his selfish policy. One by one the merchants of Manchester removed to Richmond, and Mr. L. was "left alone in his glory," to retail the old remnants from his shelves, with no inducement to replenish them.

Manchester continued to decline until no trade remained, but its great command of water power, its cheap property and its comparative exemption from taxes, began to revive it after some years.

It now contains two extensive cotton mills, two flour mills of large size, a foundry, a machine-shop, and several large tobacco factories, and the town in its corporate capacity having a right to half the water-power of James River, can furnish an additional number of mill-sites. Its ruinous old houses are being vamped up and new ones built, and should it obtain a communication with Richmond, untaxed by tolls, it will probably attract many residents to its handsome hills and heights, and mechanics to occupy the streets below them.

Having introduced a freshet, I will conclude this chapter with a

A DROUGHT AND A SNAKE STORY.

In the year 1804 or '5 an unprecedented drought prevailed in Virginia. The small streams in the country were nearly or quite dried up, and scarcely any mills could grind between the Roanoke and

27

James rivers. Only one in Manchester and one in Richmond were at work, and these were flour mills; but "necessity has no law," or rather, necessity resorted to law, and insisted that not only one pair, or two pairs of stones, should be employed as usual in grinding meal, but as many pairs as were required to give dispatch to applicants.

Wagons thronged to the mill at Manchester from a distance of fifty or sixty miles, and the vacant grounds in the vicinity were covered with their encampments. The people of the country were starving in the midst of plenty. It was distressing to see them "waiting for their turns at mill," according to the rule "first come, first served." Some would feed away to their teams, half their corn, before their turn came to get the other half ground. Slow as the process of "beating hominy" is, it was a great resource, as was the eating of it for lack of hoecake.

James river was then so low as to permit pleasant promenading in the falls, but for the rugged or rounded surface of the rocks, and active persons could cross it dry shod.

It was curious to see how the solid granite had been worn away and bored into holes from the size of a hat to that of a hogshead, by the action of the pebbles, from small to large, which had been rolled down in freshets, and lodging in fissures would there revolve by the action of the water, until both the active and passive rocks had worn each other away, and the debris was lodged at Sandy bar.   A larger pebble would be washed into the cavity formed by a small one, and so on *ad infinitum*, or until the granite was entirely worn away.   In some places it was evident that two or more neighboring cavities had been worn until they united and formed one, of irregular shape and of great size.   In many of them the active agent could be seen, resembling a cannon ball. This abrasion of the rocks has been very great, but I will not undertake to calculate when they will be entirely worn away.   The sand market will continue to be supplied until then from this great mill of Nature's construction.   It is very curious to take a walk on the northern shore of Belle Isle when the river is low.   One can look across to the Richmond side without seeing a drop of water, but only billows of rocks, between which it flows in deeply worn channels.

A truthful old friend told me, that in the course of a walk near the spot I have mentioned, on a spring morning, he saw a pyramid or rather a large ball of snakes, so coiled and entwined together as to form one mass, the heads of all projected to the exterior, forming a living head of Medusa.   He dared not approach for fear of dissolving the union and of being attacked by the separate members.

CHAPTER XXXII.

BANKS AND INSURANCE COMPANIES.

THE reader need not fear that he is to be bored with an essay on banks. As a piece of news to most of my readers, I will state that there was a bank established in Virginia before the Revolution, the first no doubt in America, called the "Virginia James River Bank." The engraved form of the notes was not adapted to that in which they were issued, as is shown by the following copy of one that I have seen. The *written* portion, most of it interlined, is here printed in *italics*:

VIRGINIA JAMES RIVER BANK,   No. 395.

We, *I, Robert C. Nicholas, Esq., Treasurer of the Colony and Dominion of* and Company Bank in Virginia, Promise to pay to, *or before the tenth day of December*, 1775, or Bearer on demand, *Twelve* Pounds, Current Money.

Witness *my Hand this first day of April*, 1773.

Cashier,   *Robert Carter Nicholas*,

Randolph.   *Treas'r*.

John Blair.

The *date of the bill* seems ominous.

The Virginia Legislature had *such a holy horror* of banks in 1803, that they refused a charter to the petitioners, as they had to previous ones, but they got over their scruples in 1804 and granted a charter to the present Bank of Virginia. About ten years afterwards they were delivered of a second; after another long interval, a third and fourth were born; but of late years it is as difficult to check the increase as it was formerly to overcome the barrenness, and each meeting of the Legislature gives birth to a whole litter of banks. In 1858 the number was about twenty-three, with sixteen millions of capital, and the last Legislature chartered about sixteen, and authorized an increase of capital for twelve branches to existing banks. The progress of banking in the United States, if tables are correct, may be thus stated:

In 1790 there were	4	Banks with $	1,950,000	capital.
" 1800 "	23	"	19,000,000	"
" 1830 "	394	"	183,000,000	"
" 1860 "	1,580	"	470,000,000	"

How much further the expansion can proceed without bursting, time will show.

INSURANCE COMPANIES.

In the former edition a chapter was devoted to an institution named by its projector "The Mutual Assurance Society, against Fire of Virginia," but the phraseology may be excused, as he was a

Prussian, and his secretary a Turk; both men of education and well qualified for the offices they held.

This institution has now existed about sixty-three years, and is likely to continue indefinitely if well conducted. Until of late years insurance companies in Virginia, important and useful as they are, were few in number, and did not attain to great age. In that branch, as in many others, we were dependant on northern or British institutions, through their agents established in our towns.

But now insurance companies shoot up at every corner, and not only in Richmond, but in our other cities, towns and villages, and· bid fair to be as numerous as banks and court-houses.

As yet the indemnity they proffer is against the risks of fire, water, storms and death—or it may be said, the four elements—as earth has its claim with the others. But we have no companies here yet, as in Europe, to insure against moral risks, such as the dishonesty of clerks and other employees, nor against theft; indemnity against both of which is certainly very desirable, and especially if the Federal and State Governments were required to have all their risks insured. This difficulty perhaps might arise, that it would interfere with the powers of appointment, or with the patronage now existing, as no prudent or safe company would insure the honesty of officials, without first ascertaining whether they possessed that qualification, and were, as Mr. Jefferson required, " honest, faithful and friendly to the Constitution." Fidelity is now required, but in a debased sense, to men, not to principles, and even that is not fulfilled.

Loss or injury by some other risks are indemnified in England. For instance, a penny will insure a passenger's limbs for a long distance on a railroad, but whether any company in this country could take such risks and pay dividends, is yet to be tried.

CHAPTER XXXIII.

MANUFACTURES AND MILLS.

THE attempts to establish *manufactories* in Richmond on the joint-stock principle, have been almost invariably unsuccessful; and not in Richmond only, but throughout the South; and I might add the North also, with the exception of those establishments which are owned by a few stockholders who look to their interests.

When England and France were vieing with each other which could commit the greatest outrages on our commerce, by their Orders in Council and Berlin and Milan Decrees, (Napoleon dating his edicts from almost any capital he chose,) and when we resorted to the terrapin policy of Embargo and Non-intercourse, to prepare for war by depriving ourselves of the means to conduct it, this among other patriotic resolutions was adopted at public meetings, that we should dress in domestic fabrics; and as homespun "was the only wear," the price of coarse mixed *Virginia cotton cloth* was a dollar or more a yard for such as is now worth twelve or eighteen cents, and many of our citizens who could afford it, especially the politicians of the Terrapin party, were thus arrayed from head to foot.

As the primitive spinning-wheels and hand-looms could not supply the patriotic demand for their productions, a resort to machinery was proposed.

A large meeting was held at the Capitol about the year 1809, to raise by subscription a sufficient sum (no trifling one) for the establishment of an extensive cotton and woolen factory. The patriotic fervor overflowed in frothy speeches, but when it subsided left no substantial residuum in cash.

Parson Blair made some fun of it in a satire commencing thus :

> "I've seen with pleasure in your patriot city,
> The appointment of a most august committee,
> To encourage manufactures of our own
> And bring Old England to her marrow bone,
> To spoil her commerce, since she's made us wroth,
> And bring her pride down with Virginia cloth."

Fortunately for the few who were disposed to subscribe for the mules and jennies, there were not backers enough to second them, and the project failed. An individual (B. J. Harris) who had twisted tobacco successfully, was the first to engage in the twisting of cotton, but unsuccessfully, and his mill was sold and converted to the more practicable purpose of grinding wheat.

Some years later, joint-stock companies were formed for the manufacture of cotton, wool, iron, paper, &c., expensive buildings were erected, the works were put in operation, and while everything was new, and improved machinery was not introduced elsewhere, some dividends were paid—but prosperity was of short duration. The raw materials were bought with cash, or if on credit, at a high rate; the manufactured article had to be sold on credit, and generally to be shipped to the North for a market, incurring heavy charges. Dividends ceased, debts were contracted, and, to wind up the concern, the establishment was sold, at a loss to the stockholders of fifty or seventy-five per cent. It now became the property of an individual, or of a few partners. Presidents, directors, agents, &c., were dispensed with. Instead of being everybody's business, it was somebody's, and each establishment in succession passed from a corporate body to an individual one, and from decay to prosperity.

The amount of capital thus sunk by stockholders

in various manufacturing establishments in almost
every town in Virginia, would count up to millions,
but it was fortunately distributed among many
parties. Their successors are rendering benefits to
the community as well as to themselves, by employ-
ing a large number of workmen, and giving occupation indirectly to the various classes of tradesmen,
farmers, landlords, &c., with whom the former deal.

The iron foundries and machine shops in Richmond are numerous, and some of them on a large
scale. The boilers and machinery for several of
the largest ships of war were constructed at the
Tredegar Works, where many cannon are made for
our ships and forts.

When the raw materials for manufactures which
our interior can supply, and the water-power extending some miles above the city, to convert them
into useful fabrics, shall be practically developed,
Richmond may become one of the largest manufacturing cities in the Union.*

---

* Although not immediately pertaining to my subject, I will
here take occasion to note, on the authority of Col. Byrd, that
Col. Spotswood, on the Rappahannock, was the first person in
America who built a furnace for making pig (or sow) iron.
There were some bloomeries in New England and Pennsylvania,
and following the Colonel's example, they introduced furnaces.
There were at that time (1732) four furnaces in Virginia, near
the Rappahannock above Fredericksburg, and the sow iron they
made was carted fifteen to twenty-four miles to boat navigation,
thence down to the port of shipment, where it was put on board

I have alluded to the Embargo and Non-intercourse which preceded the war of 1812 with Great Britain. The destitution of the country of many articles of the first necessity, caused by these precedents, was very severe, for they operated to prevent importations before war was declared; whereas the utmost facility should have been given to obtain abundant stocks of articles of the first necessity to prepare for the coming contest.

Salt sold in Richmond at one period of the war at twenty-five dollars per sack, and some persons undertook to make it along the sea-shore, by boiling the salt water in large kettles, others in vats, by solar evaporation. Brown sugar sold at twenty-five cents or more per pound, coffee at forty or fifty cents, and almost all imported commodities in proportion.

The supplies we obtained were not so much by importation as by capture from the enemy. Our privateers were numerous, daring and frequently successful in getting their prizes into those ports which the enemy could not easily blockade.

---

vessels for England, at a freight of 7s. 6d. per ton (in lieu of ballast), which with the other charges on it amounted to 20s., and it was sold at 120s. per ton. At that date so few ships sailed from Philadelphia for England that makers of iron in Pennsylvania had to work it up for home use. At that time, says Byrd, "Great Britain imported from Spain, Holland, Denmark, Sweden, and Muscovy, *no less* than 20,000 tons yearly.' Great Britain now produces 3,600,000 tons.

The exports from Richmond, Petersburg, &c., were chiefly by way of Amelia Island, at the northern extremity of East Florida, then a Spanish colony and neutral. Tobacco, the principal and almost the only article, was transported partly in small vessels through the inlets and sounds of North and South Carolina and Georgia, partly by wagons, at an enormous expense and risk, and with great labor and trouble—but all these were well compensated by the price of four or five shillings per pound for such as got safely to market, the first cost being about as many cents.

The central position of Virginia was most unfavorable for this forced trade. The New England States resorted to Eastport, in Maine, on our north-eastern boundary, where there seemed to exist a good understanding with their opposite neighbors and enemies. They each obeyed the injunction, "Love your enemies." The same vessel was repeatedly captured and re-captured, and the prize money on both sides was divided between the amicable belligerents—friendly spoliations being made by previous arrangements.

The dangerous coast of North Carolina was deemed a safeguard by some enterprising men, who relied on the fleetness of their clippers and the dangers of their coast, to carry on trade with Cuba, &c.

Virginia had to depend chiefly on hard knocks,

and Norfolk rejoiced now and then in the arrival of some captured ship, a prize to her Saucy Jack or daring Roger. A similar recourse for supplies and a similar employment for our vessels will not, I hope, recur.

The first grist mill in Richmond was built, I am told, near the spot where *Haxall's* mills now stand, or run. It was a mere wooden shanty, built on the rocks in the river, and approached by planks laid from one rock to another. The machinery was a common tub wheel, propelled by a natural rapid, and gave motion to a pair of mill stones, which served to grind corn for the inhabitants. Twenty-two pair now grind eight hundred barrels of flour per day, more or less, according to circumstances; and from the extensive additions to the buildings recently made, perhaps some ten or twenty pair more may be added to the establishment.*

As early as the year 1789, (David Ross who " could see as far into a mill stone " or a mill site as any man,) secured from the owner Samuel Overton, the ultimate possession of this great water power, embracing about one half of the width of the river, and about seven acres of land along its margin; and in 1793, he obtained it

---

* The miller says 1,500 bbls. flour have been made in one day (1860) and additional buildings are in progress.

28

complete and forever in consideration of an annual rent of 2,000 bushels of corn. This now constitutes the chief income of Overton's descendants. How much the property is worth to Ross's successors, I will not venture to conjecture.

In the long interval between the erection of the shanty and of Haxall's mills, the site of the latter was occupied by *Ross's mills*, which were swept off by a freshet and re-built. They then acquired celebrity as *Gallego's mills*, the first of the name, and resisted the floods to fall a victim to the flames, as did the next generation of mills on the same spot.

The Gallego mills changed their locality to a site on the canal, some miles above the city, and these twice shared the fate of their predecessors. Then was erected by Peter Chevallie, a much larger establishment on the basin, which after a few years was also destroyed by fire. The enterprising owners Warwick & Barksdale, nothing daunted, re-built them on even a more extended scale, and are now erecting another building of greater dimensions, twelve stories high, machinery in which can be propelled by the same water-power repeated. These and the Haxall are probably the two largest mills in the world.

A portion of the *Armory* has been converted (like the sword to a ploughshare,) into a flour mill; but I believe the State is not a partner, and may

permit it on the ground that it is better to manufacture food than fire-arms. A large flour mill*
has been erected at Tredegar, a short distance
above the Armory, and here grain is ground and
cannons are cast in close proximity. This, however, as well as two flour mills, *Taliaferro's* and
Bragg's † on the *Manchester* side, are all of recent
construction, and do not belong to by-gone days;
but those do which preceded them and occupied the
same ground, to wit:

The Tredegar Iron Works are on the spot where
Colonel Harvie erected at the close of the last
century a flour mill, a brewery and a distillery.
Whether any beer or whiskey was made there I
know not, but the mill was first occupied by a Mr.
Arthur, and bore his name (a short time only) until
he died, and the establishment fell into the hands
of Mr. Radford, who very judiciously obtained
Mr. Rutherfoord as a partner in the business in
1803, but tempted by speculation in Western
lands, he sold his interest in the mills to Mr.
Rutherfoord. They were burnt and re-built, and
became the property of Mr. Cunningham. The
same water power was applied a second time at a

---

* Now being converted into a woolen mill, with a capital of
$150,000—one of the effects of the Harper's Ferry murders.
1860.

† Now Dunlop, Moncure & Co's. and J. Brummel's.

lower level to propel the machinery of a cotton mill erected by Cunningham & Anderson, who made it a joint stock (and consequently a losing) concern. It was burnt as were the flour mills, and the site of mills, brewery, &c., is occupied by rolling mills, cannon and other foundries, machine shops, locomotive works, and in short for all sorts of iron operations, besides which Crenshaw's flour mill (now the Woollen mill) has risen in the midst of the forges and furnaces.

Mr. Rutherfoord converted Harris's cotton mill two miles higher up the river, into a flour mill, which suffered the fate of Sebastopol, by bombardment, in the process of blasting rock to widen the canal.

To a stranger, a walk along the banks of the canal is well compensated by a view of the Armory, the Tredegar Iron Works, the mills, the Water works, Belle Isle, (where there are also Iron works,) and the Rapids; and though last, not least, the Hollywood Cemetery.

The exportation (1860) of steam sugar mills, saw mills, and locomotives, railway wheels, and all work of that sort from our several factories is very extensive, and a large establishment for making pig iron from the ores on James river, is about to light its fires at Westham. But it would be tedious, except to parties interested, to dilate on the subject. Already more has been said than will be

read. One line more only to say that new enter-
prizes are starting up daily, which by judicious
management may remove from Richmond—from
Virginia—the opprobrium that she is dependant
on other States or countries for everything she
requires except bread and tobacco.

CHAPTER XXXIV.

TOBACCO WAREHOUSES.

WHERE *Tobacco* is in the mouth of almost every
man and boy, either for mastication, fumigation,
inhalation, or discussion, and where it constitutes
one of the most important commercial staples, it
seems proper to notice it, though I fear that my
fair readers, if I have any, may turn up their
pretty noses at it, instead of turning it up their
pretty noses, against which latter turn I enter my
protest, as well as against the practice of *dipping*,
which I will not explain, lest an Eve-like, and evil
curiosity might induce some now sweet lips to try
the experiment, and I won't play the serpent to
tempt them.

Tobacco is now an universal medium of introduction among those who are addicted to its use;
but in the early days of Virginia, and until the

last seventy or eighty years, it was a *circulating medium* in the place of money. Even the parson's salary and fees were rated at so many pounds of tobacco, estimated at two pence per pound.

The *Tobacco Warehouses* or Inspections in Richmond, fifty years ago were, *Shockoe*, a mere cluster of wooden sheds; *Byrd's*, of brick, opposite to the present Exchange hotel; and *Rocketts*, of which a portion of the walls is now standing, their aspect from the river having the appearance of an old fortification. The two latter ceased their vocation long since, as has also one of later date, below Rocketts, called *Powhatan* from being built near the wigwam of that King. It is now converted into a number of dwellings, and serves to shelter other heads than hogs-heads. In later years, the *Public Warehouse* on the basin became an Inspection and *Seabrook's* was established in the valley.[*]

In old times a furnace stood near each warehouse, and tobacco unfit for export, was treated as heretics were at an *auto-da-fé*, as being unfit for salvation—both were burned; and now both are suffered to pass for what they are worth.

The primitive mode of transporting tobacco to market was curious. The cask containing it was

---

[*] Dibrell's, near the Dock, is a recent establishment, and Mayo's is being erected on land of new formation, based on the granite of an island, over which the river flowed, since my remembrance, in slight freshets, (1860.)

actually rolled on its own periphery, through mud
and stream. A long wooden spike driven into the
centre of each end, and projecting a few inches
beyond it, served for an axletree, a split sapling
was fitted to it for shafts, and extending in rear of
the cask, where the parts were connected by a
hickory withe; a few slabs were nailed to these, in
front of the cask, forming a sort of foot board, or
box, in which were stowed a middling or two of
bacon, a bag of meal, a frying pan, a hoe, an axe,
and a blanket, for the bipeds; the whole covered
to some height with fodder, for the quadrupeds.
If the distance to market was moderate, the hogshead was rolled on its hoops, which were stout and
numerous; but if fifty to a hundred miles, or more
were to be traversed, rough felloes were spiked on
at each end or quarter of the cask, and these rude
tires served to protect it from being worn through.
Rough fellows also were the conductors.

The *tobacco roller*, as the driver (often the owner)
was called, sought no roof for shelter, during his
journey, sometimes of a week's duration and of
severe toil; at nightfall he kindled a fire in the
woods by the road side, baked a hoe cake, fried
some bacon, fed his team, (I omitted to mention
the bag of corn,) rolled his blanket around him,
and slept by the fire, under the lee of his cask.

When he reached the warehouse, his tobacco was
inspected, a note or receipt expressing the weight,

etc., was handed to him, and he then sallied forth
into the streets in search of a purchaser; calling
out as he entered a store, "Mister, do you buy
tobacco?" When he had found the right "Mister,"
and obtained his money, and a few articles to carry
to his "old woman," he strapped the blanket on
one of his horses and rode home. These men
generally travelled in small parties, and if the
weather and roads were good, had a merry time of
it; if bad, they assisted each other when obstacles
occurred.

The journey from beyond the Roanoke, which
then consumed six days, is now performed in as
many hours, and for the labor of two hundred and
fifty horses, and almost as many men and boys,
(for a boy usually accompanied each man,) during
ten days going and returning, is now substituted
a train of railroad cars, with some four or five
men, for half a day, and at one-fourth of the
expense.

It were superfluous to draw the contrast of those
days with the present. Tobacco rollers are an
extinct species. Instead of them, tobacco buyers
throng the warehouses. Manufactories of the
weed have sprung up in every direction. The
largest buildings in the city are, with few exceptions, tobacco factories, and I may venture to say
that more tobacco is manufactured in Richmond
than in any other place in the world. Such vulgar

terms as *negro-head* and *pig-tail* are discarded, and fanciful ones substituted, such as "*Honey-dew*," "*Christian's-comfort*," "*Heart's-delight*," "*Perfect-love*," "*Rose-bud*," and "*Cousin-Sally*." Artists are employed to design and execute embellishments for the packages, and various sweets, spirits, spices, and essences, are used to give a good flavor or to conceal a bad one.

Italy, Spain and France furnish thousands of boxes of liquorice and of olive oil to sweeten, and to brighten the quid—but they do not accept a *quid pro quo*, by permitting the importation of "Christian's-comfort," or "Heart's-delight," or any other of the consolations prepared abroad, for the lovers of tobacco. About seventy-five factories are in operation, requiring 3,500 to 4,000 hands, male and female, and working up some 25,000 hhds. of tobacco annually.

NOTE.—The following advertisement, which does not include Liquorice, Rum, Olive Oil, Sugar and Syrup, will give an idea of the condiments used in preparing tobacco for mastication.

"To Tobacconists—500 lbs. large black Angustura Tonqua Beans; 200 lbs. Oil of Cinnamon, Cloves, Peppermint, &c. ; 1,000 lbs. good Gum Arabic, in bales, low priced; 25 bottles English Essential Oil Bitter Almonds; 1,000 lbs. Cloves, All-spice, Nutmegs, Cassia, &c. ; Oil of Sweet Flag Root, Branding Paint, red and blue; a large assortment of copper bound Branding Brushes; Varnish; Spirits Turpentine, and every article used about a factory, at low prices."

CHAPTER XXXV.

THE VISIT OF LAFAYETTE.

THE greatest popular enthusiasm I ever witnessed was excited by the *visit of Lafayette* to the United States in 1824, when in his sixty-seventh year, but erect in person as in principle, and apparently with his mental and physical powers but little impaired. In 1777, at the age of nineteen, he first came to this country to volunteer his services.

His ovation was very different from that which is conferred on a political favorite of the day, in which one party only feels an interest, and many members of that party from interested motives. Nor was it like the triumph bestowed on a military or naval hero, which the blaze of glory kindles. Lafayette was welcomed and honored by the promptings of gratitude, which feeling he had in his youth inspired in the hearts of our fathers, for his disinterested and officient aid in obtaining our independence, and by our admiration of his subsequent course in seeking to establish freedom in his native land, without violence or bloodshed.

The whole American nation seemed to love and

honor him. Wherever he appeared every demonstration of these feelings was exhibited in the most conspicuous manner. In Richmond, people from all parts of the State assembled to see him, to cheer him and to touch his hand. Many a Revolutionary soldier left the comforts of home to welcome one who had partaken of the same dangers and hardships, and mothers brought their children, to see and to impress on their youthful minds the memory of the man who was beloved by Washington.

The pageant was all that its actors could devise and execute. The only alloy to their gratification was the fatigue it imposed on its beloved object. The arm of the old soldier was almost shaken from its socket, and his hand was bruised and benumbed by the grasp, not always gentle, of the thousands that sought to press it. Every window of the streets through which the long procession passed, was filled with the smiling faces of mothers and daughters. Handkerchiefs waved like the leaves of a forest in a gale, and shouts of welcome arose, drowning the music of the martial instruments.

No apartment in the city was sufficiently capacious for the ball which was to be given, where the ladies might have the privilege of saluting Lafayette hand to hand, if not lip to lip. The entire area embraced in the quadrangle formed by the surrounding buildings and galleries of the

Eagle Hotel, a space of about eight thousand square feet, was floored over and covered with awnings and flags, to form a ball-room, and large as was the space it was well filled.

Lafayette's memory was sufficiently tenacious to enable him to recognize many of those whom he had known during the war, from brother officers down to the faithful black servant James, who was again ready to wait on him after a lapse of forty-five years.

The honors shown to Lafayette did honor to the country, inspired as they were by gratitude for his services and admiration of his character. How different from the incense offered to party leaders, who are ready generally to lead whichever party can furnish the most numerous troop of followers; or how different from that which follows in the train of a successful candidate, whose office confers patronage, and is apt to confer it on those who have been the most ready tools for his promotion, not on those whose integrity and capacity would ensure a faithful performance of their duties.

CHAPTER XXXVI.

THE WASHINGTON MONUMENT.

In February, 1816, the Legislature of Virginia applied to Bushrod Washington for permission to remove to Richmond the remains of his illustrious relative, over which they desired to erect a suitable monument. Judge Washington was constrained by the will of his uncle to decline the request.

On the 22d February, 1817, the Legislature authorized the opening of subscriptions throughout the State, to raise a fund for the erection of a monument to WASHINGTON, limiting the sum of each individual subscription to twenty dollars.

The enthusiasm in Richmond was such, that several gentlemen evaded the limitation by inscribing the names of their wives and children with twenty dollars affixed to each.

Official agents were appointed in each county to obtain subscriptions. Some did not take the trouble to act, and perhaps some found it more convenient to retain than to report the sums collected, and due accountability was not enforced. So it was, however, that out of $13,063 collected,

29

about four-fifths were obtained in Richmond, if my memory serves.

It is mortifying to record such apathy on such a subject. Can it be fairly ascribed to the absence of party stimulants? Would apathy have prevailed had the glorification of some hero of the day, who could reward his followers, been the object, instead of a token of gratitude to *the man and the hero, not of the day, but of all time?*

This paltry sum (considering that Virginia was the donor) was deposited in the Treasury, and there it remained idle, or was supposed to remain; but when other moneys were missing, it was reported that the monument fund was gone. The State, however, very properly assumed the responsibility; but the fund lay dormant until the 22d February, 1828, when a resolution was adopted, ordering it to be placed at interest. Thus it remained until 1848, when it had accumulated to $41,833, with the aid of a new general subscription, which did not prove large.

On the 22d February, 1849, the Historical Society of Virginia, or influential members of it,* stimulated the Legislature to enact that a monument should be erected on the Capitol Square in Richmond, and 'to appropriate such sum as should be required, in addition to the funds collected, to make an aggregate of $100,000.

---

* Conway Robinson, Esq., was one of the most active.

On the 22d February, 1850, (action always appropriately recurring on that day) the *corner stone of the monument* was laid in the Capitol Square, in the presence of General Zachary Taylor, President of the United States, of a throng of the civil and military, of associations of all descriptions, of officials, of mothers and their children, such as never before assembled in Richmond, and foremost of all, the surviving soldiers of the Revolution, few in number, but attracting general attention.

The premium for the best model was judiciously awarded to *Crawford*, the sculptor, who, after giving instructions for the granite work, proceeded to Rome to model the statuary, and thence to Munich to have it cast in bronze. Thus far he has . succeeded most admirably, and the work bids fair to establish his fame on a higher pinnacle than it had previously attained.

Not so fortunate was the first appointment of a superintendent of the granite work, and of the disbursements pertaining to the erection of basement, columns and pedestals. The person who, by some means, obtained the appointment, proved unworthy of confidence.

This trust—which it was almost sacrilege to abuse—was thus victimized to misfeasance and malfeasance in its inception, in its progress, and in a portion of its execution. It is to be hoped

that it will arrive at completion without further
defilement.

Much anxiety existed for some time lest an
ignoble party feeling might exclude from either
of the six pedestals which surround the elevated
one occupied by WASHINGTON, a statue of his
friend and biographer, MARSHALL—a noble im-
personation of the Judiciary; but a *Wise* decision
has done justice to the memory of the man who
holds a place second only to Washington in public
love and estimation. The constellation surrounding the central luminary will be formed by Jefferson, Henry, Marshall, Gov. Nelson, George
Mason and Andrew Lewis—a glorious assemblage
of patriots, each one conspicuous for his peculiar
attribute, as well as his other talents.

P. S.—The equestrian statue of WASHINGTON
arrived in Richmond from Amsterdam at the close
of 1857, but the sculptor did not survive to see
it erected, nor to complete those which are to
surround it. Crawford died in the zenith of his
fame, and his works will perpetuate it. The in-
auguration of his statue of Washington was celebrated on the 22d February, 1858, attended by
an immense assemblage, undeterred by a snow
storm which prevailed until the statue was unco-
vered, when the sun saluted it with a bright beam.
The figures of both horse and rider are considered
unsurpassed. The height from the plinth to the

the crown of Washington's hat is 20 feet, and total height from the ground 60 feet. Washington is represented as in command and checking his horse in full career, while he points to some distant object, which seems to excite his horse also into intense animation.

The statues of Henry and Jefferson were placed on their pedestals soon after that of Washington, for which they had been waiting, and the statue of George Mason was erected soon after its arrival in February, 1860. It is a personification of firmness and decision. These statues are nine feet in height.

The selection of these characters was peculiarly appropriate. *Lewis* was the frontier warrior who drove the Indians beyond the Ohio in 1774, and served most gallantly during the Revolution; *Henry* set the ball in motion; *Mason* was the author of the Bill of Rights; *Jefferson* of the Declaration; *Nelson* was the Financier, and *Marshall* personifies the Judiciary.

CHAPTER XXXVII.

THE MUSEUM.

SYDNEY SMITH, not the hero, but the man of wisdom and of wit, tells us how the dynasty of the Neapolitan throne was changed by the antic capers of Mr. Isaac Hawkins Brown at a Court Ball: and the second effort to introduce in Richmond an establishment connected with the fine arts, was caused by the fracture of a dancing-master's leg. The sufferer by this disaster was a votary of the Graces and of the Muses. The aid of music was required to inspire and to regulate the movements of the dance. The former obeyed the action of his hands and the latter of his feet, simultaneously, and by their congenial operations he sought to confer grace on his pupils, and to inspire them with " the poetry of motion;" and moreover by these means to provide bread for his family.

The fracture of the leg spoiled his dancing, but nothing daunted by being compelled to relinquish the service of Terpsichore, he sought, instead of dancing, the favor of a sister art, that of painting, and to substitute the brush for the fiddle-stick. His success in the newly adopted vocation was remarkable, considering the disadvantages under which it

was attained; but as the emolument derived from
it was small, he determined to invoke the aid of all
the arts and sciences at once, by establishing a
museum.

The Legislature granted him permission to erect
a building for the purpose, on the Capitol Square;
but a location was unfortunately assigned for it,
which obstructed the entrance to the Square from
Franklin street on the east, and worse still, after
the Museum was removed, the obstruction was
rendered permanent by the erection of the State
Courthouse on the same spot.

The effort to erect a Museum, which at any
other time would have been hopeless, was made in
the *Flush times* of Richmond, and succeeded. The
funds were raised by subscription and a building
quite capacious was erected. As the fantastic
order of architecture prevailed at that time, the
Museum partook of that character, but it was quite
commodious in its arrangements. One apartment
was appropriated to paintings, another to statuary,
and as the specimens of the latter consisted chiefly
in plaster casts of ancient master-pieces, many of
them in a nude state, that apartment was considered by the fastidiously modest, as forbidden
ground, unless it could be visited privately and
without the risk of encountering bolder spectators.

Other apartments contained the usual assortment
of stuffed birds, beasts and reptiles, a fair display

of butterflies, spiders and other insects; also specimens of minerals, &c., &c.; but the department of
conchology was the most complete, and on the
whole the collection was very creditable, considering the limited means of its founder.

The only living specimen was a rattlesnake, and
he came to his death in a remarkable manner. A
mouse was introduced into the cage for his breakfast, on which he did not make an immediate
assault, either because the weather was cool, or his
appetite not keen. The mouse watched his motions, and as soon as he began to coil, leaped on
his head and nibbled away so industriously as to
cause his death. The valor of the mouse was
recorded in the papers of the day.

After the novelty of the sights in the Museum
wore off, the visitors to it became "small by
degrees and beautifully less," for children constituted the far greater number. The gods, goddesses and heroes began to show the dust of antiquity as if they belonged to it, and here and
there the loss of a limb might be observed, to
which the statue was fairly entitled according to
the original.

In this decline of the fine arts, when even the
door-keeper neglected his duty, or found his office
a sinecure, unlike most sinecures without pay,
a party of playful girls having provided themselves
with some cast-off toggery, waited on the goddesses

in the quality of hand-maidens, and arrayed them in trim to receive the most fastidious visitor. Imagine Venus in a checked apron and necker-chief, Ceres in a straw hat and jacket, and Diana in a fur tippet and petticoat; Apollo wearing a cocked hat, like the Indian chief who made a visit to one of our officers in that *full* dress.

The heathens retained their unclassical raiment for some short time before the masquerade was known, so few visited their shrines; but when it was rumored abroad, a perfect rush was made to see the celestials in their new or rather old attire, appareled as mortals. It was their last appear-ance—degraded in the eyes of those whose heathen progenitors had worshipped them, they would no longer expose themselves to ridicule. Instead of an apotheosis, they are probably resolved into their original elements. The dust of Ceres scattered on the fields and turned to grass, may have been con-verted into a cow, and have fattened on the fields her remains had fertilized.

Venus reduced to her original element, may have nourished myrtles and fed her doves on the berries all unconscious of their celestial food; or perhaps some love-sick swain may have eloped with her in her entirety, (as Kossuth would say,) to nourish his passion and to worship her as the image of his lady-love.

One of the mortals who was a companion of the

heathen deities in this terrestrial Olympus, suffered
the fate of mortality, and *his* clay being mortal
can be traced. A resurrectionist conveyed Lao-
cöon's body to the medical college, whether as a
subject for the professor's knife, or as a study for
anatomy and extraordinary development of the
muscles, this deponent saith not.

CHAPTER XXXVIII.

GAS AND WATER.

RICHMOND may claim the honor of being among
the first, if not the very first city lighted with gas.
An adventurer, or a philosopher named Henfrey,
in the infancy of the present century visited Richmond, and induced some of its citizens, scientific
or curious, to witness his process of pouring flame,
instead of steam or water, from the spout of a tea-
kettle. His experiments with a better apparatus
were also successful. Money was raised by subscription and *a light-house* (an octagonal tower of
brick) was erected on the then highest point easily
accessible on Main street; which was in front of
where the American Hotel now stands at the inter-

section of Main and 11th streets. A large lantern with many jets surmounted the tower at the height of some forty feet. The gas was generated in a kind of still in the basement and conducted by a pipe to the burners. The experiment on the first night and for several subsequent ones, was more successful than we would now think possible, comparing the simple apparatus then used, with the complex one and the large and numerous structures now required. Like a recent and not more successful projector in Washington, (whose light on the summit of the dome of the capitol was to enlighten the wide extent of space around it constituting the city,) Mr. Henfrey's light was to shine along the extent of Main street, and to send its superfluous rays to the Capitol and the Basin.

The novelty expired and so did the light; but the tower long remained—a monument of enterprise, if not of science and wisdom, and we may now boast that although our gas did not burn well, we were the first to light it. *Sic transit gloria*, &c.

Some years later the line of Main street was lighted according to the system of those benighted times, but this also was done by private subscription, and diligent ones were wanting to keep the lamps trimmed, mischievous boys broke them and the lights ceased to shine.

Thus also by private subscription, water was

conducted from the Basin in wooden pipes as far as the Market bridge, with hydrants at several corners, always flowing and very convenient for many purposes. Myriads of minute eels would ascend the moist wall of the Market bridge and wriggle their way to the very spouts of the hydrants. By similar pipes, water was conveyed from the Bloody Run Spring (not then a sanguinary stream) as far as the Bell Tavern. Some of these yet serve as conduits for a short distance from their source. In excavating the streets, the pipes are found free from decay, after fifty years interment of those laid from the Basin to Main street.

About twenty-five years after the wooden pipes had been laid, and when the increased population of the city had rendered many of the wells unfit for use, the river was put in requisition to pump a portion of its own water to an elevation higher than the city, and from its *reservoir* there, to circulate by subterranean channels to each domicile, though not always in a transparent state, and these water works have from time to time been increased to keep pace with the increase of the city.

About half a century after Henfrey's light went out, a new and more permanent one was kindled, and this had been burning only a few years, when the cry of "give us more light" caused the erection of new and more extensive *Gas Works* on the outskirts of the city near Rocketts, which will probably suffice for two or three generations, as would its predecessor have done for the present one.

A FISH STORY.

The mention of young eels losing their way in the Main street in *ascending* to their summer quarters to seek their natural though not native homes, reminds me of a similar mistake made by a brood of young shad in *descending* James River, from above the falls, in the course of their migration to the ocean, or to their winter quarters. On one occasion, and one only that I have known, a vast shoal of these fish, which had attained to the size of a large minnow, missed their way down the river, and entered the canal at Westham. They followed its course down to the basin, and there their progress was arrested. There were no locks through which they could descend and no mills through which they might take the chance of being ground in passing over the water-wheel. They appeared to be in great distress. The surface of the basin exhibited myriads of them, leaping out of the water and sparkling in the sun ; a beautiful but painful sight. This continued for a number of days, but the young navigators who had thus lost their reckoning, soon after lost their lives. Although not fish out of water, they were out of their proper course, and died in immense numbers ; the shores

30

of the basin were covered with them, and were rendered offensive to the olfactory organs.

It seems remarkable that this mistake of the young brood should have occurred but once, as if nature had cautioned them not to repeat it, for none survived to tell the tale.

Whether there were any operations going on above the locks at Westham, whether the water was very low in the river and a larger portion than usual was diverted to the canal, I am unable to say; but can ascribe the wandering of the lost tribe only to some such cause.

CHAPTER XXXIX.

THE COLORED ARISTOCRACY.

THE servants belonging to the old families in Virginia and especially those pertaining to domestic households, were as proud of their position as if the establishment was their own. I do not speak of the New Negroes, as the imported Africans were called, but of their descendants.

The house servants acquired something of the polite and respectful demeanor which prevailed among the gentility, and in their intercourse with each other they aped it in the ludicrous style of "High life below stairs,"—*Mister* Jupiter would inquire of *Mistress* Venus how *Master* Cupid was, —but in addressing those servants who were some years their seniors, Uncle and Aunt were the respectful terms used, and these were adopted by the white children of the family; for they would have been thought disrespectful and ill-bred to speak to old servants without giving the appellation of Uncle Adam or Aunt Eve.

The coachman in an old family felt as proud of his position on the box as he could have felt had he been inside, and he would issue his orders to the footman and the stable boys in as authoritative a tone as if he occupied the cushioned back seat.

Besides the pride of station, there was a strong attachment generally on the part of servants to their masters and mistresses, and this descended to the next generation and was mutual. The changes which have been brought about in the breaking up of families, by death, misfortune, remote intermarriages, &c., have greatly diminished the number of these ancient and respectable domestic establishments; but many yet exist on the tide-waters of Virginia; some have been transplanted to the upper country, and it is to be hoped that this beautiful patriarchal system will, in spite of the mischievous and wicked interference of abolitionists, extend, instead of being further contracted.

The most prominent member of the black aristocracy of my early years was *Sy. Gilliat*, (probably Simon, or Cyrus,) the leading violinist (fiddler was then the word,) at the balls and dancing parties. He traced his claim to position to the days of vice-royalty, having held office under Lord Botetourt when govenror, but whether behind his chair or his coach, is in the mist of obscurity.

Sy. Gilliat flourished in Richmond in the first decade of this century, and I know not how many of the last. He was tall, and even in his old age, (if he ever grew old,) erect and dignified. When he appeared officially in the orchestra, his dress was an embroidered silk coat and vest of faded lilac, small clothes, (he would not say breeches,) and silk stockings, which rather betrayed the African prominence of the shin-bone, terminating in shoes fastened or decorated with large buckles. This court-dress was coeval with the reign of Lord Botetourt, and probably part of the fifty suits which, (according to the inventory he left) constituted his wardrobe; to complete this court costume, Sy. wore a brown wig with side curls and a long queue appended. His manners were as courtly as his dress, and he elbowed himself and his fiddle-stick through the world with great propriety and harmony.

Belonging to the vice-regal family, Sy. belonged of course to the Church of England; this was one qualification for the office of sexton, (not grave-digger,) and his residence being very near the church in Richmond, was an inducement for the wardens to confer on him the appointment; although strict constructionists might have con-sidered, like Ephraim Smooth, that he was "a man of sin, rubbing the hair of the horse against the bowels of the cat;" he filled the office for some time, but was impelled to resign it in a fit of un-righteous indignation, excited by hearing that he was suspected of partaking of the wine without the other ceremonies of the sacrament. His declara-tion, that he had drunk Lord Botetourt's best wine long before his accusers knew the difference be-tween Malaga and Malmsey, whilst it vindicated Sy.'s connoisseurship, did not obtain for him abso-lution from the charge, and he left the service of the church highly indignant.

Sy. could not have many associates without com-promising his dignity, for there were few of the old aristocracy remaining; but in addition to those few, he permitted the intimacy of some of the leading stewards, coachmen, and head cooks of the best families.

His cotemporary, *Bob Cooley*, had also served the nobility at Williamsburg, and when that city lost it pre-eminence, Bob was fain to follow a republican governor to Richmond, where for many years he was intrusted with the keys of the capitol, and flourished his besom over its floor and furniture. His court-dress was a time-honored suit of black velvet, ample in skirts and flaps.

If Sy. was the Chesterfield, Bob might be called the Burleigh of his day. Sy. acquired his courtly and elegant demeanor by frequenting balls and parties, and Bob his solemn deportment by attending in council chambers and courts of justice. By dusting the judge's cushion he seemed to have acquired the solemn aspect of the dignitary who sat on it. Bob did not, however, attach a handle to his name, to indicate the dignity of office—but one was assumed by his successor, who appended the initials K. K. C., indicating keeper of the keys of the capitol.

Nick Scott, another member of the colored aristocracy, kept his coach for many years, without pride or insolence or imposition, and he took his seat on the box, thus setting an example of humility to his children.

Before the female province of pastry was usurped by the countrymen of Napoleon, there flourished in Richmond a lady of the dark aristocracy, *Mrs. Nancy Byrd*, a name that carries its own passport to distinction. No dinner nor supper party could be complete unless Nancy had a finger in the pie. She held undisputed sway over the dessert, with the rolling-pin for her sceptre, and considered herself as pertaining to the under-crust of gentility.

While I write these closing pages in the winter of 1855–56,* the severest, in the long duration of extreme cold, that I can remember; the river closed for eight weeks in almost its entire length, and the earth covered with a coating of snow of nearly equal duration ; the black servants and slaves are provided with food, fuel and clothing, while our poor-houses and other receptacles for the destitute or dissipated whites, are crowded to overflowing, chiefly with foreign paupers ; contributions are raised in every mode that can be devised for the relief of destitute whites, for many of whom we are indebted to our philanthropic brethren of the North, who seek to entice our slaves to the same destitute condition there—perhaps, on the principle of reciprocity. Whether similar charity would be extended to them there, if destitute, as to the whites here, is a doubtful question.

A fair friend furnishes this anecdote of what came under her own observation :

An old negro, who was considered so entirely "one of the family," as to be in the habit of

---

* Thus in the first edition, which may be repeated in the second, as applicable to the winter of 1856–7.

calling one of his young mistresses cousin, when addressing her, was asked by the lady, "Why he did not, as formerly, attend the meeting-house of his brethren on Sunday?" His reply was, "that when he could sit by Mr. Wickham's Bob and Judge Marshall's Jack, he liked to join *siety*, but now he never knew who he *sot* by, and he stayed at home."

This same individual, during this degenerate time, being invited to a party, was induced to attend, and furnished with a *pass* till eleven o'clock that night. Arriving at the house where the festival was held, he was exceedingly disgusted by finding himself surrounded altogether by *parvenus*, and being under the impression that he must not return home till the hour designated in his pass, he retired to an adjacent room, locked the door, remained there till the hour of eleven arrived, and then returned to his domicil, mourning over the great lights which had been extinguished ere his own had gone out.

Like their betters, the negroes of the present day have their mock-gentility, and like them, they sustain it chiefly in dress and pretension. In the streets on Sundays, plainness of attire is now-a-days rather an indication of gentility. Dashing satin bonnets now cover woolly false curls, a handsome veil conceals a sooty face, which is protected from being sun-burnt by a stylish parasol. A silk

dress of gaudy colors sweeps the ground, concealing a splay foot with receding heel. The beau
who struts beside this chamber-maid, is attired in a
talma or shawl, pants whose checks or stripes
exceed the circumference of his leg, and a vest in
which every color vies for brilliancy. He twirls
his watch-chain and his cane, and might almost put
a Broadway dandy to the blush. These gentry
leave their visiting cards at each other's kitchens,
and on occasion of a wedding, Miss Dinah Drip-
pings and Mr. Cuffie Coleman have their cards connected by a silken tie, emblematic of that which is
to connect themselves, and a third card announces,
" At home from ten to one," where those who call
will find cake, fruits, and other refreshments. And
this is not an exaggerated picture of the hardships
and miseries which the domestic blacks suffer, and
from which their abolition enemies seek to relieve
them.

VALEDICTORY.

And now kind readers, that have travelled with me to the end of this journey, I again bid you Farewell. We shall not meet again, and a year ago I little anticipated this meeting. If you did not skip occasionally along the path, you must have plodded over some very dry and barren places, where perhaps you took a nap, but on the whole, I hope you have found your journey a pleasant one, as I have found mine, tho' toilsome.

One parting word to the subject of these pages—the lovely city of Richmond! In infancy beautiful by nature, and the abode of talent and refinement, of elegance without ostentation, of hospitality without extravagance. Some alloy to these precious qualities may have been introduced in later years; but the beautiful has been retained and enhanced in the progress to maturity. On this bright May morning, when the trees that shade and the flowers that embellish every homestead display their richest hues; when the vista which terminates almost every street gives a glimpse of the country, its forest and its farms; when the river glistens through the foliage of wooded islands, and as it rushes amid the islets and rocks, makes music even with its roar, whoever is conscious of the charms of nature, must exclaim, this is beautiful!

Not only the beauties of nature excite our admiration at the present time, but the improvements of art, which are now manifested in the erection of a greater number of substantial and elegant edifices than at any former period, and in the preparation for others yet more imposing.

Should one of the boys of the present day undertake, fifty years hence, the task I now close, he will have a vastly wider field for the exercise of his pen, (if pens shall then be used,) and if these pages shall then be extant, he may amuse his readers by the contrasts to be drawn between now and then.

This is my farewell tribute to the home of my boyhood and of my old age, and of many friends, some of whom remain, but many have departed, and I shall soon follow them.